MEDIEVAL WOMEN AND URBAN JUSTICE
COMMERCE, CRIME AND COMMUNITY
IN ENGLAND, 1300–1500

Teresa Phipps

Manchester University Press

Copyright © Teresa Phipps 2020

The right of Teresa Phipps to be identified as the author of this work has been asserted by them in accordance with the Copyright, Designs and Patents Act 1988.

Published by Manchester University Press
Oxford Road, Manchester M13 9PL

www.manchesteruniversitypress.co.uk

British Library Cataloguing-in-Publication Data
A catalogue record for this book is available from the British Library

ISBN 978 1 5261 3459 2 hardback
ISBN 978 1 5261 7179 5 paperback

First published 2020
Paperback published 2023

The publisher has no responsibility for the persistence or accuracy of URLs for any external or third-party internet websites referred to in this book, and does not guarantee that any content on such websites is, or will remain, accurate or appropriate.

Typeset by
Servis Filmsetting Ltd, Stockport, Cheshire

GENDER IN HISTORY

Series editors:
Lynn Abrams, Cordelia Beattie, Pam Sharpe and Penny Summerfield

The expansion of research into the history of women and gender since the 1970s has changed the face of history. Using the insights of feminist theory and of historians of women, gender historians have explored the configuration in the past of gender identities and relations between the sexes. They have also investigated the history of sexuality and family relations, and analysed ideas and ideals of masculinity and femininity. Yet gender history has not abandoned the original, inspirational project of women's history: to recover and reveal the lived experience of women in the past and the present.

The series Gender in History provides a forum for these developments. Its historical coverage extends from the medieval to the modern periods, and its geographical scope encompasses not only Europe and North America but all corners of the globe. The series aims to investigate the social and cultural constructions of gender in historical sources, as well as the gendering of historical discourse itself. It embraces both detailed case studies of specific regions or periods, and broader treatments of major themes. Gender in History titles are designed to meet the needs of both scholars and students working in this dynamic area of historical research.

Medieval women and urban justice

Manchester University Press

OTHER RECENT BOOKS
IN THE SERIES

The state as master: gender, state formation and commercialisation in urban Sweden, 1650–1780   Maria Ågren

Love, intimacy and power: marriage and patriarchy in Scotland, 1650–1850   Katie Barclay (Winner of the 2012 Women's History Network Book Prize)

Men on trial: performing emotion, embodiment and identity in Ireland, 1800–45   Katie Barclay

Modern women on trial: sexual transgression in the age of the flapper   Lucy Bland

The Women's Liberation Movement in Scotland   Sarah Browne

Modern motherhood: women and family in England, c.1945–2000   Angela Davis

Women against cruelty: protection of animals in nineteenth-century Britain   Diana Donald

Gender, rhetoric and regulation: women's work in the civil service and the London County Council, 1900–55   Helen Glew

Jewish women in Europe in the Middle Ages: a quiet revolution   Simha Goldin

Women of letters: gender, writing and the life of the mind in early modern England   Leonie Hannan

Women and museums 1850–1914: Modernity and the gendering of knowledge   Kate Hill

The shadow of marriage: singleness in England, 1914–60   Katherine Holden

Women, dowries and agency: marriage in fifteenth-century Valencia   Dana Wessell Lightfoot

Catholic nuns and sisters in a secular age: Britain 1945–90   Carmen Mangion

Women, travel and identity: journeys by rail and sea, 1870–1940   Emma Robinson-Tomsett

Imagining Caribbean womanhood: race, nation and beauty contests, 1929–70   Rochelle Rowe

Infidel feminism: secularism, religion and women's emancipation, England 1830–1914   Laura Schwartz

Women, credit and debt in early modern Scotland   Cathryn Spence

Being boys: youth, leisure and identity in the inter-war years   Melanie Tebbutt

Queen and country: same-sex desire in the British Armed Forces, 1939–45   Emma Vickers

The 'perpetual fair': gender, disorder and urban amusement in eighteenth-century London   Anne Wohlcke

Contents

LIST OF FIGURES AND TABLES	*page* vi
ACKNOWLEDGEMENTS	viii
MAP	x
Introduction	1
1 Women, town courts and customary law in context	21
2 Commerce, credit and coverture: women and debt litigation	45
3 Law and the regulation of women's work	90
4 Violence, property and 'bad speech': women and trespass litigation	113
5 Public disorder, policing and misbehaving women	153
Conclusion	185
BIBLIOGRAPHY	199
INDEX	220

List of figures and tables

Figures

1.1 Percentage of debt and trespass suits in Nottingham, Chester and Winchester, fourteenth and fifteenth centuries. — 33

2.1 Female debt litigants in Chester, Nottingham and Winchester, separated according to those who acted alone and those who pleaded jointly with their husbands. — 66

Tables

2.1 Debt and trespass litigation in Chester, Nottingham and Winchester. — 48

2.2 Female litigants and debt litigants in Nottingham. — 53

2.3 Female creditors and debtors in Nottingham. — 55

2.4 Female litigants at Winchester City Court. — 59

2.5 Female creditors and debtors at Winchester City Court. — 59

2.6 Female litigants at Chester's Pentice Court. — 62

3.1 Trading offences presented before the 1395–6 Nottingham Mayor's Court. — 94

3.2 Trading offences recorded in Winchester City Court (across six sample years). — 95

3.3 Assize of Ale, Nottingham 1369–70. — 99

3.4 Presentments for brewing and selling ale in Winchester. — 102

4.1 Women and trespass in Chester, Nottingham and Winchester. — 122

5.1 Assailants and victims of affray in Nottingham. — 158

5.2 Assailants and victims of violence in Winchester. — 159

LIST OF FIGURES AND TABLES

5.3 Individuals against whom the hue and cry was raised at Winchester.   166
5.4 Raisers of the hue and cry at Winchester.   167
5.5 Scolds in Nottingham and Winchester.   171

Acknowledgements

The completion of this book brings the opportunity to reflect on how many people have supported me over the years, all having their part to play in the completion of this project, and on how lucky I am to be surrounded by such intelligent, caring and encouraging people. In the difficult periods of writing and research, especially towards the end of a project such as this, it is easy to lose sight of the many reasons to be thankful, but it is a pleasure to be able to take some time to express this here. First, I am grateful to the Department of History at the University of Nottingham and, while at Swansea, to the AHRC for funding my research. I had many fruitful and enjoyable visits to the local archives in Nottingham, Chester and Winchester, and am thankful for the invaluable work that these bodies and their staff do in preserving our heritage. I am grateful to MUP, especially Meredith Carroll, for astonishing efficiency, open communication and making this process as easy as possible. I would also like to thank the anonymous reviewers for their useful and attentive feedback at various stages of preparing this book. Thank you to Fiona Spooner for creating the map, as well as answering numerous questions about basic stats.

On a personal level, there are many people who have all played a part in shaping and supporting this project. Richard Goddard has been unfailing in his support of my research and career since introducing me to the joys of studying medieval urban society and medieval women's history as an undergraduate at Nottingham. In supervising my postgraduate research, he was always engaged, full of questions, and I thank him for treating me as a colleague and expert and providing me with the freedom to mould my own research path. In addition, Ross Balzaretti encouraged me to push the boundaries of my research and consider bigger questions that undoubtedly improved and refined my findings. Gwilym Dodd also suggested the comparison of towns that pushed this research to a new level. Cordelia Beattie has offered ongoing support, interest and advice on my work since examining my PhD thesis and has been particularly generous in offering feedback throughout the writing of this book. I am incredibly grateful to Deborah Youngs for providing the opportunity to develop my research within the luxury of a project (Women Negotiating the Boundaries of Justice) that was so perfectly aligned with my research and without which this book would not exist. Additional thanks are due for reading so much of my work over the last few years, offering new critical insight to my research and writing, for many fruitful and enjoyable discussions about women and the law, as well as ongoing support and advice. I have benefited hugely from being part of the project team, including collaboration and discussion with Emma Cavell and Rebecca Mason, who have been sounding boards for ideas and for the finding of common ground across our different research contexts.

There are many others with whom I have discussed this and other aspects of my work, including Sparky Booker, Sara Butler, Jeremy Goldberg, Maryanne Kowaleski, Alexandra Shepard, Matthew Stevens and Tim Stretton. They have all helped to refine my ideas and strengthen my arguments and have made me feel part of a community of scholars to which I hope I can add a valuable contribution.

The importance of being part of a community and having a sense of place and belonging has been of great importance over the many years during which this book has evolved. At Nottingham I am grateful for the PhD community, and in particular Emily Buchnea, Gemma Evans, Siobhán Hearne, Emma Lautman and Maroula Perisanidi, who all read or discussed various iterations of my work, but more importantly provided inspiration, friendship and fun throughout the PhD and beyond. At Swansea, Sam Blaxland, Catherine Rozier and Charlie Rozier (and Daisy!) offered friendship, support and a listening ear on many occasions. Away from work, Team Outcast of CrossFit Swansea have provided community, relief and a huge amount of fun that allowed me to survive and thrive in a new and unfamiliar place.

Thank you to my family and particularly my lovely mum, Jacqui Phipps, for being a constant source of love and support, for always seeming to have an answer to my worries, and giving me the space to pursue my interests, even without a clear sense of where they will take me. Finally, I thank Jess Hughes for being a source of inspiration and belief, for much needed moments of joy and adventure, and for giving me perspective at the times when I needed it the most.

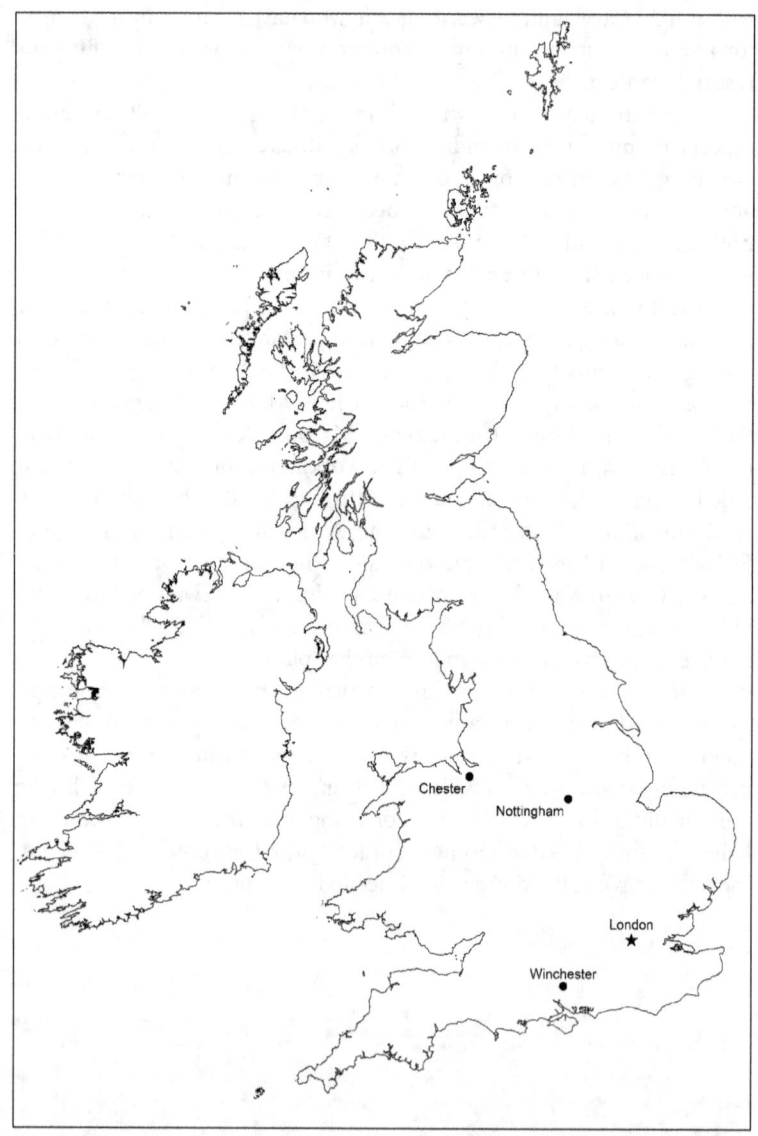

Map 1 The locations of Nottingham, Chester and Winchester within Britain.

Introduction

In May 1325, Margery Bridgford and Adam del Park faced one another in a suit brought before Nottingham's borough court. Bridgford alleged that Park had assaulted her in her house, beating, wounding and maltreating her, as well as wounding and killing three of her sheep. She claimed damages of 20s. Park brought a countersuit that recalled a different version of events. He claimed that he had attempted to impound the sheep, as they had been unlawfully grazing and destroying vegetables on his land. In response, Bridgford had defamed Park, calling him a false man, a thief and an infidel, and tearing his clothes. He sought damages of half a mark (6s 8d). Despite the parties' denial of the allegations, the jury reported that both were guilty of the respective offences, with the court awarding damages of 2s 6d to Margery Bridgford but only 6d to Adam del Park.[1] Bridgford secured compensation for the physical assault as well as the monetary loss resulting from the damage to her goods (the death of three sheep), while the defaming of Park's reputation and Bridgford's physical attack were also quantified in monetary terms, though at a lower sum. The court apparently agreed with the relative severity of the two attacks as claimed by the two litigants and reflected this in the damages that were eventually awarded.

These pleas were typical of those heard by the courts that governed England's medieval towns, illustrating how relatively trivial, mundane disputes between neighbours could result in physical or verbal violence, and ultimately in litigation in the local court. Both women and men readily resorted to law to seek redress and to enforce obligations. The surviving records of these complaints provide an insight into urban women's access to justice, revealing their standing under the law, as well as rare access to the details of their lives, interactions and relationships. In the context of medieval patriarchal society, where the identities and activities of the vast majority of women went unrecorded, local court records represent a crucial source through which we can access the lives of ordinary women. Furthermore, town court records reveal the activities of ordinary working women, in contrast to the more exceptional elite women who left their own records (such as the Paston women) or whose political roles saw them documented in contemporary histories. They allow us to access the occasions when women used the courts to claim and perform their legal identities, or when the complaints of others forced women to answer for their actions, and as a result offer an unparalleled insight into women's lives and relationships. As illustrated by the cases cited above, we are able to glimpse their actions as both plaintiffs and defendants, their complaints and grievances, and the assessments of value and harm that these involved. The records of these complaints reveal women's behaviour, interactions and altercations, instances of violence, their obligations and expectations, and sometimes their words, among many other intricacies and idiosyncrasies of urban life. They also reveal more quotidian details, such as the fact that Margery Bridgford and Adam del Park were neighbours, that she owned (at least) three sheep, and that he grew vegetables on the land surrounding his home. The court records also allow us to test and measure the experiences of real women against models or theories about the position of women in premodern society, allowing us to build a greater understanding of the lives of real women.

These women, their litigation and other legal actions, lie at the heart of this book, which seeks to understand how ordinary urban women engaged with and were defined by the legal systems that governed the late medieval urban communities of Nottingham, Chester and Winchester, c.1300–c.1500. England's medieval towns were notably litigious places, and the pleas that were so common within local courts reflected many key urban characteristics: they were dynamic, evolving places that were densely populated and were at the centre of local trade and exchange, where people worked in a wide range of occupations. These factors combined to increase the propensity of urban residents to use and engage with local justice. Through civil complaints of debt, detinue (the detention or withholding of goods) and trespass, residents used their local courts to enforce commercial agreements and obligations, to complain about the poor quality of goods or services, and to seek compensation when the misbehaviour of others caused harm to individuals, property or reputations. Local officials also used the powers granted to them to police and punish misbehaviour and enforce local bylaws and regulations. As a result of this broad scope, a large proportion of the urban population came into contact with local justice at some point in their lives, many doing so frequently.[2] In 1377, 1,477 people in Nottingham were eligible for the Poll Tax (adults over 14 who were not classed as poor); two years earlier in the year 1375–6 (Michaelmas to Michaelmas), 469 different individuals used the borough court, approximately a third of the taxable population.[3] Of these individuals, 19% were women. Interaction with various arms of urban justice was a common, ordinary experience among the residents of England's towns, and town courts were popular forums through which to resolve disputes and restore relationships.[4]

INTRODUCTION

The high volume of litigation and presentments dealt with by these courts created a wealth of documentation that allows us to access the social and economic lives of ordinary women and men who rarely featured in other written records of the period, shedding light on the legal actions of thousands of people as they negotiated urban life, its challenges, opportunities and conflicts. This book examines the active nature of women's experiences of and engagement with local justice, rather than the ways in which they were defined or punished by the law. This is in part a reflection of the sources used (particularly civil pleas) but also the approach to these records, centring women as individuals with choices and personalities, rather than simply as subjects of legal and official authority or statistics to be counted. While this study also serves as a detailed insight into the nature of late medieval urban justice, the focus here is not on the institutions that delivered this justice but on the individuals (specifically the women) who engaged with and were subject to the mechanisms and customs of local justice in the course of their everyday lives. The urban records therefore serve to expand our view of women's legal experiences to incorporate the many ways that they engaged with the law in everyday life.

There is much to learn about the lives of ordinary women from the court rolls: details of their work, their commercial contacts, what they bought and sold and from whom, their interpersonal relationships and how these broke down, where they lived and even what possessions they had. We know, for example, that Nottingham's John and Alice Sutton were wholesalers who dealt in large quantities of garlic and onions; that Agatha Spycer and Alice Mercer were both known as merchants in Winchester; and that Matilda Lok accused Ralph de Ravensecroft, a chaplain, of assaulting her in Eastgate Street in Chester's city centre.[5] Individually, these complaints offer a fascinating insight into the details of women's everyday lives. However, when studied together in detail, the court records also allow us to consider important questions regarding women's access to justice within the urban community. This book asks why, how and in what circumstances local law enabled women to complain about the actions of others who had harmed or wronged them, as well as the extent to which they were expected to account for their own behaviour through the complaints and reports of their neighbours and local officials. It represents a new, comparative focus in the study of medieval urban women, and of women's roles in litigation, allowing us to consider patterns beyond individual places and courts, and to place the urban experience within the wider legal context of late medieval England. As Laura Gowing has argued, going to court was a rare occasion when ordinary women could have their actions and words documented, in a period where written literacy levels among the working population were low, though increasing in relation to pragmatic matters.[6] Even if they were able to, there was no need for women (or men) to record who they might have had an argument with, who had stolen from them or insulted them. Most everyday commercial transactions were not recorded either, so occasions where a payment was not made on time did not get recorded unless they resulted in legal action.[7] Court records therefore bring these moments into view, allowing us to reconstruct aspects of women's legal actions and the everyday lives from which these actions stemmed. It is this which offers historians the opportunity to examine the law not just from an institutional perspective – as a system of rules that was imposed on the population for them to adhere to – but from the litigant's perspective, as a series of principles and actions that was negotiated by individuals in the ways in which they told their stories.[8] The fact that these stories were written down (to varying degrees) granted them a sense of formality and posterity that was rare in the lives of ordinary people, particularly women.

Town courts represented the lowest level of law and justice, and were thus the most accessible and relevant courts in the everyday lives of medieval women and men. This book examines and compares the records of urban justice from Nottingham, Chester and Winchester, using a combination of quantitative and qualitative analysis to compare the legal status, roles and experience of ordinary, middling status women living in these towns across the fourteenth and fifteenth centuries.[9] It does this by combining the analysis of six sample years for each town (discussed in greater detail in Chapter 1) with a broader survey and discussion of women's legal actions and experiences across the period c.1300–c.1500. This was a period during which town courts developed to become key institutions for the administration of justice in England, as well as one of demographic and economic development and upheaval. The women at the heart of this study all lived in medium-sized towns and made their living by buying, selling or making various goods, or providing different services. We cannot, however, assume that all townswomen, their status or their experiences were the same. A key finding of this study is that, despite shared characteristics, each town and its court(s) were different, and women's experiences of and engagement with the law were a product of local interpretations of legal practice, as well as their own personal lives and personalities. All of these factors intersected to create a unique experience of the law for every individual woman that is discussed within this book, as well as many thousands more who are not, a fact which speaks to the instability of 'woman' as a category. Moreover, the late medieval period was one of many turning points, meaning that the context in which women's legal action took place was not static. It was a time of demographic and economic upheaval, but also a period of evolution and growth in the legal systems of England, and of continuing development of town governance, rights and customs, resulting in increasing interaction with the law by ordinary people.[10] The courts examined here were still relatively new at the beginning of the fourteenth century when this study begins, but by the end of the fifteenth century were well established as central components within the machinery of local justice. The fact that this study spans and surveys legal records covering the period c.1300–c.1500 therefore allows for consideration of continuity and change in women's legal experiences and status over time. As a result, this study is characterised as much by differences and contrasts as it is by common factors that applied to women as a group.

The context for each town and its court is established in detail in Chapter 1, though it is useful to set out some key characteristics here. They were all medium-sized, provincial towns, with good collections of surviving records from courts that can be loosely classified as 'borough courts'. The towns were of comparable size, but in geographically separate regions of England, as Map 1 displays. Each had its own unique status, though by the fourteenth century none was nationally important in terms of politics or trade, meaning that they might be considered relatively 'ordinary' urban centres, in a separate category to major cities like London, York, Norwich or Bristol. Importantly, each town has a good collection of surviving court records from across the fourteenth and fifteenth centuries, recording comparable types of litigation between residents and regulation and policing by civic officials. The Nottingham records are the richest and best surviving, so are drawn on the most throughout the book, with extensive comparison to those from Chester and Winchester. This comparison is crucial to understanding the wider context of women's legal action and the variables that defined it.

Borough courts and urban justice did not exist in a vacuum, and the varied array of legal options that existed in this period are now widely acknowledged. These customary courts sat within a complex web of overlapping, competing jurisdictions. Disputes could take various paths, giving individuals or groups a degree of choice over where to bring their complaints. This study illuminates the structures, customs and practices that governed urban women's lives through the operation of local justice, and considers how these varied from one town to another. As Chapter 1 explains, there were many common factors that spanned all local town courts, though each court operated according to its own set of customs and traditions. Comparison between different town courts therefore identifies the ways in which these differing customs had an impact upon women's experiences of the law, and the examination of thousands of cases and presentments serves to enhance our understanding of how law and justice operated at the local level in medieval society. Throughout this book, the practices of the three towns are also contextualised against existing studies of other jurisdictions, helping to provide a more complete picture of women's litigation across the legal network of medieval England. Wider comparisons with evidence from across Britain (Wales and Scotland) and Europe also offer opportunities to consider aspects of a shared legal culture as it impacted on and was experienced by women across national and jurisdictional boundaries.

The legal lives of medieval urban women

This study rests on several decades of scholarship on medieval women, particularly that which explores their lives in towns and their status under the law. Much of the history of urban women has focused on their work, a defining feature of urban life. The intrinsic commercial functions of towns make the consideration of women's work central to the broader understanding of their lives and status within urban communities, but this was also tied to – or indeed the root of – much of their legal action, as Chapters 2 and 3 demonstrate. Various studies, including those of Maryanne Kowaleski, Jeremy Goldberg and Caroline Barron, have drawn upon a range of legal and official sources to study women in towns including Exeter, York and London, as well as Lincoln and Shrewsbury.[11] However, these studies have largely used court records to examine women's work, and consideration of the details of women's legal status and the nature of their litigation offers a background rather than the focus of these studies. There have been a handful of studies on women's involvement in debt litigation, but none of their roles in trespass pleas.[12] More research exists on Scottish townswomen's legal actions, due largely to the work of Elizabeth Ewan.[13] English court records have instead been mined for details of women's working activities, occupations and economic status. As a result, we know that women played essential roles in urban economies, working to generate their own incomes and supplementing the earnings of their husbands. However, they often inhabited marginal positions, were involved in low-value trade, low-skilled work and were less likely to work in specialised occupations than men, instead intermittently working across many areas.[14] Kowaleski's study of women's work in Exeter outlines the low status of women's work in particularly stark terms, drawing upon their actions in the borough court as evidence of work and trade in five main areas: service, brewing or selling ale, retailing, prostitution, brothel-keeping and a small number of crafts.[15] These activities are all represented in the court rolls examined here, along with many other tasks.

Some studies take a more optimistic stance on the position of women within urban society, emphasising their shifting status and positing periods of enhanced opportunity. Caroline Barron famously – and somewhat controversially – suggested that there may have been a 'golden age' for working women in late medieval London, particularly in the aftermath of the Black Death. Due to the customs of London that recognised women's separate commercial activities, married women who acted as *femmes sole* were even said to have been 'working partners in marriages between economic equals', while the independence of widows was described as being 'even brighter'.[16] Jeremy Goldberg's analysis of Yorkshire women also contended that there was a growth in employment opportunities for women as a result of the profound demographic downturn in the century following 1348. Like Kowaleski, he also noted the intermittent and fluid nature of women's working identities, while acknowledging that they could nevertheless build up a range of skills and played important roles in running the household and bringing in money through by-employments.[17] This has led to Barron and Goldberg being grouped together as proponents of the 'golden age school', though Goldberg has never used this term. But the idea that women experienced enhanced status and opportunities has been challenged by other historians, most notably Judith Bennett who has argued for the continuity of women's low economic status over several centuries under the 'patriarchal equilibrium' by which there was change but not transformation in women's status in relation to men.[18] Most recently, Matthew Stevens' work on London women has returned to the 'golden age' debate to suggest that a rise in women's economic litigation may have been a result of increased opportunity, but that, overall, women's capacity to access justice declined from the fourteenth to the fifteenth centuries.[19] These arguments all draw on a variety of administrative and legal records to reconstruct the activities and experiences of medieval women, and to trace any changes in this position over time. These patterns of change also feature throughout this study, though not with the intention of identifying or disputing the existence of a 'golden age'. Women's access to justice was never 'golden' – they were always in the minority of litigants – and though in some courts and in some situations women did have significant capacity to use the law to their advantage, the act of converting women's legal actions into broad narratives of continuity or change serves to mask the unique experiences and stories of individual women.

In the popular imagination, medieval women had few or even no legal rights, their encounters with the law were limited to 'female' acts of witchcraft or prostitution, and their behaviour punished by the ducking stool and scold's bridles. While this is, of course, not an accurate depiction, the historiography of medieval women's legal position does not offer much in terms of women's equitable access to justice. Early histories of the English law painted a rather bleak picture of women's legal status, based on general descriptions of female subordination, particularly when married, drawn from legal treatises. These outline the position of women in theory, including striking statements that saw women characterised like children and outlaws, whose lack of legal capacity and obligations meant that they were not under the law.[20] Eileen Power, for example, drew attention to the subjection of woman to man, and the law's failure to view a woman as 'a complete individual [or] a free and lawful person'.[21] Women's inferior legal status within marriage under the principle of coverture, and their husbands' legal responsibility for their actions, was a particularly prominent theme in these early discussions.[22] But none of these studies examined the actual legal actions of medieval women, or recognised the possibility that there may have existed a notable gap between women's legal rights and actions in theory and in practice.

This is where the true value of studying court records lies – in what these documents reveal about the practice, rather than theory or ideals, of law: how legal action and disputes played out in court, and in the context of everyday life; the interests, value and strategies of those involved; and how people behaved to each other. They tell us the things people could get away with, what other people thought to be out of line, and what could be done about this. All of this involved the explicit and implicit invocation of legal, customary and local norms.[23] This access to law in action is particularly fundamental to understanding the position of women, whose status under the law was characterised by notions of inferiority in relation to men which resulted in long lists of things that women (especially married women) could not (theoretically) do. Court records allow us to assess the implications of these ideas in everyday life.

The most notable and powerful convention that defined women's legal status – and has dominated much of the historiography – was the common law doctrine of coverture, which limited, or even removed, married women's legal status. The influence of coverture on legal practice is a key theme that runs throughout this book, so it is worth spending some time setting out its parameters and treatment by historians here. This principle set out, in the most basic of terms, that married women did not have an independent legal or financial identity, but instead were 'covered' by their husbands, a phenomenon which defined women's legal and economic status from the middle ages to the passing of the Married Women's Property Act in 1870.[24] As a result, much discussion of women's legal capabilities has focused on what a woman *could not* do: she could not 'own or control property, enter into contracts, make a will, or bring or defend a lawsuit without her husband'.[25] Coverture was also a defining principle for the status of non-married women, as it characterised the status of women in relation to whether they were or were not married. Furthermore, marriage was an expectation (though not always a reality) for adult women, meaning that the idea and power of coverture was something that impacted on the lives of all women. Coverture therefore created different categories of women, defined via their marital status as either maids, wives or widows.[26]

These classifications can be traced in the various legal treatises of the premodern period, revealing how lawyers interpreted the status of women under English common law. The treatise known as Bracton outlined the dual nature of coverture under common law: husband and wife are a 'single person, because they are one flesh and one blood', and men were the rulers of their wives and custodians of their property.[27] This meant that wives were unable to bring or answer complaints independently, except in a few extreme circumstances such as the murder of their husband.[28] This has led to some historians making broad statements on the power of coverture and the disabilities or invisibility of married women. Sue Sheridan Walker highlighted the rights that came with widowhood, stating that 'the legal reality of the wife is largely subsumed by that of the husband and only revived upon his death'.[29] Marjorie McIntosh suggested that, under common law, it is rare that historians are able to spot the presence of married women in court behind their husband's name.[30]

We might not, therefore, expect to find wives in court records. However, these notions of extreme disabilities for married women in particular have been tempered by analyses of the 'reality' of coverture by numerous historians. In their seminal text on English legal history, Pollock and Maitland cautioned against assuming a uniform understanding of coverture: 'we must be on our guard against the common belief that the ruling principle is that which sees an "unity of person" between husband and wife … a consistently operative principle it can not be'.[31] However, it is only recently that various studies have analysed women's legal actions across a range of contexts, drawing on the records of legal practice to assess the day-to-day impact of coverture.[32] These studies have revealed many grey areas within the 'doctrine' of coverture, suggesting that it was often more of a cultural guiding notion than a fixed set of rules. Tim Stretton has argued that coverture was a fiction which, in practice, did not mean that wives were not legal persons or completely unable to wage law. Instead, the essence of coverture lay in the power of a husband over his wife and her property, and the assumption that a wife acted under the coercion of her husband.[33] Surveying the invocation of coverture in the late medieval year books, Sara Butler has also argued that medieval courts were reluctant to definitively proclaim the 'civil death' of the wife.[34] While coverture is dominant in our perception of women's legal status, Tim Stretton and Krista Kesselring have cautioned that in fact many of the rules pertaining to coverture and women's legal status did not guide every transaction, but were only called upon in particular instances of crisis.[35] As we will see throughout this study, these rules were also applied and interpreted in various ways according to the practice and jurisdictions of different courts.

Historians have mined the records of numerous jurisdictions in seeking to understand the nature and extent of women's legal actions in the medieval period. The publication of three separate volumes on women's status across the premodern period in the last decade marked a new phase in the historiography. These studies treat the broad assumptions about the impact of coverture to close scrutiny, revealing that some women had more options than theoretical limits of the law might suggest, and that the power of coverture has perhaps been overplayed.[36] Examining the records of legal practice, these collected studies have served to capture how 'women's legal agency was marked by variation and depended on marital status, jurisdiction and region'.[37] This recent historiography shows varying capabilities of women in court, though this was consistently informed by the culture and tradition of coverture that delineated women by marital status; but it was in local courts, such as those of manors and boroughs, that communities and officials turned abstract legal ideas about women into reality through the process of litigation.[38] Matthew Stevens found that in London there was ample scope for married women to litigate despite the conventions of coverture.[39] Cordelia Beattie has also highlighted the potential for women to negotiate the restrictions of coverture, particularly in relation to household management and the provision of necessaries.[40] Miriam Müller has problematised assumptions about the power of medieval coverture in the rural context, arguing that it is inadequate in explaining gender relationships and female subordination in the medieval countryside.[41] Beyond England too, historians have noted the capacity of married women to engage in legal action, adding various caveats to theoretical legal constraints. In Scottish towns, as Elizabeth Ewan has argued, though the *Laws of the Burghs* stated that men could answer for their wives, the law did not say that men *must* represent their wives.[42] Like Matthew Stevens on London, Cathryn Spence has demonstrated the prominence of married women in early modern Scottish burgh courts, their presence being indicative of their important economic roles.[43] In Ruthin, in the Welsh marcher lordship of Dyffryn Clywd, Stevens has noted the presence of married women in court and in presentments, including many who did not appear in conjunction with their husbands.[44] In Caernarfon too, married women appear in the medieval borough court rolls, sometimes without their husbands, though mostly in relation to interpersonal violence.[45]

Others have drawn different conclusions about the legal status of women according to marital status, particularly in relation to their economic capabilities. Craig Muldrew's study of Great Yarmouth's borough court in the seventeenth century has highlighted the restrictions on women's litigation, with married women unable to sue or be sued in their own names. Unlike the Scottish burghs, this obscured their involvement in networks of credit and debt.[46] Chris Briggs' analysis of women's debt litigation in medieval manorial courts has also emphasised the limitations on married women's legal action. Though acknowledging that the principles of coverture 'did not completely prevent married women's practical experience of credit matters', wives are nevertheless shown to have rarely been involved in manorial debt litigation.[47] Taken together, these studies highlight flexibility in the determination of women's legal status, particularly at the local level, and make it clear that some women exercised more legal agency than common law doctrine or legal theory would suggest. Yet, as one volume on married women and the law acknowledges, there is much work still to be done in continuing to challenge the old view that women, particularly married women, were hidden from view in legal materials.[48] This book aims to make a significant dent in this task within the context of town courts.

Though they operated according to their own customs, English borough courts existed within the broader culture of the common law, which included the influence of the culture of coverture. Sara Butler has argued that coverture was so entrenched in the laws of England 'that courts freed from the constraints of this legal fiction still sometimes imposed it'.[49] But the ways in which coverture was interpreted and imposed were not consistent. As this study will show, the customs of each town developed in unique ways, varying from place to place, over time and according to different situations, and this was reflected in ideas about women's status at court and within urban society.[50] One specific variation in the customs relating to women's legal status was the existence of *femme sole* status, which has been the focus of some historiographical attention. These customs allowed married women who registered as *femmes sole* to trade and appear in court as though single, rather than the typical *femme covert* status of married women.[51] The potential power of this custom to tip the usual rules of coverture and wives' lack of independence on their head has led to it being overemphasised as one of the few ways in which married women could exercise independence: the 'go-to' exception to married women's powerlessness. But *femme sole* customs were rarely adopted, and most towns did not offer this status to married women – though, as we will see, this did not mean that there were no other options for women to negotiate trade and justice within their communities. The court rolls reveal marital partnership, cooperation, support and ties of honour, deepening our understanding of women's commercial and legal lives beyond basic notions of husbands' authority that dominate legal theory and doctrine. By continuing to examine the legal actions of real women – married and not married – across a range of legal actions, this book therefore makes a direct contribution to the discussion on the nature of coverture in the medieval period, and to our understanding of women's agency within the legal systems that underpinned much of their everyday lives.

While the historiography may be increasingly recognising women's legal agency and their possibilities for action, particularly in the case of married women, this does not disguise or negate the fact that women were subordinate subjects under the multiple jurisdictions of medieval England. In the borough courts, at the lowest level of the law, women never accounted for more than around a fifth of litigants.[52] Judith Bennett has highlighted the disadvantages women faced before their local courts, with legal practice marking women as 'second-rank constituents' in almost every aspect of civil litigation.[53] Chris Briggs has argued that women's limited involvement in manorial litigation indicates 'little empowerment among women'.[54] The statistical evidence for women's litigation certainly represents their marginal status in the legal management of credit ties, but the extent to which litigation can be used as a measure of female empowerment is rather more tenuous, as Chapter 2 will discuss.

Though the numbers of women in court may be low in comparison to men, this book focuses on the nature of women's legal actions and the roles they played in litigation and other cases, rather than concentrating simply on statistics and comparisons with the actions of men. A purely quantitative analysis might lead the legal actions of women to be disregarded as exceptional without questioning why their numbers were so low, and masking many of the more subtle and complex aspects of women's experiences of the law. A wholly quantitative approach also serves to wipe away the stories and experiences of those women who *did* engage with the law, as well as limiting our capacity to understand why other women did not do so. As Garthine Walker has argued, quantification of male and female presence in legal records repeatedly shows us that women were a minority group within these records, particularly as those prosecuted for crime or wrongdoing, and therefore leads to women being counted and subsequently discounted.[55] Measuring women against men in this way, particularly in statistical terms, will always serve to emphasise gender difference over what women actually did, and the ways in which their behaviour was understood by various legal systems. The highlighting of gender difference has been a particularly prominent feature of studies that consider women's involvement in crime, underscoring notions of legal action being something which, on the whole, did not involve women. Karen Jones' study of petty crime in Kent draws on a range of local jurisdictions in presenting a case for distinctly gendered patterns of virtue, (mis)conduct and criminal activity and the resultant ways that men and women were drawn into local law courts, the law serving to propagate negative images of women.[56] Louise Wilkinson's analysis of women's involvement in crime in Lincolnshire also emphasises gendered patterns of violence, with women's criminal behaviour rarely featuring in the Lincolnshire Eyre records of the thirteenth century.[57]

While quantification and consideration of gender difference is important and illustrative of some broad trends, there is more that can be said by paying attention to the presence of those women who *did* appear in borough court litigation and in the presentment of other offences, and the context within which these appearances occurred. We are able to recover important details of women's actions or misbehaviours and how these brought women into contact with the law, serving to create a better understanding of the functioning of legal practice as a whole.[58] This evidence demonstrates the ways that women were integrated into the legal systems of their local communities, claiming a legal voice and being held to account for their actions, rather than experiencing the law in distinctly female ways, or being classified as a passive minority or 'other' group over whom the law governed.

Women and urban justice

Townswomen came into contact with the law in various ways, through individual and joint litigation and the regulation and punishment of behaviour by officials. These legal actions determine the structure of this book. This involves drawing on both civil litigation and the records of misconduct, making it possible to examine and compare a wide range of women's legal action within and across urban communities and identifying the role that law played in different aspects of women's lives. However, before turning to the legal records in detail, some background is required in order to understand the details and significance of women's various legal actions. Chapter 1 therefore sets out the urban context and legal framework that underpinned both the specific courts studied here and urban jurisdictions in general, discussing the towns, the functioning of their courts and the nature of their records. It also discusses the methodology for this study and the way that the court records have been used to provide both quantitative data (via sampling) and qualitative examples that provide insight into individuals' experiences of the law.

Turning to the records of law in practice, Chapter 2 examines women's involvement in commercial litigation. Pleas of debt and detinue and disputes over broken contracts (and either the withholding of payment or of goods) provide an insight into women's work and trading relationships and reveal their ability to take action or be held to account when the obligations underpinning these relationships were not fulfilled. Though this litigation was a major component of court business across all three towns, women's involvement in these complaints was not consistent. The ability of married women to litigate over debt and detinue was considerable in some places, marking a certain malleability in the nature of coverture. However, other towns enforced a strict understanding of coverture that prevented women from taking part in this litigation. These patterns also changed over time. Chapter 3 builds on this analysis of the intersection of women's commercial life and their legal status to examine when and in what ways they were drawn into local regulatory mechanisms concerning weights and measures, the price and quality of goods and other marketing regulations. These presentments, made by local officials, represented a different form of legal action whereby individuals were held accountable for their behaviour through the simple listing of their names and issuing of fines. Together, these two chapters document the different ways in which women both used the law and were subject to its controls in the governing of local commercial activity and trading relationships.

In Chapter 4 the focus shifts to women's misbehaviour and the trespass litigation that arose from wrongdoing and the breakdown of interpersonal relationships. Pleas of trespass encompassed a wide range of misbehaviour, including physical and verbal assault, theft and damage to property. The chapter examines the nature of this misconduct, with women's involvement in a wide range of misbehaviour, as both perpetrators and victims, transcending gendered patterns of honour and wrongdoing. It also explores how the use of litigation was an important part of the process of restoring damaged reputations and publicising the misdemeanours of others. Chapter 5 takes an alternative perspective on women's misbehaviour, using the records of urban policing to recover women's wrongdoing in relation to affray, bloodshed and moral offences such as prostitution. In these presentments made by local officials, the disruptive use of women's voices also becomes more visible, in line with other studies of women's misbehaviour.[59]

Across the various chapters, this study of law and life in three English towns extends our understanding of the 'legal lives' of medieval townswomen in a number of ways. The detailed analysis of a range of legal actions highlights the extent and range of women's experiences of the law, despite the restrictions it placed upon them. This broad focus suggests that women's engagement with the law was greater than often assumed, being a regular feature of urban women's lives rather than an exceptional event or experience. The focus on women in provincial towns, and the comparison between different places, brings the examination of local custom and practice to the fore, revealing that no one place can be understood as 'typical' in defining women's experiences of the law. Instead, examination of the local context must be central to our evaluation of women's negotiation of justice, highlighting both continuities and difference. Following many other recent studies, it also sheds new light on the role that marriage and coverture played in defining the status of urban women, revealing differences across jurisdictions and various legal actions that suggests multiple possibilities beyond the binary frameworks of coverture and *femme sole* status. These factors, when combined, mean that no one woman typified 'the female litigant', emphasising the importance of paying attention to the circumstances and experiences of individual women. Borough courts could offer women considerable legal agency, though differences in local legal custom resulted in variations in the ways in which women's litigation and legal status was understood and performed in local courts.

Notes

1 Nottinghamshire Archives (hereafter NA), CA1259 rots 17d, 20. Both complaints follow common practice whereby high sums of damages were claimed but never awarded by the court.
2 Patricia Turning has also shown that a wide spectrum of people negotiated justice in the courtrooms of medieval Toulouse. See Turning, *Municipal Officials, Their Public, and the Negotiation of Justice in Medieval Languedoc* (Leiden: Brill, 2013), p. 11.
3 The Poll Tax of 1377 covered all adults over the age of 14 who were not paupers (though various issues of tax avoidance that mean this figure should only be taken as a rough indication of the actual eligible population). There were 1,477 taxpayers for Nottingham in 1377 and 469 different individuals can be identified from the borough court rolls of 1375–6; 326 of 409 pleas concerned debt or detinue. For Poll Tax figures, see Alan Dyer, 'Ranking of towns by taxpaying population: the 1377 poll tax', in D.M. Palliser (ed.), *Cambridge Urban History of Britain*, vol. 1 (Cambridge: Cambridge University Press, 2000), p. 758.
4 On choice of legal forums, see Daniel Klerman, 'Jurisdictional competition and the evolution of the common law: an hypothesis', in Anthony Musson (ed.), *Boundaries of the Law: Geography, Gender and Jurisdiction in Medieval and Early Modern Europe* (Aldershot: Ashgate, 2005), p. 149.
5 NA CA1279 rot. 12; Hampshire Record Office (hereafter HRO) W/D1/37 rot. 3d; HRO W/D1/37 rot. 8d. Cheshire Archives and Local Studies (hereafter CALS) ZSR 21 rot. 7d.
6 M.T. Clanchy, *From Memory to Written Record: England 1066–1307* (London: Edward Arnold, 1979), pp. 258–265; J.L. Bolton, *Money in the Medieval English Economy: 973–1489* (Manchester: Manchester University Press, 2012), pp. 199–202.
7 James Davis, *Medieval Market Morality* (Cambridge: Cambridge University Press, 2011), p. 348.
8 Laura Gowing has argued that the telling of 'stories' by women in legal actions gave them 'both a formal cultural agency – a time in which their words were written down – and a way of putting themselves, as actors, at centre stage'. Gowing, *Domestic Dangers: Women, Words and Sex in Early Modern London* (Oxford: Clarendon Press, 1996) p. 234.
9 For more on the methodology and approach to court records used in this study, see Chapter 1.
10 John Hatcher and Mark Bailey, *Modelling the Middle Ages: the History and Theory of England's Economic Development* (Oxford: Oxford University Press, 2001), pp. 26–30; Richard Goddard, *Credit and Trade in Later Medieval England, 1353–1532* (London: Palgrave, 2016), pp. 97–129; Anthony Musson, *Medieval Law in Context: The Growth of Legal Consciousness from the Magna Carta to the Peasants' Revolt* (Manchester: Manchester University Press, 2001), pp. 84–120.
11 For example, Maryanne Kowaleski, 'Women's work in a market town: Exeter in the late fourteenth century', in Barbara A. Hanawalt (ed.), *Women and Work in Preindustrial Europe* (Bloomington: Indiana University Press, 1986), pp. 145–164; Diane Hutton, 'Women in fourteenth-century Shrewsbury', in Lindsey Charles and Lorna Duffin (eds), *Women and Work in Pre-Industrial England* (London: Croom Helm, 1985), pp. 83–99; Marjorie Keniston McIntosh, *Working Women in English*

Society, 1300-1620 (Cambridge: Cambridge University Press, 2005); P.J.P. Goldberg, *Women, Work and Life Cycle in a Medieval Economy: Women in York and Yorkshire c.1300-1520* (Oxford: Clarendon Press, 1992); Caroline M. Barron, 'The 'golden age' of women in medieval London', *Reading Medieval Studies*, 15 (1989), 35-58; Matthew Frank Stevens, 'London women, the courts and the 'golden age': a quantitative analysis of female litigants in the fourteenth and fifteenth centuries', *The London Journal*, 37 (2012), 67-88; Louise J. Wilkinson, *Women in Thirteenth-Century Lincolnshire* (Woodbridge: Boydell and Brewer, 2007), pp. 92-115.

12 On debt litigation, see Chris Briggs, 'Empowered or marginalized? Rural women and credit in later thirteenth- and fourteenth-century England', *Continuity and Change*, 19 (2004), 13-43; Matthew Frank Stevens, 'London's married women, debt litigation and coverture in the court of Common Pleas', in Cordelia Beattie and Matthew Frank Stevens (eds), *Married Women and the Law in Premodern Northwest Europe* (Woodbridge: Boydell and Brewer, 2013), pp. 115-132.

13 Elizabeth Ewan's work on Scottish urban women and law includes 'Scottish Portias: women in the courts in mediaeval Scottish towns', *Journal of the Canadian Historical Association*, 3 (1992), 27-43; 'Divers injurious words': defamation and gender in late medieval Scotland', in R.A. McDonald (ed.), *History, Literature and Music in Medieval Scotland* (Toronto: University of Toronto Press, 2002), pp. 63-86; 'Disorderly damsels? women and interpersonal violence in pre-Reformation Scotland', *Scottish Historical Review*, 89 (2010), 153-171.

14 These general characteristics are described in a number of studies of women's work: see, for example, McIntosh, *Working Women in English Society*, p. 4. See also Hutton, 'Women in fourteenth-century Shrewsbury' pp. 83-99; Kay E. Lacy, 'Women and work in fourteenth and fifteenth century London' in Charles and Duffin (eds), *Women and Work*, pp. 24-82; Rodney Hilton, 'Women traders in medieval England' in Hilton, *Class Conflict and the Crisis of Feudalism* (London: Verso, revised edn, 1990), pp. 132-142; Peter Fleming, *Women in Late Medieval Bristol*, Bristol Branch of the Historical Association Local History Pamphlets, 103 (2001).

15 Kowaleski, 'Women's work in a market town', p. 148.

16 Barron, 'Golden age', 40-41.

17 Goldberg, *Women, Work, and Life Cycle*, pp. 335-7.

18 Judith M. Bennett, *History Matters: Patriarchy and the Challenge of Feminism* (Manchester: Manchester University Press, 2006), pp. 61-62.

19 Stevens, 'London's married women', pp. 73, 80.

20 Frederick Pollock and Frederic William Maitland, *The History of English Law before the time of Edward I*, vol. 1 (Cambridge: Cambridge University Press, 1895), p. 482.

21 Eileen Power, *Medieval Women*, ed. Michael M. Postan (Cambridge: Cambridge University Press, 1975) p. 2.

22 Power described how a married woman's rights 'slipped out of her hands' for the duration of the marriage. *Medieval Women*, p. 30. See also Pollock and Maitland, *English Law*, vol. 2, p. 405; William Blackstone, *Commentaries on the Laws of England*, book 1, chapter 15 (Oxford: Clarendon Press, 1765-9), pp. 430-433.

23 Chris Wickham, *Courts and Conflict in Twelfth-century Tuscany* (Oxford: Oxford University Press, 2003), p. 5.

24 On the continuities of coverture, see Tim Stretton and Krista Kesselring 'Introduction: coverture and continuity' in Stretton and Kesselring (eds), *Married Women and the Law: Coverture in the Common Law World* (London: McGill-Queen's University Press, 2013), pp. 3–23.
25 Stretton and Kesselring, 'Coverture and continuity', pp. 7–8.
26 On medieval classificatory systems, see Cordelia Beattie, *Medieval Single Women: The Politics of Social Classification in Late Medieval England* (Oxford: Oxford University, 2007), pp. 1–12, 15–24.
27 *Bracton on the Laws and Customs of England*, trans. Samuel E. Thorne, vol. 4 (Cambridge, MA: Belknap Press, 1977), p. 287 (hereafter Bracton). On the writing of the treatises see J.L. Barton, 'The mystery of Bracton', *The Journal of Legal History*, 14 (1993), 1–142.
28 Bracton, vol. 2, p. 353.
29 Sue Sheridan Walker (ed.), *Wife and Widow in Medieval England* (Ann Arbor: University of Michigan Press, 1993), p. 4.
30 McIntosh, *Working Women*, pp. 95–96.
31 Pollock and Maitland, *English Law*, vol. 2, pp. 405–406.
32 For example, Sara M. Butler, 'Discourse on the nature of coverture in the later medieval courtroom', in Stretton and Kesselring (eds), *Married Women and the Law*, pp. 39–40. See also Cordelia Beattie, 'Married women, contracts and coverture in late medieval England', in Beattie and Stevens (eds), *Married Women and the Law*, pp. 133–154; Stevens, 'London's married women', pp. 115–132. On early modern women, see Cathryn Spence, '"For his interest"? Women, debt and coverture in early modern Scotland', in Beattie and Stevens (eds), *Married Women and the Law*, pp. 173–190; Joanne Bailey, 'Favoured or oppressed? Married women, property and "coverture" in England, 1660–1800', *Continuity and Change*, 17 (2002), 351–371; Amy Louise Erickson, 'Coverture and capitalism', *History Workshop Journal*, 59 (2005), 116; Margot Finn, 'Women, consumption and coverture in England, c.1760–1860', *The Historical Journal*, 29 (1996), 703–722.
33 Tim Stretton, 'Coverture and unity of persons in Blackstone's Commentaries' in Wilfred Prest (ed.), *Blackstone and his Commentaries: Biography, Law, History* (Oxford: Hart, 2009), pp. 112, 115; Stretton, 'The legal identity of married women in England and Europe 1500–1700' in Andreas Bauer and Karl H.L. Welker (eds) *Europa und seine Regionen: 2000 Jahre Rechtsgeschichte* (Cologne: Böhlau, 2006), p. 312.
34 Butler, 'Discourse on the nature of coverture', pp. 30–32.
35 Stretton and Kesselring, 'Coverture and continuity', p. 8.
36 These volumes are Beattie and Stevens (eds), *Married Women and the Law*; Bronach Kane and Fiona Williamson (eds), *Women, Agency and the Law, 1300–1700* (London: Pickering and Chatto, 2013); and Stretton and Kesselring (eds), *Married Women and the Law*.
37 Kane and Williamson, 'Introduction' in Kane and Williamson (eds), *Women, Agency and the Law*, p. 7.
38 Marie A. Kelleher, 'Later medieval law in community context', in Judith M. Bennett and Ruth Mazo Karras (eds), *The Oxford Handbook of Women and Gender in Medieval Europe* (Oxford: Oxford University Press, 2013), p. 144.

39 Stevens, 'London's married women', p. 131. Barbara Hanawalt has also identified the presence of married couples pleading in London's Mayor's Court. Hanawalt, *The Wealth of Wives: Women, Law, and Economy in Late Medieval London* (Oxford: Oxford University Press, 2007), p. 171.
40 Beattie, 'Married women, contracts and coverture', pp. 133–154. See also Butler 'Discourse on the nature of coverture', pp. 24–44.
41 Miriam Müller, 'Peasant women, agency and status in mid-thirteenth- to late fourteenth-century England: some reconsiderations', in Beattie and Stevens (eds), *Married Women and the Law*, pp. 91–113.
42 Ewan, 'Scottish Portias', 29.
43 Cathryn Spence, *Women, Credit, and Debt in Early Modern Scotland* (Manchester: Manchester University Press, 2016), p. 53.
44 Matthew Frank Stevens, *Urban Assimilation in Post-Conquest Wales: Ethnicity, Gender and Economy in Ruthin, 1282–1350* (Cardiff: University of Wales Press, 2010), p. 127.
45 Deborah Youngs, 'The townswomen of Wales: singlewomen, work and service, c.1300–1550' in Helen Fulton (ed.), *Urban Culture in Medieval Wales* (Cardiff: University of Wales Press, 2012), p. 165.
46 Craig Muldrew, 'A mutual assent of her mind? Women, debt, litigation and contract in early modern England' *History Workshop Journal*, 55 (2003), 54–57.
47 Chris Briggs, 'Empowered or marginalized? Rural women and credit in later thirteenth- and fourteenth-century England', *Continuity and Change*, 19 (2004), 21–25.
48 Beattie and Stevens, 'Uncovering married women', in Beattie and Stevens (eds), *Married Women and the Law*, p. 10.
49 Sara M. Butler, *Divorce in Medieval England: From One to Two Persons in Law* (Abingdon: Routledge, 2013), p. 12.
50 Mary Bateson wrote that 'the borough customs pursue an erratic, unsteady course, and the variations can be ascribed to no difference of race, or even to differences of principle carefully thought out by the legislators. Much may have turned on the character and personal experience of the officer of the court who had most legal knowledge at the time when borough customs had to be interpreted in a case of practical difficulty.' Mary Bateson (ed.), *Borough Customs*, vol. 2 (Selden Society, Vol. 21, London, 1906), p. c. See also Tim Stretton, *Women Waging Law in Elizabethan England* (Cambridge: Cambridge University Press, 1998), p. 176.
51 Stretton, *Women Waging Law*, p. 30; Marjorie Keniston McIntosh, 'The benefits and drawbacks of *femme sole* status in England, 1300–1630', *Journal of British Studies*, 44 (2005), 410–438.
52 For more on the proportions of female litigants, see the figures in Chapters 2 and 4.
53 Judith M. Bennett, *Women in the Medieval English Countryside: Gender and Household in Brigstock Before the Plague* (Oxford: Oxford University Press, 1987), pp. 27–28.
54 Briggs, 'Rural women and credit', 13–43.
55 Garthine Walker, *Crime, Gender and Social Order in Early Modern England* (Cambridge: Cambridge University Press, 2003), p. 4.

56 Karen Jones, *Gender and Petty Crime in Late Medieval England: The Local Courts in Kent, 1460–1560* (Woodbridge: Boydell and Brewer, 2006). Sandy Bardsley has also noted the gendering of men's and women's speech as interpreted by church and local courts in the late medieval period, a 'legal devaluation' of women's speech as part of the negative construction of women's voices. Bardsley, *Venomous Tongues: Speech and Gender in Late Medieval England* (Philadelphia: University of Pennsylvania Press, 2006), pp. 69–70.

57 Wilkinson, *Women in Thirteenth-Century Lincolnshire*, pp. 160–161, 164.

58 Alex Shepard has similarly highlighted the need to look at women's commercial activities in order to understand the early modern economy, not just comparing women to men within male-centric models or emphasising the extent to which women were handicapped by patriarchal structures and practices. This approach can apply to the study of women's legal actions too. See Shepard, 'Crediting women in the early modern English economy', *History Workshop Journal*, 79 (2015), 1–24.

59 Notably Bardsley, *Venomous Tongues*.

1

Women, town courts and customary law in context

When medieval women engaged in legal action, they did so through a system that was characterised by the existence of multiple overlapping and competing jurisdictions. The late middle ages was a period of increasing legal consciousness and litigiousness, which saw women frequently drawn into litigation or facing the punishment of local regulatory systems. The records created by these systems are central to our understanding of urban women's interaction with the law, and their day-to-day experiences more broadly. It is through the records of town courts that we are able to identify women as traders and consumers, their role in crafts and business, aspects of their interpersonal relationships, claims over property and their illegal activities. But despite this, town courts are often only discussed in passing in histories of medieval law, categorised as 'borough courts' among lists of various non-royal courts, with little attention paid to how they operated in practice. Though they were certainly not the most powerful courts in England, they are significant for their broad jurisdiction and the fact that they may have offered the most frequent interaction with the law for many, if not a majority, of the residents of England's towns. They dealt with disputes and issues that arose from everyday life and trade, rather than exceptional acts of crime or high-value financial disputes. It is this 'ordinariness' that makes these courts notable. Despite a wealth of records, urban court records remain relatively underused, and there is no existing overview of the practical nature of these courts and their records, nor the actions of women within urban justice in medieval England.[1] This chapter therefore serves as an essential introduction both to town courts and to the specific places that are the focus of this study. It surveys and describes the towns and courts that lie at the heart of this book, the nature of the legal process, and the records that this created, before setting out the way that these records have been approached in compiling this study, thereby establishing the context within which urban women accessed and engaged with the legal system.

Towns and courts

This study intentionally focuses on 'middling' status late medieval English towns. Nottingham, Chester and Winchester sat somewhere in the middle of the country's urban hierarchy, smaller in population and of lesser political and economic stature than large cities such as London, Bristol, Norwich and York, but more developed and urbanised than the hundreds of small towns that bridged the gap between urban and rural society. The focus is therefore on the experiences of those women and men who lived at the more 'ordinary' level of the medieval urban experience, though of course there were variations in social status and wealth within each place. Each town had a local court (or courts) that met regularly and dealt with a range of litigation, complaints and offences arising from the interactions, rhythms and disturbances of urban life. The towns were governed by a group of officials selected from among the leading merchants of each town and often drawn from networks of families, the men of which held various offices over multiple generations. The right to elect these officials was usually granted via a town's charter and was a key component of self-governance that made towns islands of limited independence from the crown, in return for the payment of an annual fee. Urban officials – mayors, bailiffs or sheriffs – presided over the courts of their towns, while lesser officials were responsible for administrative jobs such as collecting the payments made to the courts (affeerers). In the court rolls of each town, we find complaints about unpaid debts, withheld goods, acts of violence and misbehaviour, presentments for common nuisances and disturbances and broken trading regulations. These seemingly mundane issues illuminate the lives and relationships of thousands of individuals of all statuses, both men and women. Despite this, the court rolls have received limited attention from historians, bar a handful of antiquarian works and short studies focusing on individual aspects of the legal experience.[2]

Each of the three towns held a unique status within medieval England, and they were also geographically spread across the south, north-west and midland areas of the country, as Map 1 illustrates. All three towns discussed here were provincial centres with markets, fairs and trade links with their hinterlands. Nottingham and Chester had populations of around 3,000–4,000 before the Black Death, while Winchester was larger at around 6,000.[3] Winchester ranked as the 14th wealthiest town according to the Lay Subsidy of 1334, and was also 14th by population under the 1377 Poll Tax.[4] It was the ancient capital of England, held directly for the king. However, the close connection between Winchester and the king's court lapsed during the latter part of Henry I's reign, and it was no longer a royal capital by the reign of Stephen.[5] As part of this decline from royal capital to provincial cathedral city, Winchester gradually came to be overtaken in wealth by other towns in the region such as Southampton, though proximity to London and the south coast meant that it maintained important political and trading connections.[6] These international links are also indicated through the appearance of numerous French and Flemish individuals in the city's court rolls.

Chester was also a site of administrative importance throughout the later medieval period. It was the centre of the county Palatine held by the earls of Chester, meaning that the county and city was excluded from parliamentary taxes after 1290, making comparison of population and wealth difficult. However, it has been suggested that Chester was perhaps 33rd largest in population size around the time of the 1377 Poll Tax.[7] As the centre of the Palatinate, Chester has been termed a 'mini-Westminster', with its own exchequer, law courts and a large number of officials.[8] It was also an important military base due to its proximity to North Wales and links to Ireland. The geographical setting of the city and its links beyond England are evident in the identities of some of those who appeared in the court rolls, where we regularly find names indicating Irish or Welsh roots. Chester was also somewhat unique in its region as the only centre to develop many of the characteristics of the large towns found throughout the north-east, midlands and south of England. Though the county was somewhat politically separate from the rest of England, the city itself had considerable independence in local government. In 1300, the citizens of Chester obtained the fee farm of the city from the earl of Chester for £100, in much the same way as other towns were farmed from the crown.[9] The governance of the city therefore echoed the administration of other medieval towns, despite the existence of the Palatinate.

Nottingham was perhaps a more 'ordinary' provincial centre. It was the 25th wealthiest town in England in 1334, and ranked 29th in terms of population under the 1377 Poll Tax.[10] After the Norman Conquest it consisted of two ancient boroughs, French (Norman) and English (Anglo-Saxon), though by the fourteenth century this division had very little impact on everyday town life and governance.[11] It was a central trading place within the midlands and was well connected to other important towns and Danelaw boroughs of Derby, Leicester, Newark and Lincoln. The royal castle was used as a residence by the king on visits to the area, and it was the site of a number of Parliaments. During the Wars of the Roses, the castle was an important military stronghold, though the town lacked the unique status of Winchester and Chester. All three towns therefore shared common features in the nature of their urban status (and, as we will see, in the structures of local justice), while possessing unique features arising from their distinct geographical and political contexts. They were large, important towns within their local areas, though less important on the national scale, and were thus characterised by ranging social structures and a diverse collection of occupations. Individuals interacted regularly at markets, fairs, shops and through the institutions of urban government – including courts.

Town courts lay at the heart of urban life, both physically and symbolically. They met in guildhalls or other civic buildings that were located at the centre of their towns, close to markets and shops, representing the close ties between urban government, law and trade. The rights of towns and their burgesses concerning justice were often enshrined in borough charters, setting out the privileges of towns and the right to collect the profits of justice. All courts were presided over by the town's leading officials, such as mayors, bailiffs or sheriffs, and met regularly, sometimes multiple times per week. They were therefore the most frequent, accessible site of legal recourse for most townspeople. These courts came into their own during the late medieval period. Most of the earliest surviving records stem from around the late thirteenth century, with the earliest English borough court rolls, such as those of Ipswich, surviving from the 1250s.[12]

Town courts provided a local, accessible and efficient forum for dispute resolution in accordance with medieval ideals of justice, governing acceptable behaviour and offering reconciliation to conflicting parties.[13] They were forums for both litigation between residents as well as presentments concerning local policing and regulation. Both forms of law involved numerous women of all statuses and life cycle stages, allowing an essential insight into the nature of women's experiences of the law within the urban community. Litigation was dealt with by courts often classified as borough courts (though not all towns were boroughs). They heard complaints which can be broadly categorised as either commercial (debt, detinue, covenant) or interpersonal (trespass, or trespass and bloodshed), which together spanned a wide range of interactions and transactions. These courts met frequently, usually on fixed days of the week (Wednesdays fortnightly in Nottingham) or on multiple days each week (Mondays, Wednesdays and Fridays in Winchester). The towns' charters and customs do not explicitly state whether each court was for the sole use of burgesses, though various statements regarding the rights of foreigners (those from outside the town) or aliens (from other countries) suggest that these were primarily courts for residents, if not specifically burgesses. Pleas arose from actions or behaviours that departed from expected codes of behaviour and obligations, and they allowed litigants to publicly express their discontent and perceived harm in the process of renegotiating damaged social and commercial ties. Those who were the subject of these complaints could acknowledge the allegations against them, or contest them and face the judgement of a jury. The majority were pleas of debt and trespass, and other suits related to land and covenants. Courts also enrolled the transfer of urban landholding rights into their official records.

Local officials also had rights over the policing and regulation of trade, behaviour and the urban environment. These can be defined as rights of leet jurisdiction under which policing and enforcement rights of the crown were devolved to local officials or lords via courts that met a few times each year. This policing usually took the form of presentments made by local jurors or tithingmen (in Nottingham they were called decennaries), whereby offences were listed noting the names of the individuals responsible and the fines issued. These were offences against the town itself – and by extension the crown – and there was usually no means for offenders to respond to or deny allegations. In exercising this jurisdiction, local officials were able to punish wrongful actions as agents of the crown.[14] The records of these presentments, concerning affrays, illegal and immoral activity, nuisances and trading offences, are generally more patchy than the correlating records of litigation, in part due to the fact that these offences were presented only periodically each year.

The evolution of borough courts was part of the broader development of the English legal system, manifesting what Anthony Musson has described as a growth in legal consciousness both among the nascent legal professions and in 'the reserves of knowledge and thought of those who experienced the law and legal institutions in everyday life'.[15] Court attendance enhanced knowledge of legal practice, and those awaiting dispute resolution might also have learned from conversations with others, observing other suits or calling on the advice of more experienced members of the community.[16] For men who acted in minor official roles, such as jurors or tithingmen, this would also have brought additional legal knowledge and experience. The numbers of litigants were high, as were the number of complaints brought at each court session. Women's actions in town courts must be considered in the context of this broader legal system. Borough courts were just one part of a complex and often overlapping court system that was relatively well-established in England by the late middle ages, offering potential litigants 'a number of different ways of skinning the cat'.[17] Though some actions were reserved for particular types of jurisdiction, the various paths that a complaint could take offered a degree of choice over whether, how and where to litigate.[18] Similarly, offences against the king's peace were also dealt with in different arenas depending on their severity and where they occurred. A relatively minor scuffle in an alleyway might be dealt with as affray and fined within a town's leet court, while a more serious altercation involving weapons, bloodshed and robbery might be classed as a felony and prosecuted in the king's courts.

While this abundance of legal action might be interpreted as evidence of a society characterised by conflict, it is important to highlight that the majority of legal action in towns was the result of minor civil complaints between neighbours rather than being a culmination of great strife and disorder. Furthermore, much of this business related to commercial agreements and debt, though of course there were also complaints of theft and violence. Litigation and legal presentments were therefore an integral means by which the social and economic relations of urban society were structured, negotiated and restored. This can present a large volume and variety of material; indeed Karen Jones commented over a decade ago that the records of civil pleas 'survive in such daunting quantity that to make much use of them would be quite impracticable'.[19] However, the high volume of pleas and vast quantity of the surviving records attest to the wide remit of urban justice and the numbers of individuals brought into it, strengthening the case for the common nature of this legal experience and highlighting the value of these records for the study of ordinary urban women, and indeed all urban residents.

There were many commonalities shared by all towns and their courts, including those that are the subject of this study. Yet each town existed in its own unique context, and the various courts operated according to specifically local practices and customs. Custom is often conceptualised as having existed 'since time immemorial', though this did not mean that it was fixed or unchanging; customary usages could alter as circumstances changed.[20] Custom varied from one borough to another, and these variations could have a marked impact on the economic and legal status of women. It has been suggested that custom afforded women more rights than the common law in relation to property and inheritance practices, though we should also consider local custom to include the more 'everyday' procedures of dispute resolution and enforcement of local regulations.[21] For women, these customs could determine if and how they were able to access the law.

Differences in practices and experiences of the law (for women and, to some extent, for men too) were not just down to local customary variations, but also regional or national differences between the legal systems that existed within medieval Britain. Though the focus here is on England, it is worth spending some time sketching out some of the key comparisons with other regions of Britain to better allow us to compile a picture of different regions, nations and their records. The later unions of England with Wales and Scotland, and the dominance of England within the historiography of medieval Britain, can lead us to forget that these areas existed under different legal and political systems during the middle ages, with varying levels of overlap with English common law and its key doctrines that influenced the position of women, such as coverture. Just as a single town and its legal system should not be read as representative of the 'national' English picture, the customs and practices of English law in the middle ages were not those of Britain in its entirety.

This is not to say that there was no permeation or export of English law across borders. In Wales, the post-conquest import of English common law after 1284 existed alongside a patchwork of marcher lordships, each with their own laws and customs that were made up of differing combinations of English and Welsh legal traditions. This resulted in notable differences in the legal system in neighbouring regions or even manors. For individuals, much of this rested on the different legal rights and status of those deemed ethnically Welsh or English, set out in various statutes and ordinances after the English conquest. This meant that the Welsh often had to adhere to different legal procedures and were barred from particular activities or obtaining positions of status, such as burgess, or from office holding in both English-ruled and marcher towns.[22] Alongside this racial differentiation, aspects of Welsh law that specifically pertained to women, such as the virginity fine of amobr, were retained in some areas until the union with England. This represented a more severe tax on women's sexual activity than the equivalent English fee (leyrwite), evidenced by the fact that many women and their male guardians tried to claim English status to avoid paying.[23] The import of English law after the conquest to English-ruled lands in the former principality of Wales had a significant and seemingly positive impact upon the rights of women who were, for the first time, able to hold land and claim their dower rights in areas where land was held by English tenure.[24] The impact of English law in both crown conquered and marcher Wales was also evident in the clear influence of the doctrine of coverture under various jurisdictions, including courts in urban areas, meaning that married women could not bring pleas independently of their husbands. However, as was true elsewhere, there were sometimes significant deviations from this rule.[25] These intersections of gender, ethnicity and place combined to create a complicated puzzle of legal status for women living in Wales, which was regularly claimed and contested, as the extant records reveal.[26]

In Scotland, the legal system evolved from many of the same influences as that of England, but has remained separate from the middle ages to today, and this separation meant that any differences between the rights and status of Scots and English were not enshrined in law in the way that they were in Wales. A key difference between Scots and English law lay in relation to coverture and the status of married women. The fact that Scottish women did not take their husbands' surnames upon marriage reflects the fact that they were not considered to be under coverture during marriage in the same way that English women were, with the position of married women instead being subject to *jus mariti*, a concept derived from Roman law that granted husbands the right to administer their wives' property, rather than the 'covering' of legal personhood.[27] Elizabeth Ewan's study of women in Scottish town courts found that, despite the theoretical constraints on women's legal actions, they 'were able to use the law for their own advantage ... [and] if they wished, to make use of it without male assistance'.[28] Women's experiences of the law were, therefore, variable according to different regions and political-legal systems that existed side by side, contextualised by the growing influence of English common law. This complex picture means that it is not possible, or indeed useful, to rank whether English, Welsh or Scots law was 'better' for women, the puzzle instead only further highlighting the need to examine the specific circumstances and evidence for each locality.

Jurisdictions, procedure and records

The intrinsically local nature of urban justice and custom is encapsulated in the unique names given to each court, its jurisdiction and its working patterns. Like manorial courts, each constituted its own localised legal system catering for its own clients.[29] The largest volume and best surviving records are from Nottingham, where litigation was heard in a court called the borough court or town court, and presentments concerning trade and misbehaviour came under the separate jurisdiction of the Mayor's Court. The borough court met fortnightly on Wednesdays and was presided over by the town's two bailiffs. Court rolls were titled '*Curia ville Notyngham*', '*Placita curia Notyngham*' or later '*Placita curia Burgensis Notyngham*', so the commonly used title of the 'borough court' is in fact one that was only used or applied later. It met in the Common Hall (later called the Guild Hall) next to the weekday cross, the site of the town's daily market. The borough court has been described as a local version of the central courts at Westminster, and the town's rights relating to law and justice were laid out in various borough charters, particularly that of Edward II in 1313. This charter set out that burgesses should only be impleaded within the borough in relation to land, transgressions (trespasses) or contracts arising in the borough, and that only pleas touching the king (i.e., felonies, breaking the king's peace) should be heard outside the borough. Assizes, inquests and juries relating to matters arising in the borough were to be made up of burgesses from the town.[30] Prior to this, the Charter of King John of 1200 stated that only burgesses could bring complaints about other burgesses. However none of the town's early charters referred specifically to the court itself but instead discussed the more general rights and privileges of the burgesses.[31] The right to hear pleas within the town was included in the 1399 charter of Henry IV which said that the mayor, bailiffs and burgesses should have cognisance of all pleas within the town, as well as profits from all fines and amercements.[32] This was a retrospective acknowledgement of practices already in place for at least eight decades, as evidenced by the extant court records which begin in the 1320s, and demonstrating the evolutionary nature of local customary law which developed over time and was only later formalised in charters. It is unclear whether the borough court was reserved solely for burgesses or whether non-burgesses used it too, even if they could not sue burgesses. Some of the surviving rolls pertain specifically to *forensic* or foreign pleas for outsiders, which were meant to have involved at least one foreigner, suggesting that those in other rolls related only to burgesses or at least residents of the town. However, many 'foreign' cases in fact involved both parties described as being 'of Nottingham'. The court shifted to recording its business in books c.1480, and these include both burgess and foreign pleas recorded under separate headings, again with some overlap in the status of litigants.

The Mayor's Court of Nottingham heard presentments concerning affrays and violence deemed to have broken the king's peace, as well as trading offences that broke local regulations. These presentments were usually made twice a year by tithingmen called decennaries and the jury of the *Magnum Turnum* (later called Mickleton Jury) of 25 men. Survival of these records is far more sporadic than those of the borough court.

Chester had two main town courts, the Pentice Court and the Portmote, plus the Crownmote which dealt with breaches of the peace and other leet offences. The Pentice Court is the focus here, as it was dominated by complaints of debt and trespass, while the Portmote was largely concerned with issues pertaining to urban real estate. This was a not a formal separation in jurisdictions, but one that developed over time. The regulation of trade and misbehaviour was recorded in the mayor's and sheriff's books, as well as other administrative business such as the admission of freemen. The rolls of the Pentice Court were headed '*Placita Penticii Cestrie*'. Its unusual name derived from the location in which it sat, a pentice which was originally a wooden extension abutting St Peter's Church. This building sat at the heart of the city and its four intersecting main streets and was the domain of the city sheriffs in the medieval period. The court met three times a week by the 1390s and dealt with all pleas except those pertaining to real property.[33] Chester received numerous charters from the crown and earls of Chester, including a 1300 charter of Edward I, perhaps granted in recognition of the city's contribution to the conquest of Wales, coinciding with a period of prosperity and development for the city.[34] The charter granted the right to hear pleas of the crown, as well rights of *sok* and *sak*, probably referring to the liberty to hold a court, hear pleas, impose fines, as well as excusing Chester citizens from suits in other courts. In the same charter, the city was also granted ancient rights to trading tolls (*tol*), jurisdiction over matters of legal possession (*theam*) and over thieves caught within and outside the city (*infangenthef* and *utfangenthef*).[35] It is from these rights that the jurisdiction and rights of the Pentice and Portmote courts stemmed. The Crownmote had jurisdiction over pleas of the Crown and also dealt with infringements of civic ordinances and trading offences until this was transferred to the Portmote in the 1450s. These offences also survive in the mayor's and sheriff's books of the fifteenth century.

In Winchester, the City Court was the venue for all legal business in the city, both civil pleas and presentments of illegal and trading offences. Its rolls were usually headed simply '*Curie tenta Wyntonie*' with the title of 'City Court' apparently being added by later historians or archivists. It acted as the executive arm of royal jurisdiction in the city and was usually held twice a week, before the mayor and bailiffs, in the guildhall near the busiest part of the High Street.[36] The site of the guildhall moved in the fourteenth century but both buildings were on or adjacent to the High Street, where market functions had become concentrated by the later middle ages.³⁷ The rooms underneath both guildhalls were rented out and used as shops, demonstrating the close ties between city government and urban trade.³⁸ The procedures for local justice in Winchester were set out in the late thirteenth-century text on the *Ancient Usages of the City of Winchester*, including the number of summons allowed for burgesses and outsiders before being attached (the arrest of a person of their goods in order to force them to appear in court), the types of plea allowed and the procedure in debt pleas.³⁹ This text provides probably the most detail on the procedures of the court and the rights of townspeople of the three towns studied here. The rights of burgesses, denizens and foreigners were differentiated, demonstrating that the Winchester court was not restricted only to use by burgesses, though they were afforded more time and chances to respond to summons than those of lesser or outsider status. The presentment of other offences was documented among the records of civil pleas, though usually grouped together. Long lists of names grouped under various headings recorded offenders who broke rules relating to brewing, baking, the selling of fish, as well as incidences of violence. As Chapter 3 discusses, the attention paid to these offences appears to have increased over the late medieval period, with far more offences being documented in the mid-fifteenth century than at the turn of the fourteenth century.

As we have seen, the various charters and customs of each town imply that there were protections in place for the use of the courts by burgesses or citizens, though it is difficult to be definitive about the extent of these rights in practice. Burgess status was generally reserved for men who were either born into or admitted to the freedom of a borough or city, but this did not preclude women and non-burgesses from using their local courts. It is likely, therefore, that the right to litigate extended beyond those entered on formal burgess lists for each town, as it was in the interests of town officials to provide accessible forums for dispute resolution and the regulation of the credit relationships that pervaded all levels of urban society.

Litigation in town courts

The choice to bring a complaint to court lay with the plaintiff. Individuals seeking redress for wrongdoing or broken obligations were proactive in entering their pleas which would then be dealt with over subsequent court sessions. Defendants were required to attend court to respond to these complaints, though they were able to enter an essoin to excuse non-attendance via sending another person in their place to deliver the excuse. If they continually failed to come to court, they might be ordered to appear (distrained) or forced via the seizure (attachment) of goods.[40] The entire process of dispute resolution usually took place over the course of several sessions. A complaint concerning the detention of a strong-box between Emma de Brinchull and Geoffrey le Lockesmyth appeared in the records of eight different court sessions at Nottingham's court in 1322–3, and may never have been resolved as Lockesmyth repeatedly refused to show up to court.[41] Maryanne Kowaleski observed that some cases in Exeter's Mayor's Court continued for as long as two years or longer.[42] However, the high number of residents who used their local courts suggests that this was not a particularly detrimental factor in the popularity of these courts. The presentments and punishments given under leet jurisdiction, meanwhile, represented a more efficient and simpler system of regulation and punishment for those who caused disorder or disobeyed trading rules. The records of these offences take the form of long lists, outlining the individuals responsible and the fines issued, often itemised in order of a town's various streets or neighbourhoods or grouped under different types of offence.

The popularity of civil litigation stemmed from the courts' inherently practical nature, as well as the increasingly litigious character of late medieval society. Their location in the centre of town was more practical, convenient and cheaper than travelling elsewhere to county or itinerant crown courts, or to the central courts at Westminster. Bringing a complaint before the local court was thus far less disruptive than travelling elsewhere to seek justice, enabling litigants to continue with everyday life and trade at the same time, even if it meant repeat trips to court. The relatively minor nature of many of the pleas heard by borough courts also meant that it was probably not worthwhile pursuing these claims at a higher court if it would cost considerable time or expense, but town courts provided an accessible forum in which to settle disputes of a local, low-key nature. It was even worthwhile pursuing debts of the lowest sums, such as the 2d that John, brother of William Coteler, sought from Thomas de Hutton at Nottingham in June 1360, or the 3d for milk that Matilda le Spenser acknowledged owing to Alice, widow of John Hammes, at Chester in 1317.[43]

The graph in Figure 1.1 illustrates how commercial disputes of debt, detinue and covenant (labelled under 'debt') dominated town courts, reflecting the importance of trade in towns and their role as the sites of the country's larger markets and fairs, as well as numerous shops and stalls. They were home to more merchants, traders and craftsmen than rural communities, all of whom were reliant on credit transactions in

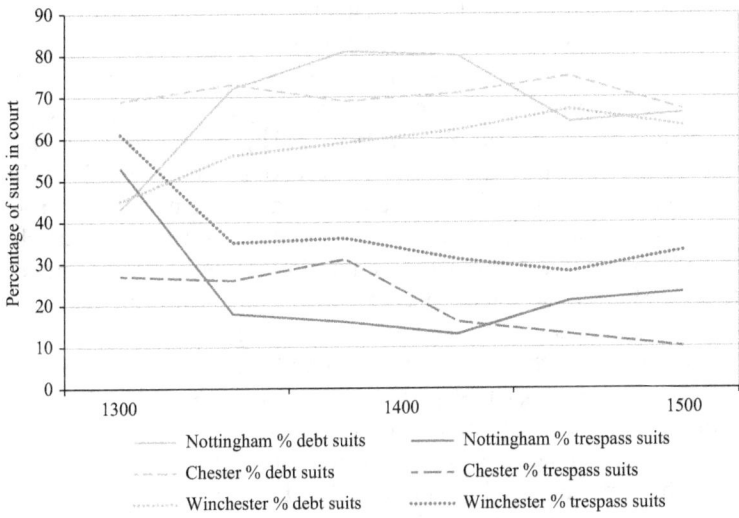

Figure 1.1 Percentage of debt and trespass suits in Nottingham, Chester and Winchester, fourteenth and fifteenth centuries.
Source: CALS ZSR 21, 81–85, 109–112, 147–155, 201–210, 369–380; NA CA 1258B, CA 1279, CA 1294, CA 1324, CA 1325, CA 1336, CA 1374; HRO W/D1/3, W/D1/13, W/D1/27, W/D1/60, W/D1/61, W/D1/64.

order to buy and sell goods and services. It has even been suggested that this was the original reason for the existence of town courts.[44] Credit dominated commercial life at all levels of society, and this led to widespread use of borough courts for the recovery of debts that were not paid on time or in full.[45] The analysis of women's roles in debt litigation thus provides an insight into their economic lives and their role in credit networks, as well as how this was represented and governed by legal action. Town courts also heard a large number of trespass complaints. This category, united by the essence of wrongdoing and defined in more detail in Chapter 4, encompassed a wide range of violent (often specified as trespass and bloodshed) and non-violent actions, including complaints of assault, theft, slander and damage to property or goods. It should not be surprising that these issues were common in towns, where people lived close to one another and were tied together by multiple commercial, familial and social networks; inevitably, these ties were not always harmonious. Through trespass litigation, we gain an insight into the ways that these interpersonal ties could break down and how this was manifested in legal action, which served as a means to redress wrongdoing and restore relationships and reputations.

Once a complaint had been brought to court (and the parties had decided to show up when required), dispute resolution could come about through various means.[46] The defendant could acknowledge the plaintiff's complaint, or the two parties could agree with the permission (licence) of the court. This could be facilitated by the grant of a 'love day' (recorded by the annotation '*Amor*'), a form of arbitration employed by the court in the hope of achieving agreement between the two parties and requiring that they come back to court at a later date. Alternatively, if the allegation was contested, an inquisition jury would be summoned to determine the 'facts' and report back to the court. Either the defendant would be found guilty and required to pay damages and an amercement to the court, or, if the jury refuted the complaint, the plaintiff would be amerced for bringing a false plea. Amercements were paid to the court, rather than the plaintiff, usually to the value of a few pence, depending on the court and the nature of the offence. Damages were sought in high sums, but never awarded. An individual might claim damages of 40s for a trespass offence, but eventually be awarded less than a shilling. These claims were therefore representations of the individual's perception of the harm caused by an offence or unpaid debt, rather than actual expectations of the sums that plaintiffs hoped to win. In some cases, both parties might be amerced, if the plaintiff was judged to have been untruthful in part of their complaint, but the defendant was still found guilty of overall wrongdoing.

Cases were regularly decided by jury, but little is known about the identities of jurors, as jury lists rarely survive. We can sometimes identify jurors by their defaults when they failed to appear in court. The jury became an increasingly prominent method of trial in many boroughs by the second half of the fourteenth century and was a common means of judgement in these towns as well as elsewhere, like the courts of Canterbury, Southampton, Norwich and Exeter.[47] Members were drawn from among the *probi homines* of the town, men of good repute who, due to their good standing and connections, would be well-informed regarding the people, activities and events of the town.[48] Unlike modern juries, their role was not to deliberate over evidence but to obtain the facts about the alleged events and report a verdict accordingly. Of course, this does not mean that what these juries reported amounted to the 'truth' of a dispute. In these relatively compact urban environments this fact-gathering may not have been an especially difficult task, as the small populations meant that many people would have known each other (or at least known about each other) and possibly also known of their extra-legal activities or failures to fulfil agreements. But this does not mean that juries might not have been open to corruption, or to reporting against individuals whom they did not like or who had bad reputations. We frequently find references to suits being delayed due to the default of jurors who did not show up to court when required, suggesting that at least some jurors did not hold this position in particularly high esteem.[49]

Litigants sometimes used attorneys to act on their behalf or perhaps to improve their chances of success. We find women using attorneys – sometimes their male relatives – but men sought legal assistance too, so this was not simply a case of female inferiority or a need for male assistance in court. Whether these were professionally trained lawyers, or simply local knowledgeable and well-connected men, is not clear.[50] The same men appeared as attorneys for multiple individuals, suggesting a degree of professionalisation, particularly as the period progressed. At Nottingham, men who acted as attorneys also held the posts of mayor and bailiff and were involved in their own personal suits at the borough court.[51] Women very rarely acted as attorneys or jurors, and did not fulfil any other official roles within urban law or government. Female litigants therefore operated within a distinctly male legal system.

Recording and reading legal practice: approaches to town court records

The overall survival of the court rolls in each of the county archives varies. In Winchester, a handful of early rolls exist from 1269–70, though the first complete set of records is from 1299–1300. There are no surviving court records between 1300 and 1361, but following this there are relatively complete rolls for much of the remainder of the fourteenth century. After 1433, standards of record-keeping appear to have deteriorated somewhat, and the survival of rolls from c.1450–1500 is more fragmentary. In Chester, the survival of Pentice Court rolls is more consistent across a longer period. The earliest is from 1298, and while rolls survive throughout the whole late medieval period, for some years this consists of only a small number of manuscripts (each one usually stemming from one court session), meaning that analysis of full year series of records is not always possible. The Nottingham court rolls offer most potential for the study of an extended period, and they also offer the most detail. For this reason, evidence from Nottingham features most prominently throughout this book. The earliest records are extracts from 1303, though the rolls begin in full from 1322. After this point, large and often complete series of rolls survive for most years during the 1320s, 1350s, 1360s, 1370s, 1390s, 1400s, 1410s, 1430s and 1440s. After this point, court records were kept in books, wherein it appears that the details of cases were edited and compiled into one entry, rather than being spread across several pages. The books are neatly arranged and include spaces apparently left for details to be added later, indicating a revision in recording practices.

In order to allow for the varying quality and survival of the records, and to enable measurable comparisons between towns, this book draws on considerable quantitative analysis of records from each of the three towns. The records have been sampled at six intervals across the fourteenth and fifteenth centuries (three per century) with specific years being chosen to reflect the best survival of each town's records, though these are not always complete rolls. This is combined with a broader collection of records to create a qualitative analysis that illuminates the actions and status of different women in more detail.

The quantitative basis for the study of each town is as follows: Nottingham 1323–4, 1375–6, 1394–5, 1433–4, 1446–7, 1491–2; Chester 1317–18, 1378, 1395, 1423, 1435, 1490; Winchester 1299–1300, 1365–6, 1385–6, 1432–3, 1454–5, 1494–5. In Nottingham and Winchester, the rolls are collated in series that run from Michaelmas to Michaelmas, meaning that the records run across two calendar years. In Chester, the records have typically been collated and catalogued according to the calendar year, and sometimes individual court sessions. In drawing upon the most complete sets of extant records for analysis, any potential seasonal variations in patterns of litigation or legal action (reflecting links between local trade and agricultural production, for example) is mitigated, though this would have been more of an issue in manorial courts than in towns. It has not been possible to compare statistics from identical years across different towns, due to the varying survival and quality of records from the three towns across the period. However, the spread of sampling across two centuries still allows for assessment of change over time within towns as well as comparison between places, in line with other studies (particularly those addressing the 'golden age' question). But the analysis included in this study is not limited to these sample years; nor, as discussed in the Introduction, does it rest solely on quantitative data. Additional records from across the period have also been consulted to enable a more detailed examination of women's legal experiences by drawing on cases that are particularly illustrative of the various ways in which women engaged with the law, and in some instances – particularly for Nottingham – to explore the legal actions of individual women over an extended period. For Nottingham and Chester, the records of local policing and trading regulation, dealt with under separate jurisdictions, supplement the records of litigation to create a more rounded picture of women's engagement with the law; in Winchester, these issues are contained within the city court rolls, alongside personal pleas.

As we will see throughout this book, the form, content and nature of the records plays a significant role in determining what can be recovered about the litigants and issues that were dealt with under local justice. The records do not necessarily reveal the whole picture concerning what happened in court, or events that happened outside it before or after a plea was heard. This does not mean that we cannot uncover any real aspects of women's experiences of the law, and of their lives more broadly, but it does mean that they cannot simply be read at face value. Town court rolls were characterised by a relatively strict and persistent structure and formula, under which those details deemed necessary by the town's officials were documented in brief and efficient ways. The legal year began and ended at Michaelmas, so series of rolls and books (when complete) tend to cover this annual time period. Court rolls (or books) were headed with the name of the court and the date, established through reference to the regnal year and nearest feast day. A typical example from Winchester's City Court thus reads 'Winchester court held there on Friday in the Feast of Saint Faith the Virgin', the year being given as 'the ninth year of the reign of King Richard the second after the conquest'.[52] By the later fifteenth century, some records give the date in full. Following this, the details of pleas and presentments were listed, often with only one or two lines per case. In civil pleas, for example, the names of the complainant and defendant were generally followed by the names of the pledges (or sureties) for each party. Some details of the alleged offence or obligation might be included at this point, or they might follow in the records of subsequent court sessions. More details are often found when an inquisition jury was summoned; its report may have followed in a subsequent session. The details of amercements and damages were listed at the end of an entry, often in the margins, or sometimes interlineated above the text.

In contrast to the processes involved in litigation, the presentment of various offences by local officials was seemingly more straightforward. When offences relating to trade or misbehaviour were presented by juries or other officials, this was not recorded in the same fragmentary nature as interpersonal pleas, as these issues were concluded in one court session. Due to the inability of offenders to contest their guilt, these records instead took the form of lists of names or brief, one-off entries, often organised by locality within a particular town. There was certainly overlap in the nature of the actions dealt with by litigation and presentment, particularly between trespasses and affrays, both of which might concern interpersonal acts of violence. However, because presentments were only made periodically and offered no opportunity for contestation or response, they did not become protracted issues in the same way that civil complaints might. Responsibility for this policing lay with local officials who reported their knowledge of misbehaviour and illegal activity within their localities.

Studying town court records requires working around their highly formulaic nature. Despite their richness and unique value, the records do not give a direct insight into what happened and why, nor can we access the 'truth' of any given dispute. This is an issue which many historians working with medieval and later legal records have highlighted, each having their own ways of conceptualising the narratives that legal records present. Much of this discussion rests on how we identify these narratives and the filters created by lawyers, scribes, the legal process, legal and cultural norms and the manipulations of litigants, and whether we can separate from these factors any sense of 'what really happened'. But there is also a question of whether this should be our aim at all, as these factors that were inherent parts of the legal process are also revealing of the way in which individuals engaged with and experienced the law. Cordelia Beattie has highlighted the storytelling aspects of court records, as the women's 'voices' that we might read in accounts of depositions or testimony are in fact products of the legal process, rather than records of what was actually said. By acting as 'translators', historians can identify the filters employed by scribes while also using these records to recover women's experiences and interactions with the law.[53] Jeremy Goldberg similarly suggests that we are, at best, accessing voices 'ventriloquized' by clerks and lawyers.[54] He also reminds us that the legal documentation upon which the historian is so dependent is only one part of the legal process, with the 'flesh and blood interactions' (sometimes literal) being either hidden, or only glimpsed through the distortion of the court records.[55] Suzannah Lipscomb has also recently highlighted the value of legal documents in allowing us to 'hear the voices of ordinary French women ... mediated, curtailed, but audible'.[56] The process of recovering and analysing these 'voices' is therefore a balancing act taking account of the details contained within the court records and the many factors that obscure and filter various aspects of these stories and voices. In her discussion of the detective work that can be involved in working with medieval legal records, Shannon McSheffrey terms them records of 'what-will-have-been': things to be remembered, not simply factual accounts. This conceptualisation of the records destabilises their meanings, but also allows us to think about the law beyond a system of rules, challenges and outcomes, as something that was also a process or tool that was flexible and vulnerable to influence.[57] Such an approach requires us to think about what was going on below the surface, why a particular legal process or action occurred, and why certain details were recorded or not recorded. All of these issues had a role to play in determining women's access to justice.

Town court records feature no formally constructed writs, oral testimony or deposition accounts, which have variously been used to gain an insight into women's thoughts, motivations, values and attitudes, as well as everyday experiences.[58] As a result, litigants' voices are harder to access via town court records than other legal sources. Nor do we find the 'storytelling' narratives that define other court records, particularly those of equity courts such as Chancery. While this might mean that the records present information in a more 'black and white' manner and are perhaps less in need of translating or dissecting, it also limits the amount of information that we can access. Civil disputes were recorded according to largely fixed language and phrases, due in part to the pragmatic desire for efficiency and common understandings of how the law should work, but probably also as a reflection of the linguistic abilities of local scribes.[59] They had to translate spoken proceedings from English to written documentation in Latin, adapting and condensing the events of court according to a common framework. Most cases ran from one court session to the next, so multiple rolls must be studied to compile the fragments of litigation to gain the fullest information about any one case. Some cases disappear from the records, perhaps because they were abandoned or settled out of court, or because the details or outcome have been lost or damaged over time. As a result, we may not always be able to recover how a debt was accrued or whether it had to be repaid, exactly how an individual was alleged to have been assaulted, or what 'malicious words' were used in defaming another. But this does not negate their value. While it might be tempting to seek out the 'truth' of the various disputes contained within the court rolls, this need not be the ultimate aim of studying legal sources. It may be intriguing to know whether Hawise and Alice Spondon really did assault Margery Dod in Nottingham's Saturday market, and with what combination of insults they allegedly called her false, a thief and whore, or whether Dod really did steal a tabard from them.[60] But even without knowing these details, the case still offers a valuable insight into the way in which women were involved in litigation, the types of offence they might be victim or perpetrator of, how these issues were brought to and recorded in court and the legal culture that was associated with these allegations.

The records do not provide a true window onto the 'lived lives', actions and relationships of those who appear in the rolls. Instead, we might approach them as though we are looking through broken glass: we cannot see the whole picture, as a result of various fractures and diffractions, but we can access fragments which can be pieced together in an attempt to better understand the situation. Clerks and scribes had the power to condense the records of proceedings through 'the twin processes of editing and translation', and the formulae and patterns involved in what they did (and did not) decide to record are indicative of the attitudes and priorities of the courts, revealing the matters perceived to be of the most importance to record for future reference.[61] Being conscious of these various hidden or diffracted aspects of events and legal process might allow us, as Garthine Walker has suggested, to use court records to both understand structures and practices of the law, but also to strive 'to hear individual women's voices in these texts, in keeping with conventional women's history that seeks to recover women's agency from a past of structural inequalities'.[62] Despite their limitations, the court records provide a window – however fragmented – onto the lives, actions and disputes of the women (and men) who inhabited England's towns, and the legal processes to which they were subjected.

Notes

1 Maryanne Kowaleski's chapter 'Town courts in medieval England: an introduction' in Richard Goddard and Teresa Phipps (eds), *Town Courts and Urban Society in Late Medieval England* (Woodbridge: Boydell and Brewer, 2019), pp. 17–42 does much to address this gap.

2 W.H. Stevenson (ed.), *Records of the Borough of Nottingham*, vols. 1–3 (London: Quaritch, 1882–9); A. Hopkins (ed.), *Selected Rolls of the Chester City Courts* (Manchester: Chetham Society, 1950); J.S. Furley, *City Government of Winchester from the Records of XIV and XV Centuries* (Oxford: Clarendon Press, 1923) and *Town Life in the XIV Century as seen in the Court Rolls of Winchester City* (Winchester: Warren, 1946). Richard Goddard has used the Nottingham sources to study debt litigation and local networks. Goddard, 'Trust: Business networks and the borough court' in Goddard and Phipps (eds), *Town Courts*, pp. 176–199. Jane Laughton provided an overview of women in Chester's city courts: 'Women in court: some evidence from fifteenth-century Chester' in Nicholas Rogers (ed.) *England in the Fifteenth Century* (Stamford: Paul Watkins, 1994), pp. 89–99.

3 On urban populations, rankings and the urban hierarchy, see Alan Dyer, 'Ranking lists of English medieval towns' in D.M. Palliser (ed.), *The Cambridge Urban History of Britain, vol.1 600–1540* (Cambridge: Cambridge University Press, 2000), pp. 747–770. On Nottingham's population, see Trevor Foulds, 'The medieval town', in John Beckett (ed.), *A Centenary History of Nottingham* (Manchester: Manchester University

Press, 1997), p. 56; for Chester, see Jane Laughton, *Life in a Late Medieval City: Chester 1275-1520* (Oxford: Oxbow, 2008), pp. 11–12; for Winchester, see Derek Keene, *Survey of Medieval Winchester*, vol. 1 (Oxford: Clarendon Press, 1985), pp. 366–367.

4   Dyer, 'Ranking lists', pp. 755, 758.
5   Martin Biddle, *Winchester in the Early Middle Ages: An Edition and Discussion of the Winton Domesday* (Oxford: Clarendon Press, 1976), pp. 29, 489.
6   See Keene, *Winchester*, vol. 1, p. 7.
7   Dyer, 'Ranking lists', p. 758.
8   Laughton, *Chester*, p. 11.
9   K.P. Wilson (ed.), *Chester Customs Accounts 1301–1556*, Record Society of Lancashire and Cheshire, vol. III (1969), p. 8; Dorothy J. Clayton, *The Administration of the County Palatine of Chester 1442–1485* (Manchester: Chetham Society, 1990), pp. 31, 59.
10 Dyer, 'Ranking lists', pp. 755, 758.
11 Administration of the two boroughs is thought to have merged with the creation of the office of mayor in 1284. Stephen N. Mastoris, 'Regulating the Nottingham markets: New evidence from a mid-thirteenth century manuscript', *Transactions of the Thoroton Society*, 90 (1986), 79.
12 Kowaleski, 'Town courts', p. 20.
13 Susan Reynolds, *Kingdoms and Communities in Western Europe 900–1300*, second edn (Oxford: Oxford University Press, 1997), p. 45.
14 On leet courts, see James Davis, *Medieval Market Morality* (Cambridge: Cambridge University Press, 2011), p. 147.
15 Anthony Musson, *Medieval Law in Context* (Manchester: Manchester University Press, 2001), p. 8.
16 Musson, *Medieval Law in Context*, p. 97.
17 Penny Tucker, 'Historians' expectations of the medieval legal records', in Anthony Musson (ed.), *Expectations of the Law in the Middle Ages* (Woodbridge: Boydell and Brewer, 2001), p. 191.
18 Judith M. Bennett and Ruth Mazo Karras, 'Women, gender and medieval historians', in Bennett and Karras (eds), *The Oxford Handbook of Women and Gender in Medieval Europe* (Oxford: Oxford University Press, 2013), p. 7.
19 Karen Jones, *Gender and Petty Crime in Late Medieval England: The Local Courts in Kent, 1460–1560* (Woodbridge: Boydell and Brewer, 2006), p. 13.
20 On borough customs and custumals, see Esther Liberman Cuenca, 'Borough court cases as legal precedent in English town custumals' in Goddard and Phipps (eds), *Town Courts*, pp. 43–45; Tim Stretton, *Women Waging Law in Elizabethan England* (Cambridge: Cambridge University Press, 1998), p. 158.
21 Stretton, *Women Waging Law*, pp. 175–177.
22 R.R. Davies, 'The peoples of Britain and Ireland 1100–1400 I: Identities', *Transactions of the Royal Historical Society*, 4 (1994), 6–7; Matthew Frank Stevens, 'Anglo-Welsh towns of the early fourteenth century: a survey of urban origins, property-holding and ethnicity' in Helen Fulton (ed.), *Urban Culture in Medieval Wales* (Cardiff: University of Wales Press, 2012), pp. 138, 141.
23 Lizabeth Johnson, '*Amobr* and *Amobrwyr*: the collection of marriage fees and sexual fines in late medieval Wales', *Transactions of the Honourable Society of Cymmrodorian*, 18 (2012), 10–21.

24 Llinos Beverley Smith, 'Towards a history of women in late medieval Wales', in Michael Roberts and Simone Clarke (eds), *Women and Gender in Early Modern Wales* (Cardiff: University of Wales Press, 2000), p. 21.
25 Matthew Frank Stevens, *Urban Assimilation in Post-Conquest Wales: Ethnicity, Gender and Economy in Ruthin, 1282–1350* (Cardiff: University of Wales Press, 2010), p. 118.
26 For example, the court rolls of the marcher lordship of Dyffryn Clwyd feature numerous references to individuals either claiming or challenging English or Welsh ethnic status in a range of cases as a means to assert the different legal rights that were tied to the different ethnicities.
27 Rebecca Mason, 'Women, marital status and law: the marital spectrum in seventeenth-century Glasgow' *Journal of British Studies*, 58 (2019), 789; Katie Barclay and Rosalind Carr, 'Rewriting the Scottish canon: the contribution of women's and gender history to a redefinition of social classes', *Études écossaises*, 16 (2013), 16; A.E. Anton, 'The effect of marriage upon property in Scots Law', *The Modern Law Review*, 19 (1956), 653.
28 Elizabeth Ewan, 'Scottish Portias: women in the courts in mediaeval Scottish towns', *Journal of the Canadian Historical Association*, 3 (1992), 29.
29 On manorial courts, see Paul R. Hyams, 'What did Edwardian villagers understand by law?', in Zvi Razi and Richard Smith (eds), *Medieval Society and the Manor Court* (Oxford: Clarendon Press, 1996), p. 69.
30 Foulds, 'The medieval town', p. 68; Stevenson, *Nottingham*, vol. 1, pp. 76–80.
31 Charter of King John, 19 March 1200 in Stevenson, *Nottingham*, vol. 1, pp. 10–13. 'Neque praeposito burgi de Notingham aliquem burgensium calumpnianti respondeatur nisi alius fuerit accusatory in causa.'
32 Charter of Henry IV, 18 November 1399 in Stevenson, *Nottingham*, vol. 2, pp. 2–11.
33 Laughton, *Chester*, p. 124. The Pentice was presided over by the mayor and sheriffs together for a brief period c.1320–1340: see C.P. Lewis and A.T. Thacker, *A History of the County of Chester Volume V: The City of Chester* (Woodbridge: Boydell and Brewer, 2005), p. 44.
34 Laughton, *Chester*, p. 24.
35 Charters recorded in R.H. Morris (ed.), *Chester in the Plantagenet and Tudor Reigns* (Chester, 1893), pp. 490–493.
36 Keene, *Winchester*, vol. 1, pp. 22, 82.
37 Biddle, *Winchester in the early Middle Ages*, p. 285.
38 Keene, *Winchester*, vol. 2, p. 593.
39 'Usages of the City of Winchester', in Furley (ed.), *City Government of Winchester*, pp. 167–177, translated in Harry Rothwell (ed.), *English Historical Documents: 1189–1327* (London: Eyre and Spottiswoode, 1996), pp. 870–878.
40 On essoins, see *Bracton on the Laws and Customs of England*, trans. Samuel E. Thorne, vol. 4 (Cambridge, MA: Belknap Press, 1977), pp. 71–146. See also Davis, *Market Morality*, p. 209 for examples of town ordinances for the recovery of debt and local court practices.
41 NA CA1258a rots 15, 16, 17, 18, 19, 22, 23, 24.
42 Maryanne Kowaleski, *Local Markets and Regional Trade in Medieval Exeter* (Cambridge: Cambridge University Press, 1995), p. 337.

43 NA CA1269 rot. 8; CALS ZSR 21 rot. 4.
44 Alan Harding, *The Law Courts of Medieval England* (London: Allen and Unwin, 1973), p. 43.
45 Richard Goddard, *Credit and Trade in Later Medieval England, 1353–1532* (London: Palgrave, 2016), p. 2.
46 On the processes of Nottingham's borough court, see Richard Goddard, 'Nottingham's borough court rolls: a user's guide', https://www.nottingham.ac.uk/ucn/documents/online-sources/nottinghamsboroughcourtrolls-usersguide2.pdf (accessed 23 August 2018).
47 Charles Gross, 'Modes of trial in the mediaeval boroughs of England', *Harvard Law Review*, 15 (1902), 705.
48 On the construction of 'good repute', see Barbara Hanawalt, *Of Good and Ill Repute: Gender and Social Control in Medieval England* (Oxford: Oxford University Press, 1998), pp. 1–2; on urban jury composition, see Marjorie Keniston McIntosh, *Controlling Misbehavior in England, 1370–1600* (Cambridge: Cambridge University Press, 2002), p. 109.
49 On the makeup of jury panels and the failure of jurors to appear, see J.B. Post, 'Jury lists and juries in the late fourteenth century', in J.S. Cockburn and Thomas A. Green (eds), *Twelve Good Men and True: The Criminal Jury in England, 1200–1800* (Princeton: Princeton University Press, 1988), pp. 65–78.
50 On the status of attorneys, see Frederick Pollock and Frederic William Maitland, *The History of English Law Before the Time of Edward I*, vol. 1 (Cambridge: Cambridge University Press, 1895), p. 213. Women were rarely named as attorneys. However, at Norwich in 1299–1300, Emma Pruding of Trowse was named as attorney of the wife of John Rodland. William Hudson (ed.), *Leet Jurisdiction in the City of Norwich during the Xiiith and Xivth centuries* (London: Quaritch, 1892), p. 51.
51 For example, John Croushawe was a bailiff, mayor and collector of the guild of All Saints in the 1380s and acted as an attorney, but also appeared in court in various suits. Similarly, Adam Payntour acted as an attorney but was also recorded as a clerk.
52 6 October 1385. HRO W/D1/27 rot. 1.
53 Cordelia Beattie, '"Your oratrice:" women's petitions to the late medieval court of Chancery', in Bronach Kane and Fiona Williamson (eds), *Women, Agency and the Law, 1300–1700* (London: Pickering and Chatto, 2013), pp. 18–20, 29. See also Joanne Bailey, 'Voices in court: lawyers' or litigants'?', *Historical Research*, 74 (2001), 406–407.
54 Jeremy Goldberg, 'Echoes, whispers, ventriloquisms: on recovering women's voices from the court of York in the Later Middle Ages', in Kane and Williamson (eds), *Women, Agency and the Law*, p. 31.
55 Jeremy Goldberg, 'The priest of Nottingham and the holy household of Ousegate: telling tales in court' in Goddard and Phipps (eds), *Town Courts*, p. 61.
56 Suzannah Lipscomb, *The Voices of Nimes: Women, Sex and Marriage in Reformation Languedoc* (Oxford: Oxford University Press, 2019), p. 4.
57 Shannon McSheffrey, 'Detective fiction in the archives', *History Workshop Journal*, 65 (2008), 73.
58 See, for example, Lipscomb, *The Voices of Nimes*, p. 5.

59 This would explain why scribes sometimes switch to recording the name of objects in English within the Latin record of pleas. An action for detinue in Nottingham's court in 1492 included a long list of household items, some given in Latin but others, like 'Frying panne', recorded in English, suggesting this was something that scribes could not or did not translate. Thomas Copeland and Margery his wife v Thomas Hygyn and Johanna his wife, NA CA1374, p. 107.
60 NA CA1258b rot. 13.
61 Goldberg, 'Recovering women's voices', p. 40.
62 Garthine Walker, 'Just stories: telling tales of infant death in early modern England', in Margaret Lael Mikesell and Adele F. Seeff (eds), *Culture and Change: Attending to Early Modern Women* (Newark, Delaware: University of Delaware Press, 2003), p. 99.

2

Commerce, credit and coverture: women and debt litigation

At Winchester's City Court in 1385, Agatha Spycer, a merchant, acknowledged a debt of 30s 7d that she had unjustly detained from Alice Mercer. The plea reveals a substantial transaction between the two women through Mercer's use of the local court to enforce payment.[1] This was by no means unusual: debt was ubiquitous in the medieval economy, with credit transactions acting as the essential mechanism by which purchases and agreements were made at all levels.[2] Towns of all sizes were important centres of provincial trade, facilitated by the existence of various markets, fairs, shops and stalls. As a result, debt litigation was a major component of the business of England's medieval town courts, often accounting for the majority of complaints. Across numerous jurisdictions, women featured as both plaintiffs and defendants in these cases. Women such as Agatha Spycer and Alice Mercer were integrated into the networks of local commerce, some being tied to others in credit agreements of a significant scale, while others bought and sold on credit of just a few pence.[3] When these agreements broke down, or expectations were not met, the parties could sue each other for debt in the local court. This litigation is generally the only record we have of these lower value trading agreements, and is an essential source that illuminates the nature of everyday trade in England's towns, as well as how individuals used the law to manage their commercial interests. This chapter examines women's involvement in this litigation, revealing a complex and often fluid intersection of their commercial, marital and legal identities, through which some women demonstrated considerable agency, knowledge and legal competency in using the law to negotiate the innumerable transactions and obligations that characterised the urban economy. Debt litigation was a central component of urban women's engagement with law and justice, making this analysis essential to the understanding of their legal experience and status within the urban community.

Women were a constant presence in urban debt litigation, though as we will see, the extent of this varied across different towns and their courts and over time. It is possible to identify patterns that indicate general trends and highlight differences between jurisdictions, as well as potential links to the changing economic and demographic context of late medieval England. Though there were some correlations in the nature of women's litigation in the courts of different towns, particularly in the apparent declining ability of married women to participate in debt pleas, the local customs and context of each court mean that it is not possible to conceive of any 'national' trends in women's commercial legal actions. The high volume of litigation that local courts heard naturally lends itself to quantitative analysis, in order to discern these patterns, but the details of women's litigation are also illuminated through the qualitative study of individual complaints. These pleas illustrate women's roles in litigation, their status and treatment by different courts, as well as (sometimes) what the complaints themselves were actually about, providing an insight into women's commercial activities. This chapter takes a combined approach in order to achieve a more rounded understanding of women's commercial litigation. After establishing the context for women's economic litigation, it deals with the records of the three towns in turn, before drawing direct comparisons between the different places and jurisdictions. A key factor in the shifting patterns of women's debt litigation was the differing status of married women in debt suits, and their ability to act as litigants alongside their husbands. As a result, the comparisons drawn between the application of coverture in debt pleas across the different towns in the later section of this chapter demonstrate the intrinsically local interpretation of this broad but flexible principle.

Credit and debt in borough courts

Distinct from the modern culture of litigation, taking action to recover debt in the medieval period should not be seen as an indication of financial crisis or complete breakdown in commercial relationships, particularly at the more modest level as represented in the borough court evidence. Rather, it often served as the final stage in the chain of credit that allowed the medieval economy to function. Martha Howell's description of the ubiquity of credit in the lives of ordinary people is particularly illustrative: 'Everyone was in debt, virtually all the time, whether to neighbours, employers, servants, superiors, fathers, brothers, mothers, or even children.'[4] At the local level this usually took the form of delayed payment for goods or services, though loans of money were also recorded among debt pleas. Urban debt litigation represented both wholesale and retail trade, with most litigants being small-scale traders and artisans.[5] Traders often needed to complete other transactions before money was available to repay their own debts, creating large, web-like networks of credit. The high volume of litigation therefore reflected this aspect of commercial life and also points to the scale of local trade, giving some measure of the general health and confidence within the economy.[6]

Appearing in court as a debtor did not, therefore, mean that someone had failed in business, and was not a symptom of economic distress or mismanagement. The most important members of urban society, including mayors and bailiffs, featured in debt pleas as both plaintiffs and defendants. Chris Briggs has suggested that, for debtors, it may even have been financially prudent simply to wait until the last moment before meeting obligations, explaining why people so regularly went to court over small debts.[7] Frequent involvement in litigation may therefore have been a symptom of greater commercial integration and prosperity.[8] Debt litigation dominated the courts of all three of the towns that are the subject of this study, generally increasing as a proportion of all litigation, as Table 2.1 illustrates. Considering the relatively small populations of each place, we see that high numbers of separate complaints were heard in each court annually. The relative dominance of debt litigation over other types of complaint was also reflected in patterns of women's litigation, indicating women's integration into broader commercial and litigious patterns. Yet despite the high volume of litigation, an unknown number of disputes or missed payments would have been resolved outside the court system, meaning that disputes heard at court only represent a minority of commercial transactions within each town.

Credit and indebtedness were therefore pervasive features of urban society, and the resulting litigation involved a large number of individual men and women, trading partners, as well as married couples. Richard Britnell estimated that in Colchester during the 1370s, there was at least one plea of debt for every eight adult residents of the borough.[9] At Nottingham, where the borough court rolls are most complete, around a third (469) of the number of 1377 Poll Tax payers (1,477) were found in court annually during the 1370s.[10] The majority of suits (72 per cent) were debt pleas. The debts that were the subject of these pleas were often small, with sums ranging upwards from a few pence and rarely reaching above the 40s limit for debt that could (in theory) be sued without a writ.[11] Some litigants appeared in just one suit while others, both creditors and

Table 2.1 Debt and trespass litigation in Chester, Nottingham and Winchester.[a]

Town	Year	Total suits	Debt suits (%)	Trespass suits (%)
Chester	1317–18	238	164 (69)	64 (27)
	1378	164	120 (73)	42 (26)
	1395	99	68 (69)	31 (31)
	1423	197	140 (71)	32 (16)
	1435	277	208 (75)	36 (13)
	1490	400	268 (67)	39 (10)
Nottingham	1323–4	268	116 (43)	143 (53)
	1375–6	453	326 (72)	83 (18)
	1394–5	316	255 (81)	50 (16)
	1433–4	479	385 (80)	62 (13)
	1446–7	319	205 (64)	67 (21)
	1491–2	438	314 (72)	87 (20)
Winchester	1299–1300	254	115 (45)	136 (61)
	1365–6	141	79 (56)	49 (35)
	1385–6	138	81 (59)	50 (36)
	1432–3	371	227 (62)	114 (31)
	1454–5	281	187 (67)	79 (28)
	1494–5	167	105 (63)	55 (33)

[a] Total suits incorporates all civil pleas of debt, trespass and covenant. Debt and trespass were the main types of plea heard by these courts, so the relative numbers of each plea are compared here to show the proportions of each type of suit and the increasing dominance of debt pleas. The Nottingham plea numbers include both burgess and 'foreign' pleas as both involved residents of the town. These only became separated from the mid-fifteenth century onwards. The number of suits counted represents only distinct complaints, not counting the repeated appearances of each plea as it progressed through the court. The varying numbers of pleas are reflective of both different volumes of business in each court as well as varying survival rates of court rolls. The percentages of different pleas should therefore be used for comparison of the relative volumes of debt and trespass pleas, rather than absolute numbers.

Source: CALS ZSR 21, 81–85, 109–112, 147–155, 201–210, 369–380; NA CA 1258B, CA 1279, CA 1294, CA 1324, CA 1325, CA 1336, CA 1374; HRO W/D1/3, W/D1/13, W/D1/27, W/D1/60, W/D1/61, W/D1/64.

debtors, came before the court more regularly. The records of these pleas are formulaic, brief and lacking detail, in many cases recording only the names of the litigants and the type of plea. For example, a Chester suit of 1395 simply tells us that Margery, servant of John Bollyn, brought a plea of debt against Emma de Byllngton.[12] However, in some entries, particularly where the outcome of a suit was decided by an inquisition jury or the debtor acknowledged the debt, more detail may be given about the value of the debt and how it arose. The response of the accused debtor might be recorded, such as the answer of John Lenton in Agnes Pys's claim of 8d for weaving in Nottingham's borough court, to which Lenton responded that he owed nothing.[13] While most debts related to the sale of goods or the provision of services, some took the form of money lending. A Chester plea of 1318 saw Alice de Ellehale accused, with her husband William, of owing 42s that she had borrowed from William le Rous, which Alice denied.[14] In April 1376, Amya Walker successfully used the Nottingham court to recover a debt of 12d loaned to William Derby.[15] As well as pleas of debt, borough courts also heard contractual complaints of detinue. These related to the withholding of goods rather than money, often citing goods that had been paid for but not delivered. However, the courts did not always draw clear distinctions between the two issues, conflating complaints of debt and detinue. Winchester's City Court often recorded debts as the detention of money, as well as using the term to refer to goods detained. For example, Petronilla Wyg acknowledged the unjust detention of 21s following a complaint of William Abbodestoun in 1362.[16]

Some suits can be traced from initiation to resolution, while others are lost in the intervening stages due to damaged records, dropped suits or settlement out of court. It could take several court sessions to resolve a debt plea, but despite its protracted nature, local debt litigation was a favourable means of managing credit ties: courts were centrally located, cheap to use and their straightforward procedures made them accessible to a wide range of the local population.[17] Many debtors acknowledged their debts in court, further indicating that litigation could simply be a routine part of many credit transactions and was not always highly contentious. Bringing a debt 'complaint' to court offered a means of recording oral transactions in writing within the official record of the town.

The nature of women's litigation

By exploring the records of debt and detinue in detail, we can examine the nature of women's litigation in order to understand the way that women participated in these pleas in their local courts and the factors that influenced their access to this form of justice. Women featured as both creditors and debtors in debt pleas in all three courts, in suits against both men and women. Many of the features of women's work, identified in numerous studies of different English towns, are reflected in these pleas. Female litigants were involved in complaints arising from transactions concerning the sale of household essentials, food and drink, petty trading and service – all identified as common forms and characteristics of women's work.[18]

In the towns compared here, women were always a minority among debt litigants, reflecting their marginal economic status and their lesser integration into local credit networks. However, the proportions of female litigants varied across different courts and over time. They accounted for between 4–17 per cent of litigants in debt pleas, with Nottingham women generally being a larger proportion of litigants than those in Chester or Winchester. This variation is also apparent in other studies of women's debt litigation, with the highest proportion of women in court in the most commercially important centres where a wider range of occupations and marketing were available to them. London women appear to have been more litigious than those in provincial towns: Matthew Stevens has shown that, in the city's Sheriff's Court, women were 26 per cent of debt litigants in 1320, declining to 21 per cent in 1461–2, though debt came to account for a larger percentage of women's actions.[19] In contrast, women's presence in economic pleas was lower in smaller urban centres. In Ruthin (Wales), women were 10 per cent (58 of 573) of debt (unjust detention) litigants in the court rolls from 1312–21.[20] Maryanne Kowaleski's study of Exeter (Devon) debt suits identified a total of 332 different female litigants, only around 7 per cent of the total.[21] David Postles' analysis of debt litigation in the small town of Loughborough (Leicestershire) similarly found that only 7 per cent (13 of 190) of cases featured women.[22] But debt litigation was not just an urban phenomenon. In manorial courts, women's involvement in debt pleas also varied from one manor to another, as well as changing over time. Chris Briggs's analysis of women's litigation in the English manors of Oakington (Cambridgeshire) and Great Horwood (Buckinghamshire) identified that women comprised 13.7 and 18.4 per cent of litigants respectively before 1350.[23] However, Judith Bennett found that only 8.2 per cent of Brigstock (Northamptonshire) debt litigants were women.[24] These varying patterns in women's litigation were a product of differences in both local context and legal practice, as the evidence from the three towns examined here demonstrates. Elsewhere in Northern Europe, women's roles as creditors and debtors have also been noted, for example in the city of Ghent. Here, women were active participants in economic acts that were recorded in the registers of the city's aldermen.[25]

The numbers of female litigants were not so low, however, that women should be considered exceptional, or their litigation dismissed without further consideration. Nor should we focus only on the numbers, and thus compare women's more infrequent suits against a 'male' norm. As outlined in Chapter 1, tracing the root and outcomes of suits can be problematic, but it is clear that women could and did win their cases, and when they came to court they were not obviously prejudiced because of their sex. When a complaint was referred to the judgement of a jury, we see that these reports could fall in favour of female litigants, with no indication that women's complaints or responses to complaints were deemed to be more or less trustworthy on account of their sex. It was, after all, in each court's interest to provide a forum for the enforcement of commercial obligations and facilitate accessible and efficient dispute resolution. These mechanisms were open to both men and women, though some women did face limitations based on their marital status, an issue that is central to the analysis of this chapter.

Women's legal action reflected their public presence in the marketplace and the wider economy, though there was not a simple or direct correlation between litigation and women's commercial lives. Numerous studies have nevertheless used women's legal action as an indicator of their 'real-life' economic activity. These studies draw links between commercial litigation and economic opportunity or status, using legal action to highlight women's commercial roles and their sometimes considerable agency. Stevens has interpreted women's involvement in 'economically orientated actions' of debt and detinue in London's courts as an indicator of their economic opportunities. The fact that these actions increased as a proportion of women's litigation after the Black Death is therefore suggestive of 'somewhat enhanced economic opportunities'.[26] Cathryn Spence has also used women's debt litigation in early modern Scotland to highlight their important role in the credit networks of the urban economy and the visibility of women of all statuses and life cycle stages.[27] Kowaleski's work on Exeter is based on the assumption that debt cases accurately reflect medieval commercial life, and Briggs has similarly suggested that there was a positive relationship between women's litigation in economic disputes and their economic activity.[28] The fact that women appeared in debt litigation in London more than they did in smaller towns (and rural manors) across the medieval and early modern periods supports the case for women's greater integration within the urban economy in London, compared to smaller centres.[29] As discussed in Chapter 1, a small number of towns and cities, including London, operated under local customs that allowed certain women to trade *femme sole*, acting as though single when they were married. These women were liable to answer plaints of debt and trespass concerning their own trade and merchandise in their own name, thereby helping to account for women's greater presence in the records of litigation.[30] The potential of this status may have contributed to the so-called 'golden age' for women in London, where the 'rosy' position of women enabled them to work throughout the life cycle, across all sections of society, and in every trade and craft.[31]

However, it has also been widely acknowledged that the patriarchal traditions that underpinned women's marginal legal status served to obscure them from view in many of the legal records, especially in the large majority of towns where *femme sole* status did not exist. This included the records of credit and debt, particularly in the case of married women whose work was hidden by their husbands, or whose financial transactions were underrepresented in court due to their husbands' legal accountability.[32] The records of local courts reveal varying interpretations of women's legal capacity in relation to their economic activity, meaning that there was not a direct correlation between women's economic activity and their involvement in debt pleas. The hidden aspects of women's lives must, therefore, be taken into account when identifying and explaining patterns in women's legal actions. This involves looking beyond the numbers and the documenting of formal customs (like *femme sole*), examining the records of litigation in practice to understand how and why women acted as parties (or not) in debt suits and considering the 'types' or statuses of women found in the records. These issues were a product of each court's individual legal customs and record-keeping practices, meaning that general statements about women's status or actions as litigants should be considered critically. Rather than a direct reflection, the records of debt litigation should therefore be understood as a representation of women's commercial activity, refracted and filtered by legal custom.

Nottingham

Nottingham women engaged in litigation in greater numbers than those in Winchester or Chester. They accounted for up to a quarter of all litigants in the town's borough court. Their involvement in debt suits was less than this, but rose over the course of the fourteenth century before declining at the end of the century and into the fifteenth century, as Table 2.2 illustrates. By 1395, the majority of women using the court (43 of 64) were debt litigants: their commercial activity was the main reason leading to legal action, reflecting the overall dominance of debt pleas at the court (as illustrated in Table 2.1). The dominance of

Table 2.2 Female litigants and debt litigants in Nottingham.

Year	A: Total unique litigants	B: Unique female litigants	C: Total debt litigants	D: Female debt litigants
1323–4	416	109 (26%)	153	15 (11%)
1375–6	469	92 (20%)	327	54 (17%)
1394–5	395	64 (16%)	280	43 (15%)
1433–4	524	67 (13%)	419	41 (10%)
1446–7	483	35 (7%)	314	11 (4%)
1491–2	590	45 (8%)	439	28 (6%)

Source: NA CA 1258B, CA 1279, CA 1294, CA 1324, CA 1325, CA 1336, CA 1374.

debt pleas in women's legal actions continued into the fifteenth century, though there was a dip in the 1446–7 sample. By this point, however, there had been a marked decline in the overall number and percentage of female litigants in all pleas. This decline was particularly marked among the records classed as burgess pleas, with more female litigants being found within the foreign (i.e., outsiders) plea rolls of the fifteenth-century court roll samples. However, many of these women were 'of Nottingham' (such as Margaret Middleton, Margery Valey and Alice Knyght), while others were drawn into litigation through their trading links to Nottingham residents, showing that these pleas were not exclusively those of outsiders. There are perhaps more women in the foreign plea rolls because these represented the pleas of non-burgesses, and women were less likely to be burgesses. However, the inclusion of women in the rolls of burgess pleas indicates that, if all of these litigants really were burgesses, this was not a status that was exclusively male, or that 'burgess pleas' did not only relate to those who held formal burgess status. The basis for the division of pleas as 'burgess' or foreign' was not therefore as clear as the two categories would suggest.

The increase in women's debt litigation, at least up to the end of the third quarter of the fourteenth century, reflects the London pattern identified by Stevens, where economic pleas came to dominate women's legal action, despite an overall intensification in the patriarchal forces that limited women's legal status and their capacity to settle disputes.[33] In other words, Nottingham women, like those in London, became less likely to go to court, but when they did they were more likely to act in pleas of debt than other complaints. If increasing volumes of debt litigation indicate a greater volume of credit in circulation and thus a healthier economy, as discussed earlier, then this pattern of female litigation points to women's integration into the credit system.[34] Furthermore, contextualising this pattern against all litigation shows that this was not a gendered development that affected only women. Debt pleas increasingly dominated the business of all three courts, as Table 2.1 has shown, demonstrating how 'economically orientated' pleas were central to the legal action of all those who engaged with town courts. Changing volumes of litigation may also have reflected the growing legal consciousness of litigants, with borough residents choosing to use the court to register or enforce business agreements instead of other, informal channels. Debt litigation could also serve as an alternative to arbitration, as court rolls frequently recorded agreements between the parties.[35] However, by the end of the fifteenth century, women's involvement in debt litigation was much rarer. The longer term pattern of women's involvement in debt pleas across the fourteenth and fifteenth centuries roughly reflects Jeremy Goldberg's argument concerning the impact of the Black Death on women's work. Goldberg argued that, in York, women's working opportunities increased in the decades of demographic recession and labour shortages following the Black Death, peaking during the first half of the fifteenth century before declining again.[36] We see a similar pattern in women's participation in debt pleas in Nottingham, though the high point in women's economic litigation occurred earlier, within a generation of the Black Death and subsequent major outbreaks of plague. While it is unrealistic to suggest that debt litigation directly correlated with levels of economic activity, the patterns and changes in women's legal actions can nevertheless be read as representative of broader shifts in women's working activities and the commercial ties that came out of various types of work, including trade, the production of various goods and service. The evidence of women's involvement in debt litigation therefore suggests that enhanced working or trading opportunities for women brought with them an increased likelihood of debt litigation, further suggesting that this litigation was indeed a sign of commercial integration, not crisis.

These shifts in women's working status must be contextualised by women's legal status within their local courts. In Nottingham, the decline in women's debt litigation across the fifteenth century can largely be accounted for by the decline of married women acting alongside their husbands in debt suits. This complicates the patterns of women's economic visibility as represented in the legal records, showing that it was in fact a product of both their commercial activity and legal status. Joint pleas of husband and wife accounted for around half of women's debt suits in the mid to late fourteenth century, but became increasingly exceptional by the later fifteenth century. Numerous couples acted as co-litigants in debt suits during the fourteenth century, such as John and Margery Coke, who were sued by William Etwell for a debt of 12d loaned to them.[37] By the end of the fifteenth century, most of the women acting in debt suits were single women, often specified to be widows, whose involvement in local credit networks (and subsequent litigation) likely arose from their independent business agreements and trading after the death of their husband, or the debts that they inherited. For example, in 1491, Isabella Couper sued Margaret Derby, both called *vidua* (widow), for a debt of 5s 6d owed for rent of a tenement in Nottingham. In the same year Elizabeth Lee, widow of Thomas Lee of Nottingham, administrator of his goods, chattels and debts, was ordered to pay a debt of 69s (presumably owed by her late husband) to John Warner junior of London.[38] These complaints were typical of women's debt litigation at the end of the fifteenth century, while a century before, numerous spouses had acted together as co-litigants in debt pleas. This shift is discussed in more detail in the second half of this chapter, drawing comparisons with the other towns examined here.

Nottingham women acted as both plaintiffs and defendants in debt pleas, revealing their roles as creditors and debtors within the urban economy. There was no discernible pattern in women's propensity to act on either side of these suits, as Table 2.3 indicates. The rise and fall in women's debt litigation was therefore comprised of an increase and then decline in actions as both plaintiffs and defendants, reflecting their role on both sides of transactions, rather than indicating a particular tendency to default on their debts.

Quantitative analysis does not, however, reveal the legal actions of individual women, some of whom were repeat or regular litigants. Some individuals were 'repeat offenders' owing many debts to different creditors, but this did not automatically make them commercial delinquents. After

Table 2.3 Female creditors and debtors in Nottingham.

Year	A: Unique female debt litigants	B: Total creditors	C: Female creditors (%B)	D: Total debtors	E: Female debtors (%D)
1323–4	15 (11%)	72	6 (8%)	94	11 (12%)
1375–6	54 (17%)	187	26 (14%)	186	28 (15%)
1394–5	43 (15%)	162	21 (13%)	168	22 (13%)
1433–4	41 (10%)	238	26 (11%)	243	30 (12%)
1446–7	11 (4%)	175	7 (4%)	162	5 (3%)
1491–2	28 (6%)	231	20 (9%)	236	15 (6%)

Source: NA CA 1258B, CA 1279, CA 1294, CA 1324, CA 1325, CA 1336, CA 1374.

all, debts were usually accrued through purchases, and the fact that a creditor agreed to defer payment in the first place suggests a degree of trust in the buyer to repay the debt at a later date – central to what Craig Muldrew has famously termed the 'culture of credit'.[39] Hannah Robb has recently argued that this sociability of credit, underpinned by reputation-based negotiations, was fundamental to the economy of late medieval England as well as the early modern period.[40] Women's litigation saw them bringing and responding to complaints concerning the sale of a range of goods and services, reflecting their active role in the urban economy. Their debts frequently concerned money owed for the selling of ale, or costs accrued through the brewing process, an area well-known as a particularly female form of production.[41] Various Nottingham women were regular debt litigants, appearing in multiple suits against different opponents, indicating their wide commercial networks. In 1375–6, 14 women appeared independently in court as debtors in 29 suits. These women were not described according to any specific marital status, so are tentatively assumed to have been single – either never-married or widows. They were responsible for their own credit transactions and were required to account for them in court. In the same year, 14 couples answered only 18 separate suits, indicating wives' more intermittent litigation. Male litigants were more likely to initiate multiple debt complaints, and this was particularly true of the town's elite. John Strelley, a member of a local gentry family, sued 14 different individuals for debt in the year 1375–6; John Samon, Mayor of Nottingham, was plaintiff in suits against 10 individuals, while John Plumptre, a future mayor, brought complaints against three separate opponents.[42] These complaints evidence both the high levels of litigiousness within the urban community, as well as the complex credit networks that many individuals were tied to.

Some women were also prolific litigants. Agnes Halum appeared in over 30 suits across the last quarter of the fourteenth century, revealing her large commercial network and involvement in what was probably 'professional' brewing. She was a long-term and regular litigant at the borough court, who appeared as a plaintiff from time to time, but was more frequently a debtor. Though she acted alone in the vast majority of these suits, she was certainly married for some of her 'legal career', and possibly all of it. But the fact that her litigation related to her independent business activity appears to have negated the supposed limits of coverture that should have seen Halum act jointly with her husband.[43] The nature of Halum's litigation reveals that the kind of work she was involved in was a typically 'female' area of the urban economy, further making sense of her independent legal action. She was regularly involved in disputes relating to the brewing and sale of ale, and a trespass complaint brought by Halum suggests that she also ran an alehouse.[44] She was named in debt suits by various individuals including William Pykard, John Alferton, John Thory, William Cotyler, William Frankleyn, William Leche and Richard and Margaret Wilford, and also brought complaints of her own. In many cases few details are recorded beyond the type of plea and sometimes the sum being sought. We know, however, that the complaints brought by William Cotyler related to an alleged debt of 6s, the detention of a pair of boots or spurs worth 18d and the breaking of two lead vessels (probably used for brewing) loaned to Halum.[45] It is this careful piecing together of the evidence, drawing on multiple cases and series of court rolls, that offers an insight into the lives and status of individual women. In the case of Agnes Halum, this also reveals that at least some of the women who pleaded alone were in fact married, not just those women who appeared with their husbands. Despite living within a legal system that, theoretically, subsumed the legal identity of wives under the coverture of their husbands, some married women could nevertheless exercise independent legal capability in certain situations, a fact that Shennan Hutton has argued for late medieval Ghent too, where women were also 'under the power' of their husbands.[46] If Agnes Halum was an exception to this pattern, there were undoubtedly other women in a similar position too.

Joan Lemeryng, a widow involved in the local coal industry, was also a regular debtor during the 1370s, and Margery Waturleder, also a widow, featured in several debt suits arising from her work in the provision of water in 1375.[47] She complained of an unknown amount owed by John de Cunesburgh in October 1375 and 13d owed for water by Matthew de Skydby in April 1376, though the inquisition jury reported that he owed her nothing.[48] Robert and Alice Waturleder alleged that Margery Waturleder owed them a debt of 10d for rent of a room for five days. The parties came to an agreement and Margery was fined 3d.[49] Joan Brailsford appeared in numerous suits as plaintiff and defendant in 1394–5, including a debt owed by Richard Brasse following a loan of 3s 11d and a debt of 7 ½d for ale owed by William Skelton junior, which he acknowledged in court.[50] She also sought £4 from John and Richard, sons of William de Etwall, owed for pots that they bought from her. The parties later agreed and Brailsford was amerced, presumably for bringing a false claim.[51]

Many of these female litigants were independent traders with multiple connections across the urban network, revealed by their repeated involvement in litigation. We know that at least some of these women were widows, and others may have been never-married single women, who were legally and commercially independent. Margaret Middleton, occasionally called the widow of William Middleton, appeared in court regularly during the mid-fifteenth century in relation to various debts owed to and by a range of men. In 1433-4, she sued six different men for debt and was herself sued by nine men, one married couple and one widow for debts she owed to them.[52] Many of these debts, as well as pleas found in subsequent years, related to purchases of cloth or the production of clothing, some of which had passed from husband to widow. William Middleton also acted as attorney for numerous litigants in the borough court prior to his death, though this collection of suits suggests some involvement in the cloth or tailoring trade too, which Margaret continued in her widowhood. When she sued Thomas Beauchamp for debt in December 1433, she complained that he had, in 1429, left two robes with William to be furred for the price of 4s, and had not paid William in his lifetime, nor Margaret after his death.[53] It was only in this instance that Margaret was specifically recorded as William's widow, despite the fact that all of her other suits in this year were also made possible by the fact that her husband had died, probably within the last year.[54] In the same year, she complained of 8s 6d owed by Robert Laurence of Radcliffe for a robe that he had bought from her.[55] This plea was not apparently a legacy of her late husband's business arrangements: she had sold the robe to Robert herself, so she was not specified as being William's widow. The selective use of this status demonstrates the mutability with which women's marital statuses were deemed significant within the written record of the court.

As these and numerous other examples indicate, women litigated against both men and other women, and in relation to debts of ranging values and nature. Complaints relating to money owed for ale were notably common, reflecting women's well-known involvement in the production and sale of ale. Though they were always a minority of litigants, women's commercial litigation was not exceptional; some women were in court more often than others, but this was nevertheless indicative of the potential for legal and commercial agency that the court afforded to Nottingham women engaged in independent commercial activity.

Winchester

In Winchester, women accounted for a similar minority of debt litigants to those in Nottingham, ranging from 12-16 per cent, as set out in Table 2.4. Debt pleas were not as dominant in Winchester's City Court as

Table 2.4 Female litigants at Winchester City Court.

Year	A: Total unique litigants	B: Female litigants	C: Total debt litigants	D: Female debt litigants
1299–1300	377	70 (19%)	170	22 (13%)
1365–6	265	49 (18%)	148	23 (16%)
1385–6	191	37 (19%)	130	15 (12%)
1432–3	379	38 (10%)	260	25 (10%)
1454–5	328	37 (11%)	212	13 (6%)
1494–5	186	17 (9%)	128	11 (9%)

Source: HRO W/D1/3, W/D1/13, W/D1/27, W/D1/60, W/D1/61, W/D1/64.

they were at Nottingham: they were up to 62 per cent of the total, compared to over 80 per cent at Nottingham (see Table 2.1). This is reflected in the general patterns of women's pleas, which were also less defined by debt suits. As was also true in Nottingham, women's participation in litigation declined, falling from 19 to 9 per cent of all litigants from the turn of the fourteenth to the end of the fifteenth century. Their involvement in debt suits rose and then declined, much like the pattern for Nottingham. By the end of the fifteenth century, Winchester women accounted for a small number of litigants in debt suits, but though the percentage of female litigants fluctuated across the samples compiled here, the average percentage across the whole period was around 11 per cent. As we have seen for Nottingham, the post-plague peak in women's involvement in debt pleas also suggests their enhanced economic opportunities immediately following the plague, followed by a return to more 'normal' levels and subsequent decline.

Winchester women were generally more often in court as debtors, as Table 2.5 indicates, suggesting that they were less likely to act as creditors

Table 2.5 Female creditors and debtors at Winchester City Court.

Year	A: Total creditors	Female creditors (%A)	B: Total debtors	Female debtors (%B)
1299–1300	86	7 (8%)	97	15 (15%)
1365–6	81	9 (11%)	78	15 (19%)
1385–6	73	6 (8%)	65	9 (14%)
1432–3	164	16 (11%)	166	11 (7%)
1454–5	117	5 (4%)	125	9 (7%)
1494–5	72	6 (8%)	72	8 (11%)

Source: HRO W/D1/3, W/D1/13, W/D1/27, W/D1/60, W/D1/61, W/D1/64.

in urban trade networks, or less often took legal action to pursue debts owed to them. The overall numbers of female litigants here are low, however, and the numbers also fluctuated from one sample to another, limiting the statistical significance of these patterns. In addition, many litigants acted as both plaintiffs and defendants in different suits, so we should not place too much weight on the differences in women's actions on either side of these suits.

Despite their more regular appearances as debtors, these appearances show that women were accruing debts through their own transactions and this again serves to indicate their status as individuals worthy of and able to secure credit. Women such as Agatha de Bertone, Agatha de Candevan, Isabella Tropinel, Joan widow of Walter Benger and Matilda de Mucheldevere, all in court over the year 1299–1300, were debtors in complaints ranging in value from 3d to 27s, representing commercial transactions and creditworthiness at a range of different scales.[56] Female creditors included Amya Uppam and Agnes Kembestre, in court in 1365 to recover debts of 4s 6d and 8s 8d respectively, both owed and acknowledged by male debtors.[57] An alternative form of credit is seen in Alice Broun's successful recovery of 12d owed to her for service by Robert Bonne, a butcher, in 1386.[58] The act of working on the assurance of later payment was itself a credit transaction. The values of women's credit varied, just as it did for men, though the scale of men's credit agreements was typically higher and greater in range. In the same year, male creditors brought complaints concerning sums ranging from the 18d owed by William Moutoun to Nicholas Fairber, to the £4 2s owed by Richard Tuttemound to John Byketoun, a prominent Winchester merchant.[59] The majority of other debts – both male and female – ranged between 2 and 6s.

Unlike the Nottingham records, debt pleas concerning sums of a few pence feature infrequently in the Winchester court rolls. Instead, it appears that higher value debts (in the range of shillings rather than pence) were prioritised in the recording of the court's business. The lesser presence of small debts also suggests that residents did not tend to go to court over these small sums, which may have meant that this was less often a form of justice used by the city's lower status workers and traders – many of whom would have been women. Instead, we have a picture of a court used by more prosperous traders and merchants in the enforcement and regulation of valuable credit transactions. Some of these high-value debts did, however, involve women, sometimes on both sides of the transaction, such as the complaint between Agatha Spycer and Alice Mercer cited at the beginning of this chapter.[60] Both of these women may have been specialist merchants (suggested by their surnames, and the fact that Spycer was additionally called a merchant in other pleas), engaged in high-value trade that went beyond household provisioning.[61] Mercer's acknowledgement of the debt suggests her willingness to repay the money owed, rather than enter into protracted litigation, despite the high value of the debt. This may not even have been a 'real' dispute, but instead simply a means of getting Mercer to pay up. In another high-value claim in 1385, Joan Cogayn accused John Braylesford of owing her 39s 3d with the merchant John Byketoun acting as her attorney, though the eventual outcome is unknown.[62] Smaller but still substantial sums were recorded in other complaints, such as the 5s 8d owed to William le Breware by Agnes, servant of Richard Rudbrigge, and 8s 8d owed by Andrew Frere to Agnes Kembestre (all in 1365–6).[63]

Another characteristic that may also be accounted for by the higher preponderance of larger debts – the domain of higher status, wealthy traders – is the fact that few Winchester women appeared in multiple debt suits, unlike their Nottingham counterparts. Most women were involved in only one suit in a given year. Agatha Spycer did, however, feature in multiple pleas, including a suit against merchant John Wynslowe of London as well as the aforementioned suit against Alice Mercer.[64] Spycer sat at the higher end of the commercial hierarchy in the city (at least in terms of women), and this enhanced status is likely to have led to a greater number of commercial ties and transactions. In contrast, some Winchester men were frequent users of the City Court, reflecting their larger economic networks.[65] Thomas Elbegate featured in at least 11 different debt pleas in 1299–1300, involving at least 10 different opponents, while in 1365–6 John Byketoun, a merchant who held many official posts during the 1350s and 1360s, brought six different complaints relating to debt, detinue and covenant to the court.[66] In other words, the court records depict commerce in Winchester as being overwhelmingly dominated by men, whose wider trade networks resulted in more unfulfilled credit arrangements, and thus more litigation. This was a court of merchants and established, prosperous craftsmen and producers, not petty traders or women who were responsible for everyday provisioning of the household.

Chester

At Chester's Pentice Court, women were less active than those in Nottingham or Winchester from the beginning of the period, though as was true elsewhere, their litigation in all suits also declined over the

Table 2.6 Female litigants at Chester's Pentice Court.

Year	A: Total litigants	B: Female litigants	C: Total debt litigants	D: Female debt litigants
1317–18	381	66 (16%)	277	38 (14%)
1378	272	33 (12%)	236	16 (7%)
1395	210	21 (10%)	117	8 (7%)
1423	294	30 (10%)	211	14 (7%)
1435	423	56 (13%)	305	35 (11%)
1490	500	57 (11%)	355	41 (12%)

Source: Cheshire Archives and Local Studies (CALS) ZSR 21, 81–85, 109–112, 147–155, 201–210, 369–380; A. Hopkins (ed.), *Selected Rolls of the Chester City Courts* (Manchester: Chetham Society, 1950), pp. 33–96.

fourteenth to fifteenth century, before some recovery in the mid to late fifteenth century (see Table 2.6). For both male and female litigants, debt pleas were the main dispute heard by the court, accounting for around 70 per cent of cases (see Table 2.1). However, unlike at Nottingham and Winchester, there was a marked decline in women's participation in these suits over the fourteenth century, and by the 1370s they accounted for less than 10 per cent of all debt litigants. The decline in women's debt litigation occurred earlier than it did in Nottingham or Winchester – most likely before the plague, with no evidence of a post-Black Death rise in women's economic activities or litigation – though the numbers recovered somewhat in the fifteenth century. The drop in the proportion of female debt litigants was a result of a notable decline in the litigation of married women. The earliest sample featured numerous married women as co-litigants alongside their husbands, such as Robert and Wladus (Gladys) de Frodisham, who complained of a debt of 20s for malt owed by Henry and Elena de Doncaster, but married women soon disappeared from the court rolls.[67]

Chester women were more often in court as debtors than creditors, following the pattern identified for Winchester. However, the declining number of female litigants means that sample size here is particularly small for some years, limiting the use of any statistical comparisons.[68] Some of Chester's female litigants appeared in more than one suit (like Margery, widow of Nicholas Goldsmyth, and Margaret Laynes, who both brought two complaints in 1423), though none appear to have been as litigious as some of the regular female litigants found in Nottingham.[69] In contrast, many men appear as repeat litigants, complaining about debts owed by numerous contacts. In 1423, Adam Wotton brought debt

complaints against five different men, and William Malpas was in four different pleas.[70]

The Pentice Court sometimes heard suits regarding much larger debts than those found elsewhere, above the theoretical limit of 40s.[71] This may have been something of a jurisdictional quirk, a reflection of Chester's position within the palatinate and its separate status from the rest of England, but may also be explained by the provision of formal evidence in cases concerning larger debts.[72] In 1317, Alice, widow of John Jamube, was accused by William le Rous of detaining 54s. William le Rous produced a tally stick in court, used to record the substantial debt, which Jamube acknowledged.[73] Another widow, Lucy Waterfal, acknowledged a debt of £6 14s 8d owed to John de Thornham.[74] She also appeared in a number of other debt pleas during the early fourteenth century.[75] The fact that these women were widows stands out here, as many non-married women were simply recorded using their full names. This suggests that their widowhood was a significant factor in relation to these particular debts and thus warranted official documentation.[76] The debts may have been accrued by their husbands, or may have represented the women's independent business transactions, facilitated by their status as widows and indicating their significant creditworthiness. The legal competence of London widows, who brought suits for recovery of dower, has been highlighted by Barbara Hanawalt; this knowledge and acumen can also be extended to widows' use of their local courts to manage their commercial interests and carry out their roles as executrices.[77] Though they may not have repaid their debts on time, they readily acknowledged them when brought to court, again suggesting that litigation could be a tool for enforcing payment, rather than being symptomatic of commercial conflict. Debt litigation also acted as a means of entering transactions into the written record of a town, and this would have been particularly useful in instances of high-value debts.[78]

Other women who appeared in court alone, but whose marital status was not specifically recorded, were also involved in substantial credit transactions. In 1378, Cecilia York was accused of owing 12s 8d to Walter le G (surname unknown) and Katherine le Noble was sued for 5s 6d by David de Strychelegh.[79] In 1395, Alice la Shermon sought 8s along with clothing worth 12s detained by Roger Aspeshagh.[80] However, this is not to say that all female debt litigants were involved in these high-value transactions. Notably small debts were also resolved at the Pentice Court, such as the 3d for milk that Matilda le Spenser acknowledged owing to Alice, widow of John Hammes, in 1317.[81] Despite the small sum, Alice still deemed it worthwhile to take this plea to court. The rarity with which these low value debts are found among the court records suggests, however, that the residents of these towns only resorted to law when substantial debts were owed, perhaps settling smaller disputes informally out of court, or that the court paid more attention to these complaints when more was at stake.

Differences in women's debt litigation: intersections of commerce, coverture and custom

There are many features of women's debt litigation that were shared across the three courts. The first of these relates to the low numbers of women acting as debt litigants. Statistically, female litigants accounted for a minority of those involved in pleas of debt and detinue across all three towns, nowhere rising above the 17 per cent peak in Nottingham. Furthermore, women's involvement in debt litigation was on a general trajectory of decline in all three towns across the late medieval period, though nowhere was this a constant downward trend. The proportion of female debt litigants in all three courts fell to around or under 10 per cent, figures that are comparable to statistics gathered for places such as Exeter, Loughborough, Ruthin and Brigstock.[82] In Nottingham and Winchester, this was a continuous decline from the latter stages of the fourteenth century, while in Chester, there was a period of decline followed by recovery. If we read debt litigation as indicative of commercial activity and status, this evidence brings into question the existence of a 'golden age' for women in the century or so following the Black Death, though the figures from Nottingham and Winchester are suggestive of a short-term, more immediate rise in women's commercial activity within a generation of so of the Black Death. But the link between women's commercial and legal actions was more complex than this, as the court records also indicate increasing limitations on women's ability to represent their commercial actions under local law. This in turn would have limited their ability to participate in credit networks and transactions, as creditors required trust both in an individual's fidelity and in a system that would allow them to seek restitution of a debt if it was not repaid when agreed.

Second, there were also commonalities in the nature of women's debt suits. Women were less likely to be repeat litigants than men, and were less often involved in transacting the highest value debts. Numerous Nottingham women were repeat litigants in debt pleas, revealing their commercial ties with a range of other individuals and suggesting a relatively 'normal' resort to litigation. However, women in Winchester and

Chester tended not to appear in multiple suits, indicating their lesser overall commercial integration while also suggesting that litigation was perhaps a more exceptional, last resort event. The Nottingham records frequently record claims for small debts, while the Winchester and Chester rolls provide less evidence for these small transactions, in part because we have less detail on the nature of specific debts from these two courts, though it is also apparent that these courts tended to be used to settle more substantial debt disputes. These smaller sums represented the lower level of trade where women were more often found.

Despite these shared characteristics, there were also significant differences in the patterns of women's litigation across the different towns and over time. To account for this, we need to consider women litigants not as one unified group, but to examine the different legal statuses and actions of different 'types' or statuses of these women. The marital status of women was a key determinant of women's litigation in commercial suits, with women's legal status being influenced by common law doctrine, even in local customary courts, as Matthew Stevens and others have argued.[83] As outlined in the Introduction, the doctrine of coverture stipulated that married women did not exist as independent legal actors but that their identities were instead merged with that of their husband. Various studies have suggested that these limitations extended beyond the common law to a range of jurisdictions including borough and manorial courts, stating that husbands would take legal action on behalf of both spouses, with the exception being married women who were trading as *femmes sole*.[84] Marjorie McIntosh has commented on the lack of understanding of the way in which towns 'that lacked formal provision for *femme sole* activity ... handled disputes arising from the independent economic dealings of married women', suggesting that their activity was probably hidden behind suits in which men only or both spouses featured as parties.[85] However, this is an issue that has not been examined in depth for medieval borough courts. The exception here is for London, where Stevens has shown that couples, during the fourteenth century, chose to bring plaints jointly as co-litigants, but that this tendency had faded by the mid-fifteenth century.[86] Stevens' study of Ruthin in Dyffryn Clwyd has also noted the underrepresentation of married women in debt suits, as they were 'eclipsed' by their husbands' legal status. Only two married women (of a total of 58 women) appeared in these suits over a nine-year period.[87]

London was not the only place where spouses litigated jointly in debt suits. Nottingham couples regularly engaged in litigation during the fourteenth century, but these pleas declined in the fifteenth century,

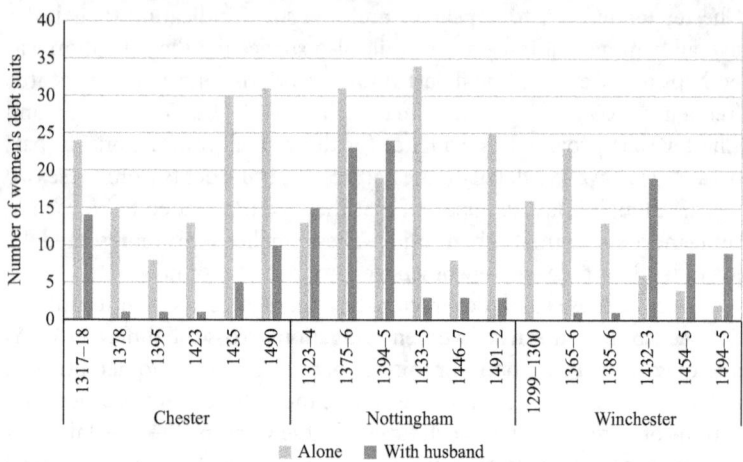

Figure 2.1 Female debt litigants in Chester, Nottingham and Winchester, separated according to those who acted alone and those who pleaded jointly with their husbands.

Source: CALS ZSR 21, 81–85, 109–112, 147–155, 201–210, 369–380; NA CA 1258B, CA 1279, CA 1294, CA 1324, CA 1325, CA 1336, CA 1374; HRO W/D1/3, W/D1/13, W/D1/27, W/D1/60, W/D1/61, W/D1/64.

as the graph in Figure 2.1 shows. The involvement of Chester wives in debt suits also declined, but this happened much earlier in the fourteenth century; while in Winchester, married women's litigation was extremely rare in the fourteenth century, though more frequent in the fifteenth century. Fundamentally, these differing patterns reveal unique and fluid understandings of wives' ability to take legal action in relation to their commercial roles, revealing each court's practical interpretation of coverture in relation to the transactions and litigation that underpinned women's engagement in the urban economy. These differences feed into the overall patterns and shifts in the numbers of female debt litigants at all three courts, revealing an additional dimension to these statistics that does not simply reflect women's commercial activity.

The data here clearly illustrates the differing local patterns of married women's involvement in debt litigation and the notable ways that this varied over time. The separation of women according to whether they pleaded alone or with their husband does not necessarily correlate absolutely with the presence of unmarried/widowed and married women in court: we have already seen from the example of Agnes Halum of Nottingham that some of these lone women were in fact married. There are also other examples of married lone litigants from the other towns, like Matilda Mucheldevere of Winchester. She was plaintiff in a debt plea against Ralph le Taillur in 1299, and was recorded only by her full name, with no indication of her marital status – a fact which is generally taken to indicate single status. She was also sued by Adam de la Pult for detaining 12d.[88] However, cross-referencing with other suits recorded in the same year reveals that she was in fact married to Roger Mucheldevere, and she appeared as co-litigant with him in an unsuccessful trespass plea against Walter Crabbeleg.[89] While these examples are rare and difficult to identify, a little lucky digging below the surface of individual pleas demonstrates that some married women could and did appear in court without their husbands, and without being labelled according to their marital status. There were undoubtedly other married women who were recorded 'as if single' within the court records, but the brevity involved in recording litigants' marital identities means that we can only be absolutely certain about the status of those specifically termed as 'wife' or 'widow'. The categories presented in Figure 2.1 nevertheless allow for observation of general patterns.

In Nottingham during the fourteenth century, debt litigation involved women of all marital statuses. Joint pleas involving husband and wife were common, and sometimes accounted for over half of all women's involvement in debt pleas, where they acted as both plaintiffs and defendants. Though wives do not appear to have brought or replied to complaints independently (apart from exceptions such as Agnes Halum), their actions alongside their husbands expand the profile of married women's commercial and legal identities beyond the general picture of invisibility under coverture painted by other studies. However, during the early decades of the fifteenth century, the litigation of spouses declined, and by the 1430s only a handful of wives appeared in these pleas. Meanwhile, in Chester and Winchester, women acting alone – many of whom would have been never-married or widowed single women – were nearly always dominant among female litigants. Spouses acted as co-litigants in Chester at the beginning of the fourteenth century, but this practice quickly declined, probably as early as the 1330s. Wives' involvement in debt suits after this point was generally exceptional. At Chester and Nottingham therefore (and as Stevens has suggested for London), the decline in the overall number and proportion of female debt litigants is largely accounted for by the fact that married women's involvement in these pleas came to be an exception, rather than part of normal practice.[90] At Winchester, however, the numbers of lone and married women in debt suits appear to have reversed from the fourteenth to fifteenth centuries. These varying patterns clearly demonstrate that broad-brush assumptions about the legal status of married women in debt suits are not indicative of the 'reality' of married women's legal experiences in various courts and in different periods.

To understand what these general patterns meant for women's litigation in practice, we need to examine the litigation of married women and the nature of their joint pleas in more detail. The litigation of married women in Nottingham in particular warrants further examination, and it is here that the sources provide the greatest insight into the nature of these pleas. Of the three towns, Nottingham was somewhat exceptional in the volume of pleas that involved married women. While adhering to the general principle of coverture that prevented married women from bringing suits alone, the court permitted – and perhaps even expected – wives' participation in legal action arising from transactions agreed jointly with their husbands, as their husbands' agents, or from wives' independent business.[91] This form of legal action was not exceptional, and was found in various other jurisdictions across premodern Britain. For London women in both the Sheriff's Court and Court of Common Pleas, 'the convention of coverture left ample scope for married women to appear before the court' in economic litigation.[92] It has also been suggested that Shrewsbury's borough court included cases where both spouses were named as plaintiffs or defendants.[93] In medieval Scotland, outside the English common law and the doctrine of coverture, married women prosecuted debtors both on their own and on their husbands' behalf, despite the fact that married women officially lacked the legal power to make contracts.[94] The extent of wives' litigation was so great by the early modern period that they were the largest group of women to appear as both creditors and debtors in Edinburgh's burgh court.[95] We see this flexible scope of coverture in evidence in Nottingham too, where joint pleas came to account for over half of women's debt litigation in Nottingham by the end of the fourteenth century, though the proportions of couples and lone female litigants fluctuated throughout the period. Wives' litigation, though theoretically unnecessary due to coverture, highlights the economic and legal agency of married women across a range of jurisdictions, bringing into question the extent to which coverture influenced married women's commercial and legal actions in everyday life.

Nottingham couples acted as both plaintiffs and defendants, revealing wives' actions as creditors and debtors and demonstrating the agency of wives in bringing complaints to court. They not only responded to the claims of others, but also took an active role in pursuing debts owed to them. What is striking about the data is that, from the fourteenth-century samples, 42 per cent of female creditors and 48 per cent of debtors were wives acting alongside their husbands, proportions that are similar to the figures for London married women's economic pleas (43 per cent) in the Court of Common Pleas.[96] Married women's actions in debt pleas were therefore a major component of Nottingham women's litigation as a whole during the fourteenth century. Wives' presence in these joint pleas was not simply symbolic or nominal, but indicative of their involvement in the initial credit arrangement. Many men who are known to have been married also appeared individually in other debt suits, representing transactions in which their wives took no part. There was clearly a distinction between litigation in which wives were or were not involved, reinforcing their important and active economic role as represented through these joint pleas.

Why were married women involved in debt litigation? What was it about certain transactions and women's roles within them that led to their being involved in debt suits in court? Answering these questions is far from straightforward, due to the nature of the details recorded about each debt in the court rolls. In Scottish burghs, Spence has used the details explaining a debt to unpick the reasons for wives' involvement in litigation, which most commonly involved both partners contracting a debt together. Other cases saw wives as principal actors, though it is assumed that they did so with the explicit or tacit permission of their husbands. Some of these cases featured the phrase 'for his interest' after the husband's name, more formally signalling his nominal role in the transaction and his legal responsibility for it.[97] The Nottingham records do not typically report in such clear ways either the individual accountability of wives, or joint agreements made by spouses in credit transactions, though these roles can often be inferred from the details that are recorded.

Spouses' debt suits related to a broad range of transactions, including those agreed by husband and wife together, as well as those made by the wife alone.[98] In February 1376, Richard Dandeson complained that Richard and Agnes Candler owed him 32d for candles, which the couple initially denied, though they later came to an agreement.[99] The nature of the debt and Richard's occupational surname suggest that both husband and wife were working together in the trade or production of candles, and it was this which brought them into court. A plea of November 1394 also suggests the joint transactions of spouses: Robert and Margery Polidod used the court to seek repayment of 22d from Richard and Alice Hawkburn, money that was owed for the purchase of ale and a cash loan. Richard and Alice were found to owe the money to Robert and Margery and ordered to pay 2d in damages.[100] The plea suggests that this transaction was agreed between both couples, though this may in fact mask an agreement made between two wives with the consent of their husbands. In some cases, this joint litigation represented couples' involvement in higher value, wholesale trade. In 1375, Matthew of Skegby complained that John Sutton (elsewhere called garleker or garlic monger) and his wife Alice owed him 10s for garlic and onions, which must have represented a large amount of vegetables. Both Matthew and Alice responded, saying that they owed nothing, though the jury disagreed.[101]

Other debts related to the independent actions of wives, undertaken with the explicit or tacit consent of their husbands. In 1374, William de Hontesdon sued Godesman Taylor and his wife Elena for a debt of 11s. He claimed that he had delivered a barrel of herring worth 11s to the couple for Elena to sell, but the couple detained the herring (or the profit from its sale).[102] In March 1391, Robert de Howedeyn and his wife Isabella complained that Tysson Braban had broken a covenant with them: Isabella had given him some thread to make into cloth for both Robert and Isabella, which Tysson had subsequently lost, thereby breaking his covenant.[103] Isabella de Howedeyn was the key agent in this transaction, though the contract concerned cloth for both spouses, so we can assume that they were already married at the time of the agreement. Others have suggested that wives' involvement in debt suits was a last resort in intractable cases, denoting these pleas as somewhat exceptional.[104] However, the wide range of married women's debt pleas in fourteenth-century Nottingham reflect their diverse roles within the urban economy, and the flexible and fluid nature of the marital economic partnership, which was well understood by the court in permitting or expecting spouses to bring and answer debt complaints jointly in order to account for the innumerable credit transactions that were required to supply a household and run a business.

These joint pleas were not unique to Nottingham, as Figure 2.1 shows. In Chester in 1317–18, 14 couples acted in joint pleas of debt or detinue. These wives accounted for 5 per cent of all debt litigants and over a third of all female debt litigants. These early joint pleas share many features with those from Nottingham, sometimes revealing wives' specific and apparently independent roles in transacting debts. In March 1318, John Cook brought a complaint against William de Forneby and his wife Christina, claiming that Christina unjustly detained payment for mutton that he had sold to her. The only place that William de Forneby was mentioned was in the initial recording of the defendants' names. It was Christina de Forneby who acknowledged and was amerced for the debt, revealing a degree of separation in the economic and legal identities of husband and wife.[105] Similarly, merchants William and Alice de Ellehale were sued by William le Rous, who alleged that they unjustly detained 42s that he had loaned to Alice. Rous produced a tally stick to prove the debt, used to record this high-value loan. The couple both denied the validity of the tally stick, though it was Alice de Ellehale who was required to swear an oath to this effect. William le Rous died before the dispute could be resolved.[106] These suits were nominally brought against both husband and wife, though the complaints related only to the wives' actions. Christina de Forneby personally acknowledged her debt, while Alice de Ellehale was required to attest to the apparently fraudulent tally stick. The nature of this litigation has many parallels with early complaints concerning *femme sole* women in London, where *sole* status was implied rather than stated, and pleas named husband and wife but only recalled debts owed by wives.[107] The Pentice Court appears to have operated a kind of informal *femme sole* custom in these earlier years, allowing considerable scope for married women to take legal action in suits relating to their commercial activity, with their husbands appearing in largely nominal roles. Married women were visible litigants, not always obscured behind their husbands, though there is no evidence that they were able to litigate completely independently without their husbands, in the way that a married man could. Other debts for everyday provisions reflected wives' responsibility for household provisioning undertaken as their husbands' agents under the 'law of necessaries'.[108] Philip and Alice Coco (Cook) were accused by John de Lynne of owing 5s for salt.[109] William and Margery de Blund sought 3s 6d from Henry and Elena de Doncaster, owed for half a bushel of malt wheat, which they successfully recovered plus substantial damages of 2s.[110]

The regularity with which couples litigated together again demonstrates the normative nature of these pleas, as well as the extent to which marriage was truly an economic partnership, which often transferred to the legal sphere. Spouses and households shared commercial networks that brought them into contact with numerous trading contacts, which could lead to couples repeatedly engaging in debt suits. In 1376, Nottingham's Robert and Margery Blyth brought complaints against both Thomas Chether and Reginald Walker, the latter concerning a debt of 16d.[111] In the same year, Richard and Margaret Wilford complained of both Agnes Halum and Joan Lemeryng, the latter of whom they claimed owed them 6s 8d.[112] Some suits involved couples on both sides, such as the plea brought by Laurence and Isabella Tyrington against Richard and Margery Grantham for a debt of 2s owed for ale. Though the defendants initially claimed they owed nothing, they later agreed and were amerced, suggesting that they did in fact detain the payment.[113] In both Nottingham and Chester, spouses' actions as co-litigants related to a broad range of commercial transactions that reflected both the commercial ties of husband and wife, and the household economy in general, as well as the independent business arrangements of married women.

As well as seeking to understand the nature of the transactions that led married women to act in debt suits, we also need to consider the timing of these transactions and the subsequent litigation. Matthew Stevens has argued that wives' actions in the Court of Common Pleas related to pre-marital debts, which became the responsibility of their husbands upon marriage, a fact also stated by Pollock and Maitland.[114] Elsewhere, such as in Ipswich and Norwich, custom dictated that husbands were also required to answer for their wives' debts accrued both before and after the marriage.[115] However, beyond a handful of examples, there is limited evidence that pre-marital debts lay behind married women's debt pleas in Nottingham or Chester.[116] In fact, there is much to suggest that couples' litigation was the result of transactions agreed *throughout* the period of marriage, such as Isabella Howedeyn's deal concerning cloth to be made for both herself and her husband.[117] The joint litigation of some couples spanned many years. Richard and Mary Hanneson can be found in debt suits covering at least a decade from 1375–86, suggesting transactions agreed during a significant period of marriage. The couple were sued by Roger Masson in October 1375, who sought various debts for wool, malt and arrears owed to the guild of All Saints. Some of these debts were said to be owed by Richard, others by Mary, and some by both Richard and Mary. The parties later came to an agreement, and Roger was fined, suggesting his complaint had been deemed unjust.[118] Many of the couple's later pleas survive in a collection of undated rolls from 1378–99. Together they sued Robert, chaplain of the chantry of William Amyas, for detention of a bronze pot worth 40d.[119] In another plea (probably in 1386), they complained about faulty washing oil bought by Mary Hanneson and warranted by John Bond of Boston, 'oylymaker', again revealing her independent purchases.[120] In both cases, Roger and Mary failed to show up at court so the suits were dropped. Richard Hanneson was Mayor of Nottingham in 1366-7 and again in 1384-5, showing that even townsmen of the highest status took joint legal action with their wives in the appropriate circumstances.[121] This pattern was not unique to the Hannesons. John and Margery Coke were involved in joint debt suits over at least seven years: in June 1372, John Averay complained that they owed him 26d; in 1375 they sought a debt owed by John Fenton and were accused of owing 12d to William Etwell, as well as another unknown debt by Richard Dandeson; and in 1379 they appeared again in a dispute over an unfulfilled contract.[122] Robert and Alice Anker and Richard and Mary de Wilford were also involved in debt pleas in 1375–6 and subsequently at least five years later.[123] Rather than incidental debts that had not been resolved prior to marriage, these pleas show that spouses were jointly accountable for a wide range of transactions agreed throughout their marriage.

As we have already seen, spouses acted as co-litigants as both plaintiffs and defendants. None of the previous discussions of custom concerning married women and debt have allowed for this possibility – that wives (with their husbands) might also proactively bring complaints about debts owed to them by others, thus representing their roles as creditors. Furthermore, when couples were part of a dispute but did not attend the court session, essoins (excuses for not attending court) were often recorded for both husband and wife.[124] These facts reinforce the notion that married women were active litigants in joint pleas. The convention of joint litigation was well established, to the extent that women could avoid litigation if it was not adhered to. In either 1386 or 1387, John de Averham brought a plea of detinue against Agnes de Akham, though Agnes replied that she was married to Alan de Acum [sic] and would not reply to the plea without him, and John was amerced 3d for an unjust suit.[125] Similarly, Agnes Palmer, said to be the widow of William Palmer, avoided answering a complaint of Adam Clerk in August 1387, claiming that her husband was still alive.[126] It has been argued that ordinary English people (men and women of all statuses) had 'an impressive level of technical knowledge' in relation to the common law, and these cases suggest that a similar claim can be made for town residents' knowledge of their local customary law, including strategies that could help them avoid facing a suit.[127] This is perhaps less surprising than detailed understanding of the common law, given that local custom was rooted and practised in the local community. Clearly these women knew enough about legal custom to use the restrictions of coverture to avoid litigation on some occasions, though we should be wary of interpreting this as particularly advantageous. These were rare instances where women challenged legal procedure, suggesting that, on the whole, litigants correctly sued both husband and wife when required.

The suits discussed here, along with many others, show that joint litigation in Nottingham and Chester was not simply a means of husbands acting on their wives' behalf, and that women were held to the same procedures and standards as male litigants. Married women were active participants in the processes of local justice and, in the right circumstances, there was clearly an incentive in bringing joint debt suits to court or choosing to sue both husband and wife. This was a pragmatic understanding of coverture that reflected wives' important commercial roles. Though their husbands may have been ultimately responsible for paying amercements and damages, the presence of wives in court should not be overlooked. Shennan Hutton and Cathryn Spence have similarly suggested that the naming of both spouses meant that they shared liability and acted jointly. In late medieval Ghent, a large group of spouses appeared before the aldermen to publicly perform legal acts together, particularly in relation to the transfer of property, in a manner in which wives were fully engaged actors.[128] Spence has shown how, in Scotland, 'the naming of a wife must have sometimes been a form of insurance on the part of the creditor', enabling recovery of a debt if one spouse died. This could also work in the interest of couples named together as creditors, enabling either to pursue a debt owed to them.[129] It is widely acknowledged that wives possessed knowledge of the trade or crafts of their husbands or households, demonstrated by their taking over of businesses in widowhood and the frequency with which husbands made their wives executors of their wills.[130] We know that widows also pursued their husbands' debts after their death, and in some instances it is possible to trace the shift from wife to widow and from joint to individual litigation. Nottingham woman Margaret Stapulton was in court with her husband Hugh in 1390, but a few months later used the court to recover debts owed to her husband after his death.[131] The fact that widows were competent in continuing their husbands' businesses is suggestive of their knowledge and partnership with their husbands prior to widowhood too. For Nottingham's court in particular, the enforcement of commercial obligations superseded adherence to gendered codes that excluded women from litigation elsewhere, demonstrating the court's balancing of its own priorities in delivering justice alongside the influence of the 'ubiquitous misogyny' of the common law.[132]

However, as Figure 2.1 shows, this was not a consistent practice. The shift in wives' litigation is clearly visible both statistically and in the changing nature of the pleas that married women acted in from the fourteenth to fifteenth centuries. The records suggest that the legal experiences and status of married women living in Nottingham were markedly different in the 1490s, compared to the 1390s. This shift occurred in the early fifteenth century, as the numbers of married women litigants had declined significantly by the second decade of 1400s. By the 1430s, their numbers were incidental. In Chester, this change happened earlier, as there was a marked decline in married women's litigation during the second quarter of the fourteenth century. In both towns, this meant that the instances where married women litigated in relation to debt by the later fifteenth century were rare, and of a distinctly different nature to the earlier pleas. The limited appearances of Nottingham and Chester wives in later debt suits often related to the estates and inherited debts of their former husbands, brought to court with new husbands once they had remarried. Scribes made efforts to record the multiple marital identities of these female litigants, in a way that served as justification for their involvement in a particular suit. We see this in the example of Elizabeth, wife of Robert Oldham, sherman, who appeared alongside her husband in a suit against John Strelley of Wodburgh, gentleman, in 1492. The couple sought £6 10s that John Strelley owed to Elizabeth's late husband, William Johnson. The sum stemmed from an agreement made over 20 years earlier in 1468.[133] We do not know when Johnson died, but we do know that Elizabeth waited until she had remarried to seek her late husband's debt. Perhaps her new husband was particularly keen to recover such a substantial sum, and his assistance may have been particularly useful against Strelley, a member of a local gentry family.[134] A similar decision may have lain behind the plea brought by Robert and Margaret Stevynson (who was the late wife of William Clemanson) against Nicholas Clemanston [sic], concerning a dispute over 40s relating to William Clemanson's testament.[135] Nicholas was likely a relative of William's, perhaps a brother or son, against whom Margaret sought the support of her new husband. The majority of Nottingham women involved in debt suits in 1491–2 were widows. Those who had not remarried, but were the executrices of their late husbands' estates, sought debts that also probably related to their husbands' testaments. Others acted in suits concerning more typical commercial transactions. Johanna Sampson, a widow, sued Jacob Heley for a debt of 2s, claiming that the sum was owed for her work in healing his leg after an injury.[136]

In Chester too the notable litigation of married women did not continue, and in fact had become exceptional by the mid-fourteenth century. As both creditors and debtors, married women disappeared from the Pentice Court and its records, apart from a very small number of exceptions. This contributed to a significant decline in the overall number of female debt litigants. This change marks an earlier 'intensification' of coverture than took place at Nottingham, and probably in London too.¹³⁷ Locating the exact point of this change is problematic. No couples feature in the extant rolls from 1320, while three appear in the 1325 rolls (though these are not complete, so it is possible that more may have been recorded).¹³⁸ It is likely that this was a gradual change, but one that began before the Black Death, not simply a result of the intensification of the ideology of coverture following a demographic crisis. By 1350, five of the eight women recorded in the one extant Pentice roll were widows (none were married), possibly reflecting the recent plague.¹³⁹ The reappearance of married women in debt suits in Chester also fits the model of remarried widows recovering the debts of their late husbands. Richard and Christina Leche, widow and administrator of the goods and chattels of Thomas Chaloner, sued Robert Hoolton for debt in June 1490. The careful documenting of Christina's legal status in relation to her late husband's estate suggests that the debt related to that same estate.¹⁴⁰

A specific change in custom did provide alternative options for some of Chester's married women. By the later fifteenth century, some women were explicitly classified as *femmes sole*, though only those trading in bread and ale. A court roll entry of 1486 claimed that this custom dated back to a time 'beyond which contrary memory did not exist', suggesting a longer history, though how far back this custom really went is unclear.¹⁴¹ This status served to legitimise debt litigation for a small number of married women, though only those of low status, in contrast to the wives who litigated in relation to large debts in the early fourteenth century. Alice, wife of John Wilkynson,¹⁴² and Johanna, wife of Thomas Fichell,¹⁴³ were both called sole merchants (*sola mercatrix*), and both appeared in debt suits independently in 1490. Other women were also called sole merchants with no reference to a husband, but they too may have been married. Agnes Huett (also known as Agnes Filenes), another sole merchant, appeared in court without any reference to her marital status, though she was certainly married at various points in the last decade of the fifteenth century.¹⁴⁴ If the adoption of *femme sole* status went back to the early fourteenth century, this might explain the disappearance of Chester wives from joint debt pleas. However, the decline in wives' litigation predates the evidence for sole merchants, and the added decline in the overall proportion of female litigants suggests that married women were not simply disappearing from joint pleas and acting in court alone, as *femme sole* women; rather, they were largely excluded from all forms of commercial litigation.

Like in Nottingham, the prevalence of widows among Chester's female debt litigants was also much higher by the end of the fifteenth century, though here there were fewer references to their roles as executrices. Instead, their debts appear to have arisen from a broad range of transactions, such as the 8d owed by Katherine, widow of Thomas Harrison, for the cost of a cart travelling from Wirall to Honbrugge (Handbridge) in Chester.[145] Also in 1490, Gilbert Kelly and his wife Johanna, the widow and executrice of Thomas Kempe, successfully sued Robert T (surname unknown) and his wife Cecilia over a debt of 2s 6d accrued by Johanna while she was sole, this status presumably referring to her period of widowhood prior to remarriage.[146] This is a rare example of pre-marital (or intra-marital) debt as the justification for a wife's legal action.

In Winchester, the joint action of spouses in debt pleas was rare. In the fourteenth century, those cases that have been identified appear as exceptions to a norm where only unmarried women appeared in court over debt. The situation here reveals an interpretation of coverture more in line with the assessments of McIntosh, Mate and Muldrew, who all highlighted the absence of women in debt pleas. Though Winchester women were rarely identified as widows or as single women, nor did they act as co-litigants with their husbands until the fifteenth century. However, this general pattern was not without exceptions – such as Matilda Mucheldevere – reminding us of the flexible nature of coverture and its various caveats.

Another instance that saw married Winchester women take part in litigation of a commercial nature was not in debt pleas but in complaints of detinue, where they did occasionally plead alongside their husbands. These related to the detention of goods (not counted in the graph), rather than monetary debts. In several cases the items detained were articles of clothing. These may have constituted forms of paraphernalia over which women possessed rights of disposal, therefore permitting or justifying their involvement in these disputes.[147] Medieval legal treatises recognised wives' limited rights over property and material goods, and though husbands were custodians of their wives' property, they could not act on their wives' behalf without her consent.[148] Joint actions in cases of detinue may have been an extension of this principle. Alternatively, these pleas of detinue may have related to the wrongful taking of property, reflecting the definition of detinue under tort law and also having parallels with the civil complaint of trespass – which married couples did take part in, as Chapter 4 demonstrates.[149] For example, Richard le Canevaser complained in November 1299 that Robert and Alice Strut detained a hood. It is clear that the presence of both Robert and Alice was required, as Alice was essoined separately.[150] The case was dropped when Richard le Canevaser failed to show up in court. Hugh Belde and his wife, Radulf, and Katherine de London and William and Lucy le Despenser were also defendants in complaints about the detention of goods in 1299–1300.[151] Richard and Dyonisa le Jay were accused by John Kyngsle in November 1365, and John and Joan Haywode were named in a suit for detention of chattels by William Wordman in January 1386.[152] Pleas of both debt and detinue had their root in claims of economic harm or loss, but in Winchester there was clearly a distinction in the perception of debt and detinue complaints and their relation to the capabilities and legal identity of married women.

The understanding of married women's ability to act in commercial suits changed in Winchester, in a way that was opposite to that of Nottingham and Chester, as well as London. From the mid-fifteenth century onwards, several married women are found pleading jointly with their husbands. These women are particularly conspicuous in the 1432–3 sample of court rolls. Of these women, 16 were plaintiffs, while 12 acted as defendants. Some were remarried widows and executrices (like Juliana, wife of John Kent, chaundeler and late wife of and executrices of William Burnham), whose legal action related directly to their widowed status, as we have already seen for Nottingham. But many others were not identified or described in this way. The lack of detail recorded in the court rolls concerning the nature of individual debts means we cannot know much about the transactions that led these women to court with their husbands, as the rolls instead focus on the legal process, recording essoins, jury summons and defaults. However, the notable rise in the number of spouses pleading together nevertheless demonstrates a shift in the legal capacity of married women in this area and a likely change in the court's interpretation of coverture as it applied to debt suits.

The variation in married women's roles in debt suits demonstrates clear differences in local courts' applications of coverture and the customs that ruled wives' legal actions. Previous studies of married women's commercial activities have suggested that customs allowing wives to register as *femmes sole*, only existing in a handful of towns, were the main means by which they might take responsibility for their credit transactions. *Femme sole* customs permitted wives to act as though single in business, and gave them independent responsibility under the law for their own debts.[153] Elsewhere, as McIntosh surmised, married women's commercial and legal identities were subsumed by those of their husbands; in the legal record, they were literally *femme covert* and therefore invisible. However, for many women this was not always the case, and we find them as active participants in litigation alongside their husbands – as partners, not as 'covered', invisible wives. As Cordelia Beattie has recently argued in relation to married women's ability to make wills, 'we need to be cautious in assuming that, just because common lawyers set out a particular position, medieval people followed it'.[154] We also need to provide sufficient space within our conceptualising of women's legal position for the variations and exceptions that existed within customary jurisdictions and practices. The changing, often contrasting picture of women's debt litigation and its intersection with marital status clearly complicates the situation beyond a simple contrast of *femme covert* (the norm) and *femme sole* (the exception).

Even without *femme sole* customs, married women were not automatically or always excluded from legal action. There is no evidence that such a custom existed at Nottingham, and nowhere in the court rolls were married women referred to as trading as *femmes sole*, either explicitly or by implication. Nor do we find instances of husbands declining responsibility for their wives' debts, as Kowaleski observed in the Exeter records.[155] But this does not mean that wives were legally invisible. Their frequent presence in commercial litigation demonstrates their ability to agree to a range of commercial transactions and take part in litigation if the need arose. Spence's comparable evidence for early modern Scotland similarly demonstrates that customary laws recognised the necessity that wives be able to make certain transactions without the explicit permission of their husband.[156] Caroline Barron even suggested that married women in London 'were frequently working partners in marriages between economic equals'.[157] However, this assessment of equality must be tempered by the fact that while men could represent themselves and their transactions independently, married women could not. In Chester, where the adoption of *femme sole* customs did arise for a limited group of low-status female traders, this did not represent legal equality or an opportunity for women to gain enhanced commercial status. Nevertheless, the presence of wives in debt litigation shows their regular involvement in business and other household functions prior to widowhood; whether acting alone or in joint agreements with their husbands, some of these business arrangements would lead to litigation. *Femme sole* status was not the only means by which married women could take responsibility for their commercial activities and negotiate the restrictions of coverture.

Conclusion

At the simplest level, the various series of court rolls reveal the sometimes significant, though not equal, ability of women to take legal action when commercial agreements, deals or transactions were not fulfilled in a manner that satisfied the creditor or seller. Women's subordinate and often marginal economic status meant that they always accounted for a minority of litigants in cases relating to credit and debt, but they were not exceptional litigants. Some women are more visible in the court rolls due to their frequent involvement in litigation, reflecting their larger commercial networks, but their litigation is nevertheless indicative of women's legal actions more broadly. Women were subject to the same processes and expectations when acting as either plaintiff or defendant, and there is no evidence that female litigants were disadvantaged when they actually ended up in court. Their pleas were recorded in the same formulaic manner, and when they were the subject of others' complaints there is no suggestion that they were discriminated against because of their sex. In addition, the courts generally showed limited concern with classifying women according to the maid–wife–widow model of the female life cycle, instead following a simpler binary version of coverture under which women were simply married (if appearing with their husbands) or not married. It was this distinction that was central to determining if or how women used the court. The exception to this pattern was in suits which directly arose from a woman's role as widow and executrix, which saw these details often being carefully recorded.

However, women's commercial activities were differently translated into legal action under the jurisdiction of each local court, and nor was their access to justice and action as litigants constant across the fourteenth and fifteenth centuries. Most notably, married women's involvement in debt suits differed significantly across the three towns examined here, suggesting that this difference is also likely to have extended to litigation in other towns. Even where married women were regular litigants, as was the case in fourteenth-century Nottingham, this was not a pattern that continued into the 1400s. Here, there was a change in the normal pattern of women's litigation when it came to their commercial activities, from regular suits involving spouses to exceptional cases arising from testamentary disputes or legacies. This change, and the comparable earlier shift at Chester, represents a restriction in married women's legal actions in line with a more orthodox interpretation of coverture.

The shifting patterns of married women's debt litigation account for changes in the overall proportions of female litigants within each court, meaning that the visibility of women in court cannot be read as a simple correlation with their economic status. Instead, it was a complex and fluid reflection of their commercial activity and their legal status as it was interpreted within individual jurisdictions, and probably each woman's personality as well. These variations limit our ability to recover women's economic identities and activities, but also offer a significant insight into the way that local officials and legal systems interpreted the legal status of married women. This was a result of each court's understanding of the way in which women's commercial activities intersected with the legal rules of coverture, which was not fixed according to a consistently agreed set of rules for married women's litigation, but rather something that appears to have been in a state of local evolution. There was, however, a general trajectory of decline in married women's litigation in relation to their commercial activities, indicative of an increasing adherence to the rules of coverture that rendered married women's formal commercial and legal action the domain of their husbands alone. In both Nottingham and Chester, married women's work and credit relationships thus came to be rendered invisible through their increasingly exceptional participation in litigation within their local courts. Litigation and court records do not provide a direct window on to the societies that they stemmed from, though they do represent many of the patterns and forces at play in those societies. Rather than directly reflecting levels of women's commercial activity, the involvement of women in litigation arising from their commercial activity should be interpreted as a minimum representation of their economic roles, which must be understood through the fluctuating refractions and distortions imposed by local applications of the principles of coverture, which varied from place to place and over time.

The legal context that underpinned the management and negotiation of credit networks may have also influenced the status of individuals within those networks. In Nottingham, particularly in the fourteenth century, the knowledge and confidence that transactions agreed with married women could be enforced at court may have enhanced their credibility within local networks. According to Barbara Hanawalt, the joint discussion of debts and deals made wives well-equipped to handle business matters, increasing the confidence of their husbands as well as their trading contacts.[158] This may in turn have altered the extent to which wives acted as their husbands' agents in business or under the so-called 'law of necessaries'.[159] But the records of debt pleas extend this agency to include wives' ability to bring debt suits jointly with their husbands, and their involvement in larger transactions that point to mercantile trade or wholesaling, suggesting that litigation could also result from wives' credit arrangements beyond 'necessaries'. In contrast, the understanding that wives could not account for credit transactions in Winchester or Chester may have limited the extent to which creditors were willing to deal with them beyond the purchase of low-value household necessaries. By enabling all women to account for their commercial activity in court, the joint litigation of Nottingham spouses may also have aided efficient and expedient dispute resolution. With both husband and wife required to attend court when summoned, both could give their account of events, rather than husbands simply being expected to report on their wives' agreements. While not diverging from the general principles of coverture, this practice allowed married women to play a more formal role in the credit networks to which they and their households were tied. By the end of the fifteenth century, however, town courts and their officials adhered to a more absolute understanding of coverture that dictated that married women had no claim over money or goods once married; customs which served to mask the commercial activity of married women when examined via the legal records.

Notes

1. HRO W/D1/37 rot. 8d.
2. Pamela Nightingale, 'Money and credit in the economy of late medieval England', in Diana Wood (ed.), *Medieval Money Matters* (Oxford: Oxbow, 2004), p. 51; James Davis, *Medieval Market Morality: Life, Law and Ethics in the English Marketplace* (Cambridge: Cambridge University Press, 2012), p. 348.
3. On women's creditworthiness and credit ties as revealed in borough court litigation, see Teresa Phipps, 'Creditworthy women and town courts in late medieval England', in Elise Dermineur (ed.), *Women and Credit in Pre-Industrial Europe* (Turnhout: Brepols, 2018), pp. 73–94.
4. Martha C. Howell, *Commerce Before Capitalism in Europe, 1300–1600* (Cambridge: Cambridge University Press, 2010), p. 25.
5. Richard Goddard, 'Surviving recession: English borough courts and commercial contraction, 1350–1500', in Richard Goddard, John Langdon and Miriam Müller (eds), *Survival and Discord in Medieval Society: Essays in Honour of Christopher Dyer* (Turnhout: Brepols, 2010), pp. 71–77; Davis, *Market Morality*, p. 206.
6. Maryanne Kowaleski, *Local Markets and Regional Trade in Medieval Exeter* (Cambridge: Cambridge University Press, 1995), p. 349; Goddard, 'Surviving recession', p. 78; Richard Goddard, 'Trust: Business networks and the borough court', in Richard Goddard and Teresa Phipps (eds), *Town Courts and Urban Society in Late Medieval England* (Woodbridge: Boydell and Brewer, 2019), pp. 176–199.
7. Chris Briggs, *Credit and Village Society in Fourteenth-Century England* (Oxford: Oxford University Press, 2008), p. 152.

8   Briggs, *Credit and Village Society*, p. 152; Kowaleski, *Exeter*, p. 349.
9   Richard Britnell, *Growth and Decline in Colchester, 1300–1525* (Cambridge: Cambridge University Press, 1986), p. 106.
10 See p. 23 above. For Poll Tax figures, see Alan Dyer, 'Ranking of towns by taxpaying population: the 1377 Poll Tax', in D.M. Palliser (ed.), *Cambridge Urban History of Britain*, vol. 1 (Cambridge: Cambridge University Press, 2000), p. 758.
11 See F.M. Nichols (ed. and trans.), *Britton: An English Translation and Notes* (Washington, DC: Byrne and Co., 1901), p. 128; John S. Beckerman, 'The forty shilling jurisdictional limit in medieval English personal actions', in Dafydd Jenkins (ed.), *Legal History Studies 1972* (Cardiff: University of Wales Press, 1975), pp. 110–117.
12 CALS ZSR rot. 109.
13 NA CA1277a rot. 7.
14 CALS ZSR 21 rot. 9d. This case is discussed in more detail on p. 71 of this chapter.
15 NA CA1279 rot. 15.
16 HRO W/D1/10 rot. 11d.
17 Richard Britnell also observed the low cost of bringing debt complaints to Colchester's borough court, evidenced by the low value of many debts (under 1s). Britnell, *Colchester*, p. 108.
18 On medieval women's work, see Maryanne Kowaleski, 'Women's work in a market town: Exeter in the late fourteenth century', in Barbara A. Hanawalt (ed.), *Women and Work in Preindustrial Europe* (Bloomington: Indiana University Press, 1986), pp. 145–164; Diane Hutton, 'Women in fourteenth-century Shrewsbury', in Lindsey Charles and Lorna Duffin (eds), *Women and Work in Pre-Industrial England* (London: Croom Helm, 1985), pp. 83–99; Kay E. Lacey, 'Women and work in fourteenth and fifteenth century London', in Charles and Duffin (eds), *Women and Work*, pp. 24–82; Marjorie Keniston McIntosh, *Working Women in English Society, 1300–1620* (Cambridge: Cambridge University Press, 2005); P.J.P. Goldberg, *Women, Work and Life Cycle in a Medieval Economy: Women in York and Yorkshire c.1300–1520* (Oxford: Clarendon Press, 1992); Caroline M. Barron, 'The "golden age" of women in medieval London', *Reading Medieval Studies*, 15 (1989), 35–58; Louise J. Wilkinson, *Women in Thirteenth-Century Lincolnshire* (Woodbridge: Boydell and Brewer, 2007), pp. 92–115; Judith M. Bennett, *Ale, Beer, and Brewsters in England: Women's Work in a Changing World, 1300–1600* (Oxford: Oxford University Press, 1996).
19 Matthew Frank Stevens, 'London women, the courts and the "golden age": a quantitative analysis of female litigants in the fourteenth and fifteenth centuries', *The London Journal*, 37 (2012), 77.
20 Matthew Frank Stevens, *Urban Assimilation in Post-Conquest Wales: Ethnicity, Gender and Economy in Ruthin, 1282–1350* (Cardiff: University of Wales Press, 2010), p. 130.
21 Kowaleski, *Exeter*, p. 349. Kowaleski identified 2,249 different adults (1,917 men and 332 women) in debt pleas for the period 1378/9–1387/8.
22 David Postles, 'An English small town in the later middle ages: Loughborough', *Urban History*, 20 (1993), 28. Figures are drawn from a broken series of court rolls from 1397–1409.
23 Chris Briggs, 'Empowered or marginalized? Rural women and credit in later thirteenth- and fourteenth-century England', *Continuity and Change*, 19 (2004), 19.

24 Judith M. Bennett, *Women in the Medieval English Countryside: Gender and Household in Brigstock before the Plague* (Oxford: Oxford University Press, 1989), p. 29. Bennett's figures are drawn from the records of 549 court sessions 1287–1348.
25 Shennan Hutton, '"On herself and all her property": women's economic activities in late medieval Ghent', *Continuity and Change*, 20 (2005), 330–334.
26 Stevens, 'London women', 83.
27 Cathryn Spence, *Women, Credit, and Debt in Early Modern Scotland* (Manchester: Manchester University Press, 2016), p. 53.
28 Kowaleski, *Exeter*, p. 348; Stevens, 'London women', 71; Briggs, 'Rural women and credit', 35–37.
29 Craig Muldrew has also identified the greater involvement of London women in early modern debt pleas, in comparison with courts in Great Yarmouth, Bristol, Exeter and Kings Lynn. Muldrew, '"A mutual assent of her mind"? Women, debt, litigation and contract in early modern England', *History Workshop Journal*, 55 (2003), 55.
30 On *femme sole*, see Marjorie Keniston McIntosh, 'The benefits and drawbacks of *femme sole* status in England, 1300–1630', *Journal of British Studies*, 44 (2005), 410–438. For London, see Barron, 'Golden age', 40.
31 Barron, 'Golden age', 47. Barbara Hanawalt has also argued that women benefited from various 'generous' laws in London, giving them a unique position and important contribution to capital formation: *The Wealth of Wives: Women, Law, and Economy in Late Medieval London* (Oxford: Oxford University Press, 2007), p. 4.
32 For example, Kowaleski, 'Women's work', p. 147; Muldrew, 'Women, debt, litigation and contract', 54–57; McIntosh, *Working Women*, p. 95; Stevens, *Ruthin*, pp. 127–133.
33 Stevens, 'London women', 79, 83.
34 Goddard, 'Surviving recession', p. 78.
35 On the growing legal consciousness of the English population, see Anthony Musson, *Medieval Law in Context: The Growth of Legal Consciousness from Magna Carta to the Peasants' Revolt* (Manchester: Manchester University Press, 2001), pp. 84–134. On litigation and arbitration, see pp. 91–92.
36 Goldberg, *Women, Work, and Life Cycle*, pp. 336–337.
37 NA CA1279 rot. 8. The couple were found to owe nothing.
38 NA CA1374 pp. 13, 143.
39 Craig Muldrew, *The Economy of Obligation: The Culture of Credit and Social Relations in Early Modern England* (Basingstoke: Macmillan, 1998), p. 2.
40 Hannah Robb, 'Reputation in the fifteenth century credit market; some tales from the ecclesiastical courts of York', *Cultural and Social History*, 15 (2018), 297–313.
41 On women and brewing, see Bennett, *Ale*; McIntosh, *Working Women*, pp. 140–181.
42 NA CA1279. For a list of Nottingham mayors, see W.H. Stevenson, *Records of the Borough of Nottingham*, vol. 1 (London: Quaritch, 1882), pp. 422–426.
43 Agnes Halum appears frequently in NA CA1279. For more on her 'legal career' and marital status, see Teresa Phipps, 'Female litigants in medieval borough courts: status and strategy in the case of Agnes Halum of Nottingham', in Goddard and Phipps (eds), *Town Courts*, pp. 77–92.
44 NA CA1280a (miscellaneous pleas from 1378–9). On women's brewing, see Bennett, *Ale*; McIntosh, *Working Women*, pp. 140–181.

45 Agnes was found not to be guilty of the detinue and broken vessels, while she acknowledged only 40d (2s) of the 6s debt. NA CA1279 17. Bennett notes the use of lead vessels for brewing, often found in the lists of possessions of brewers. See *Ale*, pp. 14, 49, 116.

46 Shennan Hutton, 'Property, family and partnership: married women and legal capability in late medieval Ghent', in Cordelia Beattie and Matthew Frank Stevens (eds), *Married Women and the Law in Premodern Northwest Europe* (Woodbridge: Boydell and Brewer, 2013), p. 168; Cathryn Spence, 'For his interest? Women, debt and coverture in early modern Scotland' in Beattie and Stevens (eds), *Married Women and the Law*, p. 156.

47 On Joan Lemeryng and Nottinghamshire coal-mining, see Richard Goddard, 'Coal mining in medieval Nottinghamshire: consumers and producers in a nascent industry', *Transactions of the Thoroton Society*, 116 (2012), 101.

48 NA CA1279 rots 2 (1d), 5, 16.

49 NA CA1279 rots 5, 7.

50 NA CA1294 rots 21, 23.

51 The suit can be traced through the rolls: NA CA1294 rots 8, 9, 10.

52 NA CA1324.

53 NA CA1324 rot. 4.

54 William Middleton appears in court rolls of 1432–3, acting as attorney for a large number of Nottingham residents. NA CA1323.

55 NA CA1325 rot. 5a.

56 HRO W/D1/3. Agatha de Bertone was sued for debts of 27s, 2s and 11d by her son, Henry. Isabella Tropinel acknowledged a debt of 3d owed to John de Laverkestoke.

57 HRO W/D1/13 rots 3d, 9.

58 HRO W/D1/13 rot. 6.

59 HRO W/D1/13 rots 1, 6.

60 '*Agatha Spycer pro iniuste detencione tresdicim [sic] solidos et septem denarios versus Aliciam Mercer prout in plena curia cognovit ideo ipse [sic] in misericordia. Et nichilominus preceptum est ei quod satisfecit predicte Alicie de denariis predictes una cum dampnus que taxantur ad* [blank] *infra octo dies etc.*' HRO W/D1/37.

61 Agatha Spycer was called *mercatori* in a complaint made by John Wynslowe de London, merchant: HRO W/D1/37 rot. 8d.

62 HRO W/D1/27 rot. 8d.

63 HRO W/D1/13 rots 1d; 9.

64 HRO W/D1/37 rots 4, 4d, 5; 8d.

65 Richard Goddard, 'Trust: Business networks and the borough court', in Goddard and Phipps (eds), *Town Courts*, pp. 176–199.

66 Called a merchant in other complaints, e.g. HRO W/D1/13 rot. 5d; see also Derek Keene, *Survey of Medieval Winchester*, vol. 2 (Oxford: Clarendon Press, 1985), p. 1182.

67 CALS ZSR 21 rot. 4.

68 In 1395, five women are found in the rolls as creditors and three as debtors.

69 CALS ZSR 149, 153d, 154.

70 CALS ZSR 149–153d.

71 Paul Brand, 'Aspects of the law of debt, 1189–1307', in P.R. Schofield and N.J. Mayhew (eds), *Credit and Debt in Medieval England, c.1180–c.1350* (Oxford: Oxbow, 2002), p. 23.

72 On the status of Chester, see Chapter 1.

73   CALS ZSR 21 rot. 3. See also A. Hopkins (ed.), *Selected Rolls of the Chester City Courts* (Manchester: Chetham Society, 1950), pp. 55–56.
74   CALS ZSR 21 rot. 5. See also Hopkins, *Chester City Courts*, p. 67.
75   CALS ZSR 27 rots 6d, 7d.
76   On the status of widows, see Hanawalt, *The Wealth of Wives*, pp. 95–115, 162–171, 174–176; Barron, 'Golden age', p. 47; Mavis E. Mate, *Women in Medieval English Society* (Cambridge: Cambridge University Press, 1999), pp. 34–38, Goldberg, *Women, Work and Life Cycle*, pp. 339–340; McIntosh, *Working Women*, pp. 31, 226, 234–235.
77   Hanawalt, *Wealth of Wives*, p. 98.
78   James L. Bolton, *Money in the Medieval English Economy: 973-1489* (Manchester: Manchester University Press, 2012), p. 204.
79   1378: CALS ZSR 82 rot. 2.
80   1395: CALS ZSR 112 rot. 1.
81   CALS ZSR 21 rot. 4. See also Hopkins, *Chester City Courts*, p. 41.
82   See p. 50 above.
83   Stevens, 'London women', 74; Sara M. Butler, 'Discourse on the nature of coverture in the later medieval courtroom', in Tim Stretton and Krista J. Kesselring (eds), *Women and the Law: Coverture in England and the Common Law World* (London: McGill-Queen's, 2013), pp. 39–40.
84   See McIntosh, *Working Women*, pp. 95, 97; Mavis E. Mate, *Daughters, Wives and Widows after the Black Death: Women in Sussex, 1350-1535* (Woodbridge: Boydell and Brewer, 1998), p. 187; on manor courts, see Briggs, 'Rural women and credit', 22. For the early modern period, see Muldrew, 'Women, debt, litigation and contract', 54–57.
85   McIntosh, '*Femme sole* status', 423.
86   Stevens, 'London women', 75.
87   Stevens, *Ruthin*, p. 132.
88   HRO W/D1/3 rot. 9, 9d.
89   HRO W/D1/3 rot. 4d.
90   Stevens, 'London women', 74.
91   On the nature of women's joint pleas, see Teresa Phipps, 'Coverture and the marital partnership in late medieval Nottingham: women's litigation at the borough court c.1300–c.1500', *Journal of British Studies*, 58 (2019), 768–786; Stevens has argued that cases in London's Sheriff's Court could not progress without the presence of both husband and wife: 'London women', 76.
92   Stevens, 'London's married women: debt litigation and coverture in the court of Common Pleas', in Beattie and Stevens (eds), *Married Women and the Law*, p. 131.
93   Hutton, 'Women in fourteenth century Shrewsbury', p. 86.
94   Elizabeth Ewan, 'Scottish Portias: Women in the Courts in Mediaeval Scottish Towns', *Journal of the Canadian Historical Association*, 3 (1992), 39; Rebecca Mason, 'Women, marital status, and law: The marital spectrum in seventeenth-century Glasgow', *Journal of British Studies*, 48 (2019), 787–804.
95   Spence, *Women, Credit, and Debt*, p. 42.
96   Stevens, 'London's married women', p. 127.
97   Spence, *Women, Credit, and Debt*, pp. 45–46.
98   For more on this, see Phipps, 'Coverture and the marital partnership in late medieval Nottingham', 778–782.

99 NA CA1279 rot. 11.
100 NA CA1294 rots 3, 4.
101 NA CA1279 rot. 12. 'Et predicti Johannes et Alicie uxor eius suum venerunt et defendere vim etc et dicunt quod nichil ei debet et hoc petunt quod inquisition.'
102 NA CA1278 rot. 22.
103 NA CA1291 rot. 13d.
104 Stevens, *Ruthin*, p. 133; Briggs, 'Rural women and credit', 26–27.
105 Chester Pentice Roll, 1317–18 CALS ZSR 21 rot. 8; see also Hopkins, *Chester City Courts*, p. 92. '*Unde queritur quod predicta Christiana ei iniuste detinet ... argenti pro uno carcose multonis sibi vendito et liberato ut mercatrici ... Et predicta Christiana non potest dedicere ... Et predicta Christiana pro detentione in misericordia ...*'.
106 CALS ZSR 21 rot. 9; see also Hopkins, *Chester City Courts*, p. 75.
107 McIntosh, '*Femme sole* status', 418–419.
108 Cordelia Beattie, 'Married women, contracts and coverture in late medieval England', in Beattie and Stevens (eds), *Married Women and the Law*, pp. 134–136.
109 CALS ZSR 21 rot. 9d.
110 CALS ZSR 21 rot. 1. For more on the claiming and awarding of damages, see Chapter 4.
111 The complaint against Reginald Walker was over a debt of 16d. The other is unknown and may have been cancelled as Chether's name in the entry was crossed through. NA CA1279 rots 11, 12, 14.
112 NA CA 1279 rots 11, 12, 13.
113 Progression of this suit can be traced through various court sessions. NA CA1279 rots 8 (9 January 1376), 9 (23 January 1376), 10 (6 February 1376).
114 Stevens, 'London's married women', pp. 118–119, 129; Frederick Pollock and Frederic William Maitland, *The History of English Law before the Time of Edward I*, vol. 2 (Cambridge: Cambridge University Press, 1895), p. 405. The seventeenth-century text *The Lawes Resolutions of Womens Rights* stated that wives' debts were only those contracted prior to marriage, implying that they would not be involved in transacting debts once married: T.E., *The Lawes Resolutions of Womens Rights* (London, 1632), p. 213. Blackstone also suggested that couples could only litigate in relation to wives' pre-marital debts and the injury to her person or property. William Blackstone, *Commentaries in the Laws of England* (Oxford: Clarendon Press, 1765), vol. 1, pp. 430–433. For more detail see Chapter 1.
115 Stevens, 'London's married women', pp. 118–119, 129. 'Usages and Customs of Ipswich', cap. 56, in William H. Richardson (ed.), *The Annalls of Ipswche: the lawes customes and governmt of the same, collected out of ye records books and writings of that towne by Nathll Bacon serving as recorder and town clark in that towne. Anno. Dom. 1654* (Ipswich: Cowell, 1884), p. 35. 'The husband shall answere for the debt of his wife contracted before or after marriage.' For Norwich, see Mary Bateson, *Borough Customs*, vol. 1, Selden Society vol. 18 (London: Selden Society 1904) p. 225. There was a caveat in Norwich that this would not be enforced if husband and wife were not on good terms, or if the wife had separated herself from her husband to 'make mischief'.
116 None of the Chester married women's suits refer to debts accrued before marriage, and only two such cases have been identified for Nottingham. For more, see Phipps, 'Coverture and the marital partnership'.

117 See p. 70 above.
118 NA CA1279 rots 1d, 3d. The poor condition of the roll prevents transcription of the full details of the complaint.
119 NA CA1279 – year unknown. 1378x1399.
120 NA CA 1280a (extracts 1387x1399) foreign pleas. The purchase was made by Margery (Mariota) on 1 August 1386.
121 For Nottingham mayors, see Stevenson, *Nottingham*, vol. 1, pp. 422–426.
122 NA CA1277a rot. 18; NA CA1279 rots 1, 7(6d), 10; NA CA1280a.
123 NA CA 1280a.
124 For example, John del Abbeye and Margery his wife had separate essoins in their dispute with Nicholas le Roper. NA CA1258b rot. 23.
125 NA CA1287.
126 NA CA1287. Agnes featured in a later suit as administrator of her husband William's goods which demonstrates that he was certainly dead by September 1388, though whether he was already dead at the time of Adam Clerk's complaint is not clear.
127 Cynthia Neville, 'Common knowledge of the common law in later medieval England', *Canadian Journal of History*, 29 (1994), 472.
128 Hutton, 'Property, family and partnership', pp. 167–168.
129 Spence, 'For his interest?', pp. 181–182.
130 Of men leaving wills in London's Husting Court, 83 per cent named their wives as executors: Hanawalt, *Wealth of Wives*, p. 120. See also pp. 95–115, 162–171, 174–176. Barron, 'Golden age', 47; Mate, *Women in Medieval English Society*, pp. 34–38; Goldberg, *Women, Work and Life Cycle*, pp. 339–340; McIntosh, *Working Women*, pp. 31, 226, 234–235; P.J.P. Goldberg, 'Some reflections on women, work and the family in the later medieval English town', in Jesús Ángel Solórzano Telechea, Beatriz Arízaga Bolumburu and Amélia Aguiar Andrade (eds), *Ser Mujer en la Ciudad Medieval Europea* (Logroño: Instituto de Estudios Riojanos, 2013), p. 192.
131 NA CA1291 rot. 4d, 5; CA1291 rot. 13d. For more, see Phipps, 'Coverture and the marital partnership', 774.
132 Sara Butler discusses the diversity of interpretations of coverture in the medieval Year Books, reminding us that other concerns also influenced the legal process. See Butler, 'Discourse on the nature of coverture', pp. 39–40.
133 NA CA1274 p. 90.
134 Sara Butler has suggested that this was a tactic used by some women. 'Medieval singlewomen in law and practice', in Andrew Spicer and Jane L. Stevens Crawshaw (eds), *The Place of the Social Margins, 1350–1750* (London: Routledge, 2017), pp. 64, 67.
135 NA CA1374 p. 145.
136 NA CA1374 p. 142.
137 Stevens, 'London women', 79. Stevens' samples are separated by a period of 140 years, however, so identifying the point of change is difficult.
138 1320: CALS ZSR 27. 1325: CALS ZSR 35.
139 CALS ZSR 62.
140 CALS ZSR 374.
141 Jane Laughton, 'Women in court: some evidence from fifteenth-century Chester', in Nicholas Rogers (ed.), *England in the Fifteenth Century* (Stamford: Paul Watkins,

1994), pp. 93-94. See also Laughton, 'The alewives of later medieval Chester', in Rowena E. Archer (ed.), *Crown, Government and People in the Fifteenth Century* (Stroud: Alan Sutton, 1995), pp. 191-208.
142 CALS ZSR 377d.
143 CALS ZSR 380d.
144 CALS ZSR 372, 376; Laughton, 'Alewives', pp. 204-205.
145 CALS ZSR 378d.
146 CALS ZSR 370d.
147 On paraphernalia, see Janet S. Loengard, 'Which may be said to be her own': widows and goods in late-medieval England', in Maryanne Kowaleski and P.J.P. Goldberg (eds), *Medieval Domesticity: Home, Housing and Household in Medieval England* (Cambridge: Cambridge University Press, 2008), pp. 164-168; Richard H. Helmholz, 'Married women's wills in later medieval England', in Sue Sheridan Walker (ed.), *Wife and Widow in Medieval England* (Ann Arbor: University of Michigan Press, 1993), p. 166.
148 On wives and property, see *Bracton on the Laws and Customs of England*, trans. Samuel E. Thorne, vol. 4 (Cambridge, MA: Belknap Press, 1977), p. 335.
149 On debt and detinue, see David J. Ibbetson, *A Historical Introduction to the Law of Obligations* (Oxford: Oxford University Press, 2001), pp. 30-36.
150 HRO W/D1/3 rot. 3.
151 HRO W/D1/3.
152 HRO W/D1/13 rot. 2d; HRO W/D1/37 rot. 6.
153 McIntosh, '*Femme sole* status', 410-438; Barron, 'Golden age', 40; Hanawalt, *Wealth of Wives*, pp. 160-184; Brian Gastle, '"As If She Were Single": working wives and the late medieval English *femme sole*', in Kellie Robertson and Michael Uebel (eds), *The Middle Ages at Work: Practising Labor in Late Medieval England* (Basingstoke: Palgrave, 2004), pp. 41-64.
154 Cordelia Beattie, 'Married women's wills: probate, property and piety in late medieval England', *Law and History Review*, 37 (2019), 60.
155 Kowaleski, 'Women's work', p. 146.
156 Spence, 'For his interest?', p. 178.
157 Barron, 'Golden age', 40.
158 Hanawalt, *Wealth of Wives*, p. 120.
159 Beattie, 'Married women, contracts and coverture', pp. 134-136.

3

Law and the regulation of women's work

The regulation of trade and enforcement of local bylaws was a key function of local justice. Jurors and officials administered systems of licensing and punishment for various offences relating to the quality of goods, weights and measures, as well as marketing behaviour. Authorities were keen to regulate the trading environment, and particularly the prices of staples such as bread and ale. Playing an important role in urban trade, particularly in the provision of victuals, women featured regularly in officials' lists of commercial rule breakers. The records of these presentments and fines offer an alternative perspective on women's interaction with the law arising from their commercial life, illustrating how their activities were documented, regulated and policed 'from above'. This provides an insight into how women's work, trade and production were understood by civic authorities, in contrast to the personal pleas brought revealing disputes between peers or trading contacts. There was usually no process for responding to or disputing allegations; instead, names were simply listed and fines issued. As a result, the regulation and licensing of trade gave women and men a different form of legal accountability to interpersonal pleas. By examining women's roles in these presentments, this chapter further investigates the ties between women's commercial activity and their legal status, and allows us to compare litigation and the regulation of trade as two contrasting, yet overlapping, means by which women engaged with the law within individual towns and jurisdictions.

The regulation of trade and the punishment of the various associated offences fell under towns' privileges of leet jurisdiction. The records of trading offences represented the local interpretation of statutory regulations, meaning that the presentments of one town held much in common with those of others.[1] For example, all towns monitored the prices and quality of bread and ale, staple products that were essential to the medieval diet. In most towns, offences and regulations were presented periodically over the course of a year, as part of a fixed regime of inspection and monitoring that took a specific form within each town. In Winchester, where offences were recorded among the pleas of the city court, trading presentments appear more frequently than in Nottingham, where they were reported twice per year, suggesting that these Winchester presentments were made on a somewhat ad hoc basis. The court and its officials appear to have paid more attention to recording a larger range of trading offences over time, with more being documented in the fifteenth-century rolls than the earlier records of the court. Offences and regulations were reported by jurors, tithingmen (called decennaries in Nottingham) or specific officials such as aletasters, who were nearly always male. However, in the list of Nottingham jurors from 1459–60, one woman, Alice Wey, was included among the men.[2] These individuals made their presentments before the mayor and/or bailiffs of their town, and their statements were considered conclusive, with no opportunity for disputation. Depending on the product or the type of trade, regulation could be imposed at the point of production and/or at the point of sale.[3] This was certainly the case for the brewing industry, where the quality of the ale produced was monitored, as were the measures and prices by which it was sold. Some brewers appear to have both brewed and sold ale, but ale was also sold by tapsters. The way in which these regulations were recorded can blur the line between production and sale, however, particularly when entries simply record that individuals or whole occupational groups had acted against the assize.

Before considering women's commercial activities, it is worth noting the scope and limitations of the sources. The records of commercial regulation and licensing survive less extensively than the litigious material. This means that they act as a form of supplementary, contextual evidence concerning women's legal involvement, rather than offering an extensive or complete view of their trading and producing activities. As suppliers of food and ale, women were sometimes found in considerable numbers within the records of trading presentments. However, as this chapter will go on to show, we cannot take the presence (or absence) of women at face value. Chapter 1 of this book noted how court records do not provide a mirror of society, and, as Jeremy Goldberg has discussed, the records of trading regulation do not offer a complete picture of all commercial activities, but only those which contravened customary law, required control and fell under the jurisdiction of the court.[4] This means that in the study of women's work and its legal implications, these records represent a minimum level of women's activity.

The understanding of the household as a legal and economic unit meant that men (particularly husbands) were often accountable for work performed by women, most notably in areas like brewing that were closely regulated but where we know that women played a major role. Women's trade and work is therefore obscured in the records of trading regulation, a fact that Judith Bennett has interpreted as 'the legal subsumption of wives under their husbands'.[5] Maryanne Kowaleski has argued that the 'lack of legal recognition of women's work was due to the vagaries of common law, which dictated that a wife was one with her husband under the law'.[6] So, while the records of Winchester's trading regulations have been described as 'a virtually complete directory of persons practising certain trades in the city', this assumption does not account for the way in which women's activities were obscured by the householding status of their husbands.[7] These lists must therefore be assessed critically, bearing in mind the complex and refracted links between women's day-to-day activity and their legal and fiscal accountability for these activities.

Historians have used the records of trading regulation to study urban commercial life, profiling the nature and range of trades and crafts within towns and attitudes to trade among urban officials. Hilton argued that urban elites and authorities regarded retailers with suspicion, and it is this which led officials to seek to control their activities, thus generating the documents that record various trading and craft activities, offences and licensing.[8] Catherine Casson has also argued that regulation of trade was part of towns' attempts to bolster their reputations and address competitive threats.[9] These records have also been used to explore the nature of women's work, highlighting their role in particular essential, but low-status, areas such as brewing and the provision of victuals.[10] Women lacked the occupational identity that was held by many men, as they tended to practise more than one trade, a fact that reflected their marginal and unstable economic status.[11] Building on these studies, the focus here is on the way in which this work brought women into contact with local legal regulation and the way that their status was defined in legal terms.

This chapter will focus on the trading offences and regulation recorded by the courts in Nottingham and Winchester, with some additional evidence from Chester. Records of Chester's trading regulations do not survive until the late fifteenth century, recorded in the city's sheriff's and mayor's books, and their survival and condition is mixed. Winchester's City Court rolls record trading presentments alongside personal pleas, while the records documenting these offences in Nottingham survive in a more sporadic and fragmented fashion than those documenting personal pleas of debt and trespass. Often, those that are extant are not complete. This means that assessments of change over time are problematic, and these records should therefore be read as indicative of the systems of regulation, rather than as definitive evidence of the entirety of these systems or their operation across the late medieval period.

The regulations found in the records of the various towns are indicative of the concerns of urban officials. Much of this focused on provision of essentials, encapsulated in the assizes of bread and ale, which regulated the prices and quality of these products (upon which the nutritional requirements of the population relied). The records of the assizes survive across numerous urban and rural centres, recording the activities of both the brewers and sellers of ale (tapsters).[12] Supplies of meat, fish and prepared foods were also monitored for quality and price, with the clear concern and understanding that bad (often described as putrid) or reheated food could bring on illness. The cooks of Nottingham, for example, were fined as a group in 1395 for selling meat and fish that had been reheated and was thus 'hurtful to the human body' (*nocivas corpori humano*).[13] It is also common to find entries like the one stating that all members of certain occupational groups were guilty of operating unlawfully, though without any specific accusations, and all required to pay a small annual fine. This has led to various suggestions that these regulations operated as a form of licensing via amercement or a more systematic means of quality control, rather than simply (or only) as a reactive form of punishment.[14] This may have been particularly true in the case of the assizes of bread and ale and the provision of other foodstuffs, with many towns often fining all brewers, butchers, fishmongers and other occupational groups.[15] Unlawful trading behaviour was also punished: those who engaged in forestalling or regrating, buying goods outside the specified hours of the market (often to sell on elsewhere), were accused of inflating the market, and were also viewed with suspicion as middlemen (or women), profiting simply by selling on the products of others.

A broad mixture of individuals and groups feature in the records, some of which were quasi-professional groups with a relatively strong occupational identity, such as bakers, butchers, fishmongers, tanners and shoemakers, as well as lower status petty traders who made their money by selling a range of low-value goods and food. For those who featured less often in commercial litigation (they may have had less extensive commercial networks), this form of regulation and licensing defined their legal experiences, meaning that law and justice was often only something *done to* them, or served from above, rather than something which they actively chose to engage in.

The range of offences

The tables below display the range of trades that were regulated under the leet jurisdiction of Nottingham and Winchester's courts (Tables 3.1 and 3.2). The fragmentary nature of Nottingham's records means that only the complete 1395 records of the Mickletorn jury have been included here, though other sections of the partial extant records from Nottingham will supplement the discussion. The numbers for Winchester are far higher, as they include presentments taken from the six samples of City Court rolls that provide the quantitative basis for this study. The tables indicate that in both towns, the greatest regulatory concern lay with the victualling trades and the production of essential food and drink. By compiling a complete analysis of the categories of offence in each court, we see the presence of women in certain areas, as well as those in which they were not active – or at least not formally accountable under the regulations. In order to examine the legal accountability of married women in commercial offences and regulation, the presentments of women known to be married (called wife) have been separated. Women were presented most often for offences relating to the brewing and selling of ale, and were also punished for forestalling. These specific activities will be discussed in detail later in this chapter.

This quantitative analysis of individuals recorded under various categories and offences does not, however, account for the offences

Table 3.1 Trading offences presented before the 1395–6 Nottingham Mayor's Court.

Offence/category	Women (no marital status)	Married women	Men	Total
Brewing	23	0	143	166
Selling ale	0	0	14	14
Baking	0	0	4	4
Forestalling/regrating	10	9	47	66
Selling faulty candles	2	1	9	12
Shopkeeping while not a burgess	0	0	2	2
Other marketing offences	6	2	1	9
Totals	41	12	220	273

Source: NA CA3942.

Table 3.2 Trading offences recorded in Winchester City Court (across six sample years).

Offence	Women (no marital status)	Married women	Men	Total
Brewing/selling ale	49	0	418	467
Tapsters/selling ale only	60	1	487	548
Hostelers	3	0	48	51
Fishmongers/selling fish	2	0	27	29
Cooks selling bad food	0	0	20	20
Butchers/selling meat	1	0	464	465
Baking	3	0	46	49
Selling bread	35	10	28	63
Forestalling/regrating	12	6	34	52
Selling oats/grain	0	0	10	10
Selling wine	0	0	7	7
Selling victuals	0	0	5	5
Other/unknown	0	0	13	13
Totals	165	17	1607	1779

Source: HRO W/D1/3, W/D1/13, W/D1/27, W/D1/60, W/D1/61, W/D1/64.

reported against whole occupational groups. Nottingham's Mickletorn jury reported in 1395 that all the brewers, bakers, butchers, fishermen, taverners, tanners, shoemakers, cooks, hostelers, weavers, fullers and dyers produced and sold their wares improperly.[16] Among this list we see additional concern for the quality of goods produced by artisan traders and craftsmen, in addition to the victuals that dominated the tables above. The jury also presented that all the hucksters of the town sold various victuals such as garlic, flour, salt, tallow, candles, butter and cheeses too dearly and unlawfully, as well as being common forestallers of these provisions.[17] This group was termed *auxiatrices*, a term apparently unique to Nottingham and translated by Stevenson, the town's most famous historian, to mean huckster as well as poulterer.[18] The feminine ending implies that this was a solely female group, and the role of women as hucksters, selling a wide range of basic goods and victuals, has been well documented in the history of women's work. Elsewhere, including Norwich and Bristol, English versions of the term (such as hukster or hokkestere) were used in official records.[19] The presentment of all Nottingham hucksters was made twice in 1395–6 using almost identical wording, suggesting that this was a regular, formulaic means of reporting and monitoring the town's hucksters, rather than a response to any specific illegal activities.[20] This itself suggests a persistent concern by officials to monitor the activities of those selling numerous low-price essentials and a perception that these 'middlemen' (or middlewomen) might attempt to deceive the people of the town by charging unreasonable prices, intercepting goods from their producers or selling poor-quality goods. Their activities were framed as being detrimental to the people of the town, with implications of intentional fraud or deception. Whether or not this 'anti-huckster ethos' actually impacted on women's access to retailing has been questioned by Goldberg; these repeated presentments sought to monitor the activities and behaviour of victuallers while recognising their essential role in provisioning the town.[21] The inclusion of hucksters among the list of other occupational groups shows that, despite not being engaged in skilled work, they were also conceptualised as group with some kind of united occupational identity in the eyes of Nottingham's officials.

We do not know the names of these purportedly fraudulent hucksters, though the relatively small size of the town's population may have meant that the identities of these women were common knowledge. However, in addition to this grouping, specific individuals were also labelled and fined for being hucksters. This included some men, showing that this was not an exclusively female role or title, but that it was certainly one with connotations of being disreputable. Roger, servant of Roger de Arnall, was presented in 1395 for holding a stall while not being a burgess, selling candles without wicks and for being a common huckster (*communis auxiator*) of cheese, butter and other victuals. The wife of William Dalayow was presented for the same offences, as were many married women who were also presented for forestalling.[22] Richard de Burfford, William Couper, John Bacefforde and Richard Hoppewell were also named hucksters, though under the feminine form '*auxiatrices*'.[23] We know that Richard Burfford was selling victuals typically associated with female hucksters, as in the same year he sued Nicholas Taylur in the borough court for 6 1/2d owed for bread, ale and victuals.[24] Perhaps the court scribe was so used to women being labelled under this category that he automatically reverted to the feminine form of the noun, highlighting that this was an identity that was largely, though not solely, associated with women.

For Nottingham, we also know the names of the jurors who reported on these issues. Some of the 17 jurors named, or their wives, worked among the trades and crafts that were being regulated, and they sometimes included themselves among their presentments, further reinforcing the idea that many of these presentments were part of a system of licensing, and that this was not something that local officeholders were exempt from. Robert de Chesterfeld was one of the decennaries of Chapelbarre, and he was also one of the men listed for brewing and selling ale against the assize in the same street. The entry records no specific fine, suggesting again that this was a form of licensing with set fees to be paid, rather than punishment. By presenting himself for brewing, Chesterfeld was in fact including himself in the system of regulation. It is also possible that it was in fact his wife who actually did the brewing, but that he was responsible as head of the household. Various other decennaries did the same.[25] John de Horton, decennary of Goosegate, made no presentments in 1395 due to the fact that he was unwell or disabled, except for naming himself as a common brewer.[26]

Bread and ale

The most frequent reference to trading regulations in both Nottingham and Winchester were presentments against the assizes of bread and ale. The basis for these assizes came from national statute, most notably the thirteenth-century Assize of Bread and Ale (thought to date from 1266–7, though established in local customs earlier than this).[27] These laws reflected the government's attempt to control trading practices, prices and supply, but specific prices were set locally in response to local prices of wheat, barley and oats.[28] While there was some variation in the other trading regulations recorded by the courts of different towns and manors, presentments against the assizes were the most commonly documented, demonstrating consistent concern for the prices and quality of these essential products.[29]

Baking was a largely male-dominated occupation, and few women were fined for baking against the assize.[30] Baking was a skilled trade (not that brewing was unskilled) and required specific equipment, namely a bread oven, which itself required capital investment. These factors meant that it was dominated by a smaller group of full-time bakers within any given urban centre. At Nottingham, the assize of bread was monitored regularly according to the price of grain sold at the market, with prices for different types of bread set in relation to this. These prices were compiled along with presentments of those deemed to be breaking the assize, often by producing underweight bread, and recorded in the rolls of the Mayor's Court periodically throughout the year, though they were presumably documented elsewhere prior to the court session. These entries do not feature any female bakers. On most occasions, no bakers were found to have broken the rules of the assize, perhaps because of such frequent and careful monitoring of prices. The four Nottingham men named for baking against the assize in the 1395–6 rolls were said to have baked bread at the wrong weights, and all were called 'baxster', demonstrating that baking was their main form of work and part of their legal and social identity.[31] Women, however, were involved in the provision of bread, if not directly responsible for adhering to the assizes. One of these Nottingham bakers, John Bond, sued Amya Huxter in the borough court in May 1395, seeking 8d owed for bread.[32] Amya's surname reflects her more marginal role in the provision of food, and perhaps some of the other unnamed hucksters were also involved in the sale of bread. Another baker, Robert Baxster, was enrolled as a burgess in 1395.[33] However, by November 1396 he had died, and his widow Matilda appeared in the borough court to recover a debt of 18d owed for bread from John Collingham, suggesting that she was carrying on her late husband's work.[34]

The Winchester rolls only document those deemed to be baking or selling bread against the assize, without details of the correct prices for various types of grain and bread. Here too, low numbers of individuals were repeatedly fined for baking against the assize, reflecting the fact that baking was a something of a 'professional' trade rather than something that many households engaged in on the side. Those who were fined (whose surnames or bynames also reflected their status as professional bakers) therefore represented a small group of bakers responsible for supplying the whole town. Women's role in the distribution of bread, and their failure to adhere to Winchester's ordinances, is revealed in the 1299–1300 city court rolls, where 42 women were fined for procuring bread to sell before noon, which was prohibited.[35] After this point, the presentments concerning baking were limited to the bakers themselves and featured very few women. In 1495–6, Mary Vyolet was presented for both baking and brewing against the assize, and for being a hosteller. All of these fines also indicated that she was selling without licence to trade.[36] Chester women also featured among lists of those who sold bread illegally within the city, usually coupled with the selling of ale, though they were probably not professional bakers but sellers of victuals and the surplus of food produced for the household. These fines reveal the role of women as intermediaries or 'middlemen', selling essential victuals and probably making a small profit for their efforts in order to supplement the household economy. Some of these women were married, others were servants, but all were individually accountable for their activities.

In contrast with baking, women were actively involved in brewing. Judith Bennett has shown that, in the fourteenth century, women did most of the brewing and selling of ale in England.[37] Some individuals may have brewed on a commercial scale, but others brewed for the household, often alongside other work, and sold their surplus. The licensing and legal regulation of brewing did not, however, always reflect this, as a result of women's subordinate household and legal status. While all towns monitored the production and sale of ale against the assizes, the ways in which women's legal status was interpreted via this regulation differed across towns and manors, as Judith Bennett has discussed in detail.[38] In Yarmouth, Janka Rodziewicz found that women were named for 74 per cent of brewing offences, demonstrating their monopoly of the trade.[39] In contrast, Maryanne Kowaleski found that women only accounted for 9 per cent of those fined for brewing in fourteenth-century Exeter.[40] The figure was similarly low in Nottingham, where women only account for a total of 14 per cent (43 of 312) of those named for ale-related offences (brewing and selling) in the extant rolls from 1369–70 and 1395–6. In the complete records of 1395–6, women were named for brewing and selling ale, listed among their male neighbours. None of these women were designated by any marital status, recorded instead by their full names, suggesting that they were not married, though this is not something that can be proven without further contextual information. While this does not mean that married women did not brew and sell ale, it implies that their husbands took responsibility for the licensing and regulating of this trade.[41] The partial rolls from 1369–70, where only the records of the assize of ale survive, also replicate this pattern, with no married women being presented for brewing or selling ale (Table 3.3). In both sets of records, the fact that numerous men were named for selling ale, some of whom clearly had other occupations and were not professional brewers, further suggests that at least some of these presentments related to the selling of the household surplus that was brewed by their wives.

The loss of further fifteenth-century assize records limits our ability to assess women's legal accountability for their involvement in the

Table 3.3 Assize of Ale, Nottingham 1369–70.

Offence	Women (no marital status)	Married women	Men
Brewing	2	0	9
Selling ale	18	0	80
Not being in the liberty	1	0	7

Source: NA CA4811.

brewing process itself beyond these two fourteenth-century snapshots.[42] However, the fines paid for licence to trade in various industries also identify the continued involvement of women in the selling of ale, if not its production. Several women classed as tipplers paid fines of 4d in 1478–9. None of these women were designated as being married.[43] However, these independent female sellers of ale were required to adhere to the system that regulated and taxed traders within the town. Some of these women appeared in multiple lists of trading permissions and of burgesses enrolled, including Alice Chadwyk and Edith Flecher, suggesting that the sale of ale could warrant admittance to the freedom of the town.[44] But these female burgesses were exceptions among the largely male lists.

The proportion of female brewers was even lower in Winchester at 11 per cent (110 of 1015). As the table below indicates, the number of brewing and ale-selling presentments increased substantially from the fourteenth to fifteenth centuries, clearly demonstrating the city's increased attention to the regulation of the ale industry. There were a total of 10 presentments for brewing and selling ale in 1299–1300; a century later there were 101 and by 1495–6 there were 266. Judith Bennett has also highlighted this increased attention to regulation in communities across England, particularly after 1350 with concern for the open advertisement of ale, and later attempts to regulate the supply of ale and to limit the opening hours and activities allowed within alehouses.[45] The regulation of ale and brewing was also a source of considerable income for the governments who controlled it, adding extra incentive to the enforcement of brewing regulations.

A handful of women were fined for ale-related offences in the earlier Winchester records, including Katherine, wife of Geoffrey de Lindicper, who was fined 12d for selling ale against the assize.[46] However, this example is somewhat exceptional, as beyond a small number of individuals, Winchester's married women (like those of Nottingham) are largely invisible among the records of all trading regulations – or at least women specifically recorded as being married were largely absent from these lists. However, cross-referencing the identities of female brewers with other court entries reveals that at least some of these supposedly 'single', independent female brewers were married. Katherine de London, fined 12d for brewing against the assize in 1300, was recorded using only her full name, but in the same year appeared in a detinue suit alongside her husband, Ralph de London.[47] We cannot know why the court's scribe chose not to record Katherine de London's marital status when recording her brewing activity, but did choose to note that of Katherine Lindicper in the same year, but this disparity once again demonstrates that the recording of marital status (or lack of) is not conclusive evidence of female status. The different legal actions and identities of Katherine de London show that she was independently responsible for her brewing activity, but that in the detinue case of the same year (in which she was a defendant), her coverture required her to plead jointly with her husband, clearly identifying the differing impact of coverture across legal contexts.

In 1433, two Winchester women were named as brewers, while more sold ale, all recorded with no marital descriptor. In the 1454–5 and 1495–6 samples, no married women were named for any trading offences. The proportions of women named as brewers and tapsters varied in the later fifteenth century, though the absence of married women tells us that this represented the absolute minimum of women's involvement in the trade. There were consistently hundreds of presentments naming men for brewing and selling ale against the assize, using incorrect measures or measures that had not been sealed. The high numbers of individuals fined, usually repeatedly over the course of a year, again indicates that this was a system of regular licensing.[48] Even by the end of the fifteenth century, 108 individuals were fined for brewing, demonstrating that the industry in Winchester had not yet become professionalised or dominated by a small group of individuals.[49] Of these, 21 were women, though none were named as married. It was this process of professionalisation which Bennett has argued marginalised women from the production of ale through the move away from smaller-scale home production to larger-scale, industrial brewing and the increased brewing of beer.[50] However, in Winchester there was actually a rise in the proportion of female brewers recorded at the end of the fifteenth century, demonstrating that there was still space for women to operate as brewers in the city at the turn of the sixteenth century.

Many of the men listed as brewers were likely to have been paying the licensing fee in relation to household brewing, which was in fact done by their wives and other female family or household members. Winchester's ancient usages set out various ordinances relating to brewing and the regulation of the assize, and the (Anglo-Norman) language used refers to these brewers as a female group.[51] However, increasing regulation across a range of victualling trades saw fewer women being presented (Table 3.4). These regulations did not formally acknowledge women's brewing (or indeed their contribution to other forms of production), a process which reflected and reinforced their marginal economic position and the authority of the male householder. In both Winchester

Table 3.4 Presentments for brewing and selling ale in Winchester.[a]

Year	Offence	Woman (no marital status)	married woman	man	total
1299–1300	brewing	2	0	4	6
	selling	3	1	0	4
1365–6	brewing	0	0	0	0
	selling	9	0	58	67
1385–6	brewing	7	0	37	44
	selling	19	0	64	83
1432–3	brewing	2	0	124	126
	selling	15	0	129	144
1454–5	brewing	4	0	97	101
	selling	9	0	170	179
1495–6	brewing	34	0	156	190
	selling	14	0	62	76
Totals		118	1	901	1020

[a] It is likely that the brewing and selling of ale was amalgamated in the 1365–6 entries, with no individuals presented specifically for brewing.

Source: HRO W/D1/3, W/D1/13, W/D1/27, W/D1/60, W/D1/61, W/D1/64.

and Nottingham, the brewing of wives was continuously and officially obscured by the legal authority of their husbands, just as Bennett found for Oxford, where Edward III had ordered that burgesses were responsible for any members of their household who sold wine or other foodstuffs to scholars.[52] While this may have been a unique example of extra regulation, the effect on the visibility of married women's work in the legal record was not unique.

In Chester, women's involvement in the brewing industry has been studied by Jane Laughton, through their use of the Dee mill to grind their malt. Women of high status, including wives of mayors, sheriffs and aldermen, were chosen to represent Chester's brewers in resisting the excessive chargers of the millers, and often supervised significant production in their own households.[53] However, by the time we turn to the surviving records of the regulation of brewing from the late fifteenth century, the involvement of elite women is less visible. Indeed, the vast majority of individuals who brought their ale measures to be sealed by the mayor, in order to adhere to the regulations of the assize, were male. Laughton argues that 'this masculine dominance was more apparent than real': when brewers were named for breaking the assize, most of these were married women.[54] There was therefore a distinction in the individual's responsibility for brewing and the householder's responsibility for warranting the size of their measures, which was itself a pre-emptive, rather than reactionary, regulatory measure.

The presentment of offences relating to brewing that survive in the Chester sheriffs' books relate to individuals who brewed or sold ale without being admitted to the franchise of the city. Most were men, though some women, both married and not, were also listed. Of the 45 individuals reported for brewing and selling ale in the extant books from 1505–10, 12 were unmarried women, 4 were married and 29 were men.[55] These figures contrast somewhat with the list of retailers recorded in 1487, studied by Laughton, which comprised 55 women (27 of whom were wives) and 46 men.[56] By the early sixteenth century (or perhaps earlier, as Laughton identifies this difference in the 1498 list), when the focus of the records had shifted from those selling too dear or using unsealed measures to retailers and brewers not being part of the franchise, far fewer women were named for their ale-selling activities. Individuals were assigned different fines ranging from 4d to 13s 4d that presumably related to the severity of the offence, suggesting that these were actual instances of wrongdoing, rather than a means of licensing. Women were rarely required to pay the highest fines, suggesting that their unfranchised brewing was on a lesser scale than that of men, or that it was perceived to be so. Agnes Marshall, Alice Monkesfeld and the wives of John Latewisse and Richard Gyle were all said to sell bread and ale that they had brewed, while not being in the franchise or guild merchant, and were fined various sums from 12 to 40d. The men that were reported at the same time were fined 40d, 8s 8d or 13s 4d.[57] The small number of Chester's married women who continued to be accountable for their unregistered sale of ale, which probably came from the surplus of their household provisions, were generally recorded as 'wife of …', reflecting their husband's accountability for these fines and the relative irrelevance of their own specific identity. Married women could trade as *femmes sole* in the provision of bread and ale, though evidence of the adoption of this status is limited. Elena Buccy (married to Henry Buccy) was recorded as *sola mercatrix* in the 1503 sheriffs' book, and she was fined the lowest sum of 4d for buying and selling bread and ale to and from foreigners, suggesting that this was not a particularly high standing or prosperous position to hold.[58] Two unmarried sellers of bread and ale were called 'huswiff', a term which probably indicated their status as householders, and thus independently responsible for their own commercial activity, rather than marital status.[59] The declining numbers of women recorded in the brewing industry may have been a precursor to the more severe restrictions that were introduced in 1540, where women were prevented from keeping alehouses and men were prevented from employing women or girls to sell ale.[60]

The contrasts across the different towns identify some important distinctions in the regulation of women's ale work, which Judith Bennett previously pointed to in her study of women's brewing. Rather than a massive disparity in the number of women brewing in different towns, these figures indicate a difference in the way that local juries and other officials interpreted married women's legal role in relation to the regulation of brewing. However, this cannot simply be explained by married women's legal disabilities under coverture and the issue of the 'disappearing wife', as the presence of wives in other legal documents complicates the situation somewhat.[61] We know that married women in Nottingham were involved in brewing, as evidence for this appears in borough court litigation, demonstrating the differing ways in which married women's brewing might be represented under the law. Isabella, wife of William Thrumpton, was in court in 1395 alongside her husband concerning a covenant that she made with Robert Feysy to brew 60 gallons of ale, and the couple also sought recovery of other debts for ale throughout the 1390s.[62] However, in the presentments of those brewing against the assize, also in 1395, only William was named. Similarly, Robert Polidod was named for brewing and selling ale against the assize in April 1396, though in November 1394 both Robert and his wife Margery were in court to reclaim a debt owed for ale, indicating that it was probably Margery who was brewing within the household, and Robert who was accountable when it came to adhering to the assize.[63] Laughton has similarly identified that many of the Chester debt suits that related to ale in fact arose from women's brewing activities, including those of married women.[64]

Many of the female brewers recorded in Nottingham and elsewhere were probably widows, which can be confirmed in some instances from contextual evidence in the borough court rolls. Joan Samon was the widow of John Samon, former Mayor of Nottingham; Margaret Briddesmouth was known as the widow of John Briddesmouth in the borough court rolls (he died sometime between January 1393 and January 1395); and Agnes Remay is found in court cases with her son, John Remay, suggesting that she was also a widow. A handful of Winchester's female brewers were described as widows, such as Elizabeth Boys and Edith Bowlond, and it is likely that others were too.[65] Kowaleski has similarly noted the 'sudden appearance of widows paying brewing fines' immediately following their husbands' deaths, and that these women must in fact have been brewing all along.[66] While we cannot know whether these examples also represented 'sudden' appearances in the records (due to the fragmentary nature of the records), they nevertheless show women continuing to brew in their widowhood, as they would have done during their marriage. It was their status as widows that made them accountable for adhering to regulations, thus making them visible in the records.

Winchester's male 'brewers' often had other occupations, recorded alongside their names in presentment lists, further suggesting that it was their wives who were responsible for the brewing and selling of surplus ale, providing supplementary income for the household.[67] Kowaleski suggested that increasing standardisation in the presentment of brewing fines led heads of households – usually male – to be more regularly assessed and named for offences against the assize of ale, but that earlier records in Exeter tended to list women as brewers rather than their husbands.[68] There is no such evidence of early legal recognition of wives' brewing in Winchester, though the court records certainly appear to become increasingly standardised by the mid-fifteenth century, with all trading offences and regulations listed together and a wider range of trades being monitored. In contrast, the presentments from the turn of the fourteenth century concerned a much smaller number of offences (only 88 in total), with a more even balance of men and women, including wives. As systems of regulation and its legal enforcement developed, so did the understanding that adherence should fall to (male) heads of households, thus marginalising the commercial activities and offences of women within urban records.

Regrating and forestalling: regulating women's work beyond the household

Women were slightly more prominent in offences that represented clear disregard for market rules, such as forestalling. This was the act of intercepting goods before they reached the open market, either outside the hours of the market or at a location outside the physical space of the market. Purchasers might then sell on the goods at higher prices in order to make a profit, and the practice also led to the evasion of tolls on the part of both seller and forestaller. As part of their attempts to foster open and fair trade, urban authorities sought to prevent forestalling in order to control prices and prevent the evasion of tolls. For this reason, presentments against forestallers often cited the detriment caused to the people of the town that resulted from these actions.[69] Regraters engaged in a similar practice, buying up food to sell on by retail, though this was condoned within strict limits concerning the types of food they were allowed to buy, and the times at which they could do so. Deceptive practices – pretending to buy food for personal consumption and then selling it to others – were also prohibited.[70] Some records conflate forestalling and regrating, while others separate them as different offences.

Forestalling was an offence that women were punished for relatively frequently. Winchester women accounted for 18 of the 34 presentments for forestalling and regrating across the sample period, while 19 of 66 presentments in Nottingham in 1395–6 were made against women. Clearly, Nottingham's officials paid more attention to forestalling than those of Winchester – or perhaps this was a more common practice in Nottingham, given that this figure is only drawn from one year of presentments. The attitude to forestalling is encapsulated in one lengthy report included in the Mayor's Court rolls from 1396, which recounts how 3 men bought up 12 quarters of corn from various men coming to the market and took it to the house of Magota Ball. This apparent conspiracy was said to have been to the 'great prejudice of the town … and of the whole community there coming to the … market'. The forestallers were later amerced 11s 8d for their offence.[71]

Across all towns, there was something of a gender divide in the products that women and men forestalled, reflecting the feminisation of the victualling trades, as a number of examples cited by Goldberg have also suggested.[72] Women were named as forestallers of dairy products, candles, poultry and other foodstuffs such as garlic, salt and flour. In Exeter too, the largest proportion of market fines against women were those relating to forestalling and regrating of dairy products, for which women accounted for a quarter of all offenders.[73] In contrast, men forestalled a wide range of other goods, usually not victuals. In Nottingham, 17 men were fined for forestalling coal in 1395, while 3 dealt illegally in items such as rods and tables. Some men forestalled fish, with one specifically selling eels.[74]

Among Nottingham's female forestallers, there was an almost even split between married and not married women. Unlike other commercial offences, this was an area in which wives took personal responsibility for their wrongdoing and disregard for the rules of the market in actions that took place away from the household. Some Nottingham women were often referred to simply as 'wife of', such as the wives of William de Ascheburnne, Ralph Pollard and John Burstall, who were all common hucksters as well as being forestallers of cheese, butter and various kinds of poultry.[75] However, we know the first names of others, such as Katherine, wife of Richard Byrforde, Ibota, wife of John Albayne, and Isabella, wife of John Hakkenay.[76] Married women were also among those who sold herring at inflated prices (five for a penny instead of six) in both Nottingham's Saturday and Daily markets.[77] These were offences that took place outside the household, meaning that these married women were named personally, though their marital and household ties were nevertheless central to their identities. Elizabeth Fisher, huswyff, wife of Richard Fissher, litster, was presented in 1500 for forestalling malt at Nottingham and taking it for sale in Derby, inflating prices in Nottingham.[78] In what was depicted as purposeful act of deception and cornering the market, Elizabeth was described first as huswyff and second by her marital status, and her wrongdoing was hers alone.

In Winchester, individuals presented for offences like forestalling were able to contest their prosecution, and several women turned to inquest juries in contesting their labelling as forestallers and regraters. Alice Carsewell, Agnes Spore, Joan Playnamour, Alice Stoke Kembestre, Alice Pouddynge and Agnes Houckstere were all fined for forestalling various victuals including eggs and 'cinnmon' in 1365–6.[79] In 1433, five women (four of whom were married) were named as regraters of butter, while male regraters and forestallers dealt in grain, oats and wheat, as well as pigs and capons.[80] Women were six out of thirteen forestallers and regraters fined across 1432–3. These were the only married women named for any trading offences in this year, suggesting that this was a distinct offence in which married women's failure to adhere to the rules of the market led to punishment, and perhaps one more associated with women and suspicion of their marketing practices. One of these women was Margery, wife of John Clyffe, here called a mercer and elsewhere a spicer.[81] These details suggest that Margery was not a poor woman desperate to enhance her profits, but the wife of a merchant who sought to supplement her husband's income through the buying and selling of victuals. A total of nine women were named forestallers (of a total of forty) in the Chester records from 1505–10, and six of these were married. Again, they were said to illegally purchase typical 'female' victuals, such as eggs, cheese, butter, grain and other foodstuffs. One woman, Katherine Calkyn, was also included in a long list of fishermen from outside the city who bought and sold illegally at Chester's market.[82] Together, the records of the three towns compile and confirm a common picture of female forestalling that was closely tied to their involvement in the victualling trades, and which held all women individually responsible, regardless of their marital status.

The recognition of women's failure to adhere to the rules of the market reveals a distinction in the legal position of married women in relation to different types of trading regulation. Married women's marketing transgressions were instances of specific illegal behaviour that took place away from the physical space of the household. For the purposes of law enforcement, this marked out women as individual, independent traders, rather than simply being members of the legal unit of the household, even if they were married. The act of forestalling took place outside the home in the 'public' space of the market or in the streets approaching the market. It was an act conceptualised to be of harm to the community of the town through the interception of goods and inflation of prices. The fact that this was an intentionally deceitful act also separated it from the more systematic licensing of other commercial activities, such as brewing, under which the identities of specific individuals were perhaps less important. Forestalling and regrating were not, therefore, household offences, nor were they ones for which married women were 'covered' by the eminency of their husband as the legal head of the household.

Conclusion

Women's involvement in work and trade was notably gendered, adhering to particular female roles and patterns that reflected their low economic status within the urban community. The records of commercial regulation provide an insight into the roles and activities of women and the implications that they faced when they did not observe the rules, or were required to adhere to systems of licensing. This focus on women's actions and activities as traders, rather than their litigious behaviour, provides an alternative perspective on the links between women's economic and legal lives. While there are commonalities in the nature of women's presentments, there are also contrasts in the way in which women accounted for their commercial behaviour under local legal regulations. This was defined by their marital and household status and also the way in which different offences and activities were interpreted. The Winchester evidence, which allows us to trace changes over time, suggests that as trading regulation became more systematic and thorough, there was increased concern for the provision of essentials such as bread, ale, meat and fish. However, as this shift occurred, there was also a concurrent decline in the number of women who were associated with this form of provisioning and victuals. This suggests a decline in women's official and legal status as traders responsible for adhering to the various regulations and assizes.

By highlighting women's sometimes conspicuous absence from the records of trade, this chapter has reaffirmed the marginal status of women workers and traders, who often lacked an occupational identity beyond the category of huckster. Women's inferiority under the male householder was reflected in their not being 'known' for a particular trade or craft. This was exacerbated by the obscuring of women's working activities, particularly for married women, under the dominance of the male head of the household. However, this chapter has identified that the situation was more complicated than the automatic ascribing of all married women's economic activities (legal and illegal) to their husbands. When we look beyond the assizes, we see that women of all statuses could be held accountable for other forms of marketing behaviour, such as forestalling. The comparison of different towns, and of different records within towns, has revealed a lack of consistency in how the principles of coverture were interpreted under the multiple jurisdictions of urban justice, and in the contrasting practices of different towns. Contextualising the records of trading presentments among other legal documents from different towns reveals that wives' commercial and legal identities were not consistently obscured by the status of their husbands as householders, but that this was dependent on the legal context and purpose for which different records were created. Because brewing fines and presentments represented a form of household licensing, these were most often attributed to the head of the household, regardless of who actually did the brewing. But this was not true across all categories of trading regulation. While all married women may have been defined by their ties to their husband, we find numerous instances where wives were held to account for flouting the rules of the market, demonstrating legal recognition of women's work – albeit only in terms of its illegal consequences.

Notes

1. James Davis, *Medieval Market Morality: Life, Law and Ethics in the English Marketplace* (Cambridge: Cambridge University Press, 2012), pp. 147–149.
2. NA CA4478, p. 1.
3. Catherine Casson, 'Reputation and responsibility in medieval English towns: civic concerns with the regulation of trade', *Urban History*, 39 (2012), 396.
4. P.J.P. Goldberg, *Women, Work and Life Cycle in a Medieval Economy: Women in York and Yorkshire c.1300–1520* (Oxford: Clarendon Press, 1992), p. 85.
5. Judith M. Bennett, *Ale, Beer, and Brewsters in England: Women's Work in a Changing World, 1300–1600* (Oxford: Oxford University Press, 1996), p. 103.
6. Maryanne Kowaleski, 'Women's work in a market town: Exeter in the late fourteenth century', in Barbara A. Hanawalt (ed.), *Women and Work in Preindustrial Europe* (Bloomington: Indiana University Press, 1986), p. 156.

7 Derek Keene, *Survey of Medieval Winchester*, vol. 1 (Oxford: Clarendon Press, 1985), p. 249.
8 Rodney Hilton, 'Women traders in medieval England', in Hilton, *Class Conflict and the Crisis of Feudalism*, revised edn (London: Verso, 1990), p. 135.
9 Casson, 'Reputation and responsibility', 389–390.
10 Bennett, *Ale*; Kowaleski, 'Women's work', pp. 145–164; Goldberg, *Women, Work, and Life Cycle*, pp. 104–118; Hilton, 'Women traders', pp. 136–142.
11 Kowaleski, 'Women's work', pp. 157–158.
12 Davis, *Medieval Market Morality*, pp. 231–248.
13 NA 3942 rot. 4.
14 Davis, *Medieval Market Morality*, p. 215.
15 On assizes as licensing, see J.A. Galloway, 'Driven by drink? Ale consumption and the agrarian economy of the London Region, c.1300–1400', in Martha Carlin and Joel T. Rosenthal (eds) *Food and Eating in Medieval Europe* (London: Hambledon Press, 1998), p. 89; Gwen Seabourne, 'Assize matters: Regulation of the price of bread in medieval London', *The Journal of Legal History*, 27 (2006), 29–52; Bennett, *Ale*, p. 100.
16 NA CA3942 rot. 3d.
17 'Item dicunt quod omne auxiatrices Notingham vendunt allium, farina, salem, sepas candelas sine cotoni interposito butturum, casios, et hujusmodi nimis caros, contra statute, ad deceptionem populi, et sunt communes forestallatores talium victualium predictorum venientium ad villam Notingham vendendorum, stantes ad exitus viarum ubi talia victualia veniunt ad vendendum etc.'
18 W.H. Stevenson, *Records of the Borough of Nottingham*, vol. 1 (London: Quaritch, 1882), p. 444.
19 Norwich: 'hukster', see William Hudson (ed.), *Leet Jurisdiction in the City of Norwich during the XIIIth and XIVth Centuries* (London: Quaritch, 1892), p. 63; Bristol: hokkestere, see Francis. B. Bickley (ed.), *The Little Red Book of Bristol* (London: Hemmons, 1900), p. 33; on London hucksters, see Marjorie Keniston McIntosh, *Working Women in English Society, 1300–1620* (Cambridge: Cambridge University Press, 2005), pp. 131–132.
20 NA CA3942 rots 3d and 4.
21 McIntosh, *Working Women*, pp. 130–132; Kowaleski, 'Women's work', pp. 148–149; Hilton, 'Women traders', pp. 135–136; Goldberg, *Women, Work and Life Cycle*, pp. 117–118.
22 NA CA3942 rot. 2d.
23 NA CA3942 rot. 3.
24 NA CA1294 rot. 7.
25 NA CA3942 rot. 3. A total of 12 decennaries from different areas of Nottingham listed themselves among those brewing against the assize.
26 NA CA3942 rot. 3. '*Johannes de Horton wrigth decenarius de Gosegate nichil presentat quia debilis est etc except Johanne de Horton qui est communis braciator et vendit cum ciphis et discis contra Assisam etc.*'
27 Bennett, *Ale*, p. 100.
28 Davis, *Medieval Market Morality*, pp. 232–234.
29 On the assizes and their implementation elsewhere, see Seabourne, 'Assize matters', 29–52; Bennett, *Ale*, pp. 99–121; Hilton, 'Women traders', pp. 136–137; Janka

Rodziewicz, 'Order and Society: Great Yarmouth 1366–1381', Unpublished PhD Thesis, University of East Anglia (2008), p. 59.
30 Maryanne Kowaleski, *Local Markets and Regional Trade in Medieval Exeter* (Cambridge: Cambridge University Press, 1995), p. 139.
31 NA CA3942 rot. 5.
32 NA CA1294 rot. 19.
33 NA CA3942 rot. 1.
34 NA CA1296/I rot. 11.
35 HRO W/D1/3 rot. 5; for the ordinance, see J.S. Furley (ed.), *The Ancient Usages of the City of Winchester* (Oxford: Clarendon Press, 1927), pp. 34–35.
36 HRO W/D1/64.
37 Bennett, *Ale*, pp. 3–4.
38 Bennett, *Ale*, pp. 164–166.
39 Rodziewicz, 'Order and Society', p. 59.
40 Kowaleski, 'Women's work', p. 149.
41 Bennett, *Ale*, pp. 103, 164–166.
42 The extant 1407–8 and 1414–15 Mayor's Court rolls only feature the presentment of affrays.
43 NA CA3350 pp. 20–21.
44 CA 4494 p. 31.
45 Bennett, *Ale*, pp. 100–101.
46 HRO W/D1/3 rot. 5; rot. 10.
47 HRO W/D1/3 rot. 9d, 10d.
48 Bennett, *Ale*, pp. 160–164.
49 On the professionalisation of brewing, see Bennett, *Ale*, especially chapter 5.
50 Bennett, *Ale*, p. 77.
51 Furley, *Ancient Usages*, p. 36. '*Derechef chescune braceresse del poier de la vile ke brace a uente face cerveise bone sulump la vente del ble e sulump la asise done, e si autrement le funt soient en la merci li rois tante feiz cume baillifs les purrunt atteindre.*' '*Derechef nule braceresse hors de franchise ne pust bracer dedenz le poier de la cite a uente si ele ne face gre as bailiffs sulump la quantite de son fet.*'
52 Bennett, *Ale*, p. 113.
53 Jane Laughton, 'The alewives of later medieval Chester', in Rowena E. Archer (ed.), *Crown, Government and People in the Fifteenth Century* (Stroud: Alan Sutton, 1995), p. 197.
54 Laughton, 'Alewives', p. 199.
55 CALS ZS/B/5 a, b, d, e.
56 Laughton, 'Alewives', p. 202.
57 CALS ZS/B/5d fol. 61.
58 CALS ZS/B/5a fol. 7. Laughton, 'Alewives', p. 204.
59 Agnes Haslyngton huswiff and Elina Pole huswiff, CALS ZS/B/5e fol. 88a v.
60 Laughton, 'Alewives', p. 208; Bennett, *Ale*, p. 108.
61 Bennett, *Ale*, p. 165.
62 NA CA1295 rot. 3d. See also William and Isabella v Robert Feyse in a plea of debt of 3s owed for ale bought from him and Isabella in November 1394. NA CA1294 rot. 15.
63 NA CA1294 rot. 3.

64 Laughton, 'Alewives', pp. 202–203.
65 HRO W/D1/64.
66 Kowaleski, 'Women's work', p. 151.
67 For example, John Byketon tailor, William Flye cook, William Baker harper, Ralph Dutton smith, John Phylpot cook and John Chepman tailor, all fined for selling ale in 1433. HRO W/D1/60 rot. 10d.
68 Kowaleski, *Exeter*, p. 132.
69 Davis, *Medieval Market Morality*, pp. 254–255.
70 Davis, *Medieval Market Morality*, p. 261.
71 '*in magnum prejudicium villae predicta et totius communitatis ibidem ad forum predictum venientis* ...'.
72 Goldberg, *Women, Work and Life Cycle*, p. 117.
73 Kowaleski, 'Women's work', p. 149.
74 NA CA3942 rot. 4.
75 NA CA3942 rot. 3.
76 NA CA3942 rot. 4.
77 NA CA3942 rot. 3d.
78 Stevenson, *Nottingham*, vol. 3, p. 79.
79 HRO W/D1/13 rot. 3.
80 HRO W/D1/60 rot. 2, 3, 3d, 11d, 12d, 13, 14.
81 HRO W/D1/60 rot. 12d.
82 CALS ZS/B/5b fol. 35v.

4

Violence, property and 'bad speech': women and trespass litigation

Urban living brought with it a fair share of interpersonal conflict and violence. Town court records reveal women's involvement in physical and verbal assault, theft and attacks on property. When Margery Dod brought a complaint of trespass to Nottingham's borough court in April 1324 against Robert de Spondon, his wife Hawise and daughter Alice, the list of alleged transgressions committed against her was long and detailed. She said that they had assaulted her in the town's Saturday market place, called her false, a thief and a whore, and accused her of stealing a tabard. As well as defaming her with these accusations, they also beat, crushed and dragged her on the floor. Margery sought damages of 20s in compensation for the attack.[1] Though the outcome of this suit is not known, it serves to demonstrate the range of physical and attacks that the plea of trespass could encapsulate, as well as the ways that members of the urban community (allegedly) caused harm to one another. In addition, trespass pleas allowed townspeople to defend their rights over property, goods and chattels, in which both financial prosperity and social status were vested. In Winchester in January 1386, Johanna Burbache complained that William Crowk, a chaplain, attacked her with force and arms using sticks and knives, entering her house against her will and stealing goods and chattels to the value of £6. Burbache claimed damages of £10 for the injury and harm she experienced, though the jury awarded only £6 3s.[2] These complaints were not simply about the direct financial loss that they caused, but the resultant damage to an individual's honour and reputation. The public nature of borough court litigation offered an ideal forum in which to voice these grievances and seek retribution.

This chapter examines women's roles in a wide range of interpersonal offences, recorded in pleas of trespass, and the representation of these offences under local law. It considers both the nature of these misdeeds as well as the choices of litigants to bring these issues to light in court and the way that these complaints were dealt with. Trespass litigation provided for the public voicing of complaints about misbehaviour and acted as a mechanism to rebuild damaged honour and reputation.[3] The claiming of monetary damages also allowed for quantification of the harm caused by trespasses, somewhat in common with the 'blame and claim' compensation culture of the twenty-first century. While criminal pleas, reserved for the central courts, represent the most severe and exceptional acts of violence and wrongdoing, trespass pleas allow us to access the more 'ordinary' misbehaviour that was a constant feature of town life. As Patricia Turning has argued for medieval southern France, the records of crime and misbehaviour, though constructed by men and often appearing to be dominated by men's transgressions, offer clues about women's day-to-day concerns and experiences of urban life, as well as the strategies they employed to fight 'for power and placement within the social hierarchy'.[4] Women's involvement in the offences that were categorised as trespass, their legal construction and repercussions, were therefore indicative of their integration into the rhythms, fractures and frictions of urban life, from which women were not precluded simply because of their sex.

The nature of trespass pleas in borough courts

The plea of trespass (*transgressio*) represented a broad category of wrongdoing, stemming from the essence of 'direct forcible injury' that caused harm to either persons, goods or land.[5] In the most basic terms, this plea simply meant 'wrong', at a level below more serious felony offences of homicide, mayhem, wounding, false imprisonment, arson, rape, robbery, burglary and larceny.[6] Trespass pleas were heard in a range of courts, both royal and customary/seigneurial, the appropriate jurisdiction corresponding to the authority whose 'peace' had been broken.[7] In towns where rights of self-governance had been farmed out from the king, trespasses which broke the 'king's peace' (often cited in court records) were therefore under the jurisdiction of borough courts. The rural equivalents of town courts in England's manors dealt with pleas of trespass that occurred on the land of their lords, causing Glanvill to state that it was within these lords' jurisdictions that the primary jurisdiction over trespass lay.[8] Common law writs of trespass typically included the formula that the defendant had used force and arms (*vi et armis*) and acted against the king's peace to abuse, wound and/or maltreat the plaintiff.[9] Trespass pleas in town and manor courts borrowed this language, though here pleas were initiated orally. After complaints concerning debts owed, pleas of trespass were the second most voluminous category of plea across all the towns examined here, a fact that contrasts with Stevens' findings for fourteenth-century Ruthin in Dyffryn Clwyd, where appearances relating to violence and trespass outnumbered those relating to debt and detention of goods.[10] The prominence of these complaints thus represents urban residents' desire to seek retribution for offences and misbehaviour that harmed either their physical person, their reputation or their personal or real property. As Hannah Robb has recently highlighted, reputation was a key commodity in late medieval England, in both the marketplace and the courts.[11] But despite their high volume, pleas of trespass have received little attention from scholars of social or legal history, as they have been overlooked in favour of criminal cases. There is some overlap with many criminal offences, meaning that trespass broadens our evidence base for the study of misbehaviour. Yet the relatively low-level nature of trespass complaints also allows for consideration of more 'ordinary' forms of misbehaviour, more common to the experiences of women and men than exceptional cases such as murder, rape and serious violent assault. In urban contexts, the focus on towns as centres of trade has resulted in attention being focused on commercial litigation concerning debt and detinue, with interpersonal pleas being somewhat neglected in the study of urban justice.

The value of trespass litigation in revealing the social interactions of the medieval town lies in the broad range of offences that fell under this category of complaint. Though quantification of the different 'types' of complaint is problematic due to the varying amount of detail recorded, many concerned physical attacks, often described using formulaic language borrowed from common law, naming weapons (commonly sticks, staffs, knives or fists), and sometimes describing the nature of a victim's beating, wounding and injuries caused.[12] The repeated use of this formula means that we should be wary of reading too much into these descriptions; deviations from formula may in fact be more illustrative of what may have happened. As trespass complaints only recorded interpersonal relationships that broke down, we may be inclined to read them as evidence of a bloody, lawless society. However, it is thanks to the pervasiveness of medieval law that we are able to recover these offences at all, even at the local level. These records can be read as both evidence of almost constant misdemeanour, and the efforts of local governments and individuals to punish and seek retribution for such misdemeanours.

As well as complaints of violence, many trespass pleas alleged attacks on property, both urban real estate and individuals' goods and chattels.

According to Barbara Hanawalt, larceny was the most common crime in fourteenth-century England, and many larcenies were in fact prosecuted as trespass.[13] The line dividing trespass from criminal offences, particularly in relation to property, was blurred. Acts of petty larceny involving the theft of goods worth under 1s were said to be actionable under the law of trespass, while offences worth over this value amounted to grand larceny. However, many instances of trespass found in borough courts concern goods well above the value of 1s, indicating, as Karen Jones has previously suggested, that litigants or courts had the power to decide whether offences would be prosecuted as trespass or felony.[14] Some of these complaints cited unwanted entry to homes, messuages or gardens, frequently coupled with the theft of goods and chattels which were often named and valued. Even when no goods were taken, plaintiffs cited the harm and damage caused and represented this in monetary terms through the claiming of damages. Other trespasses concerned verbal assaults, with allegations concerning moral and commercial fidelity, as well as specific accusations of theft, illegal activity such as cutting purses, or sexual impropriety. Less common, but still illustrative of some of the problems of urban living, were complaints citing the misbehaviour of animals, for which their owners were held responsible. Cows, pigs and sheep could be classed as 'vagrant' when they trampled upon neighbouring gardens, destroying plants or breaking down fences. These complaints remind us of the presence of certain 'rural' characteristics within medieval towns, particularly small–medium sized urban centres. The most exceptional complaints concerned the abduction of women – wives, daughters and servants – complained about by men but constructed as part of the theft of property rather than as the felony of rape or abduction.[15]

To understand the nature of trespass pleas, both individually and as a category of complaint, we need to think about the intended outcome: what were complainants hoping to achieve as a result of bringing their complaint to court? The impetus for legal action came directly from the plaintiff, not legal officials or the crown. Punishment for a guilty defendant was rarely imprisonment or another form of physical correction. Instead, plaintiffs sought monetary damages as recompense for wrongful behaviour, and this was the perhaps the key distinction in the origin of trespass and its separation from felony.[16] These damages were cited in each plea, and were always significant sums that were sometimes accompanied by a description of the harm, loss or shame experienced as a result of a trespass. The jurisdictional limit of trespass pleas in local courts (both town and manor) was, theoretically, the value of damages below 40s. Claims above this sum were to be brought before the royal justices.[17] However, as we will see, town court trespass pleas did sometimes concern damages over 40s, though these sums were never awarded. Where a plea related to damaged or stolen goods, the damages claimed typically went far beyond the value of these goods; and in instances of physical or verbal assault, plaintiffs also claimed significant sums though they had experienced no tangible financial loss. Rather, trespass pleas and the damages claimed intended to represent the loss to honour or reputation that victims experienced. An attack on a person's property, goods, body or character constituted an attack on their worth, standing or credit within the community, and, as Elizabeth Ewan has argued, in a society in which so many transactions were made on credit, a good reputation was essential to livelihood.[18] Rather than cover up these attacks through shame, the public nature of trespass litigation therefore offered an opportunity for the reconstructing of honour, through both social and financial recompense.

Outcomes could be determined by the defendant's acknowledgement of their offence, or the seeking of a 'licence to agree' between litigants (always followed by the defendant being amerced, suggesting another means of acknowledgement). If the defendant denied the accusation, the case would usually be referred to the decision of an inquest jury, which reported on the guilt of the accused party and was also involved in the assessment of damages. Plaintiffs (male and female) never won the damages they sought, with courts typically awarding a small fraction of the original sum. For example, Agnes Solyan of Chester claimed damages of 20s following an attack 'with force and arms' by John Smale in 1423, and while the jury agreed that Smale was guilty, she was awarded only 6d as compensation.[19] In Nottingham in 1410, Edmund de Wheteley complained that Richard Fletcher had committed trespass by destroying various plants in his garden, as well as using a ladder to strip his garden wall of stones. He claimed damages of 100s, though the jury eventually assessed damages of only 4d.[20] Six months later, in March 1411, Wheteley complained that John Hodyngs and his wife Elizabeth had also torn down the wall of his close, using pick axes and spades (a significant feat given that the wall was apparently eight foot high), taking away the stones as well as tearing down a fence. This time he cited damages of 10s, and the couple were ordered to pay 2s in compensation.[21] That this discrepancy between damages claimed and awarded was a common part of legal practice must have meant that plaintiffs would have known this would happen, but nevertheless used the claiming of large sums as symbolic representation of the harm experienced or perceived. Some complainants were explicit about their loss of credit as a result of the actions of others. In 1324, Richard Baldok of Nottingham complained of Richard le Couper and Juliana, his wife, claiming that Juliana had assaulted him, called him a false man and an infidel and accusing him of stealing malt from John le Colier's house along with a woman called Margery Brewood. Baldok claimed that he had, as a result, lost credit of Richard le Marescall to the value of half a mark. After numerous delays, Baldok failed to appear in court to prosecute his plea, and so was amerced for bringing an unjust suit.[22] This insight into the alleged implications of public slander demonstrates the way that reputation played out within urban communities, and how this was commodified and converted to legal damages by individuals.[23]

Many trespass complaints do not allow us to trace the outcome of a particular dispute, and the amount of detail recorded for each offence varies. This was something that was true for much of the litigation recorded in town court rolls, not just trespass pleas, though there were some factors that related specifically to trespass. This may be because a complaint was dropped, settled out of court, or because scribes did not deem the details of who said what, or exactly how an assault was reported to have happened, as necessary details to document. Some records may simply have not survived to reveal the details of a plea or its outcome. Of the courts examined here, the Winchester records offer the least detail on the nature of trespasses, particularly by the later fifteenth century when usually only the names of litigants and the type of complaint are recorded. While this can frustrate the storytelling element involved in reconstructing these pleas, answering questions of guilt is not the essential aim here. The construction, procedure, content and recording of each complaint is valuable in itself for what it reveals about litigants' and officials' attitudes to misbehaviour and justice, so those cases where the outcome is not known have not been dismissed. It is also important to bear in mind that just because a jury reported that a defendant was culpable (or not), this may not represent the 'truth' of the dispute of the offence itself. Both these judgements and the court records more widely are only partial representations of what 'really' happened.[24]

Both men and women were part of this process of misbehaviour and retribution. Women acted out trespasses as well as being on the receiving end. When they were 'victims', they used local justice to seek retribution and restore damage to personal or household worth. By bringing their complaints to court, litigants were actively claiming and seeking to repair their credit – both social and financial – in public.[25] Patricia Turning has also emphasised the public nature of much of the misbehaviour and criminal actions in medieval Toulouse – including that involving women.[26] Together, these two public aspects of misbehaviour and retribution reveal the crucial role that the negotiation of justice played in the making and breaking of social ties and status within the urban community.

Gendered analyses of honour, reputation or *fama* have often emphasised a dichotomy of gendered honour and status, under which female honour was based on sexual reputation, while male honour was derived from economic and occupational identity, household status and physical prowess.[27] For example, Shannon McSheffrey has argued that women's value was more closely tied to their marital status, marriageability and sexual repute than men's.[28] A woman's good name was constructed largely through others' knowledge about her sexual behaviour which related to her governance by male authority, though sexual misconduct was also damaging for men as it demonstrated a lack of good governance and control over the self.[29]

The evidence of women's involvement in misbehaviour, criminal or otherwise, sits somewhat at odds with this binary understanding of honour. Trespass pleas reveal women as active participants in actions that were linked to the breaking and re-making of honour in ways that had much in common with interpersonal relations between men. Honour was something that could be both accrued and taken away through an individual or household's actions, and through legal action. This is something that has also been highlighted in other studies of women's misbehaviour and legal action. Both Elizabeth Ewan and Patricia Turning have argued, for medieval Scotland and Toulouse respectively, that women were unafraid to take action in defence of their rights and their honour, both in court and on the streets.[30] For Turning, women's legal action demonstrates that they 'actively protected their own honour both through the judicial system and in their neighbourhoods', taking active roles in court rather than passively standing beside their husbands.[31] Garthine Walker has also debunked notions of female dependency and passivity as an explanatory factor for women's lesser involvement in crime, highlighting the proportions of married female assailants in non-lethal violence.[32]

Traditional views of male and female 'types' of misbehaviour have also been tied in part to this gendering of honour, leading 'female' offences to be written off as marginal.[33] Barbara Hanawalt, in the 1970s, emphasised the differences in women's patterns of criminality as compared to men: they were involved less often in crimes against the person and usually acted alongside male accomplices in these attacks, as well as in property crimes.[34] The varying amounts of detail recorded in relation to trespass pleas make quantification of the specific nature of offences problematic, but it is clear that women featured in every type of complaint, illustrating their integration into the full spectrum of misbehaviour that fell under the plea of trespass. Furthermore, these were marked by a lack of gendered verbal assaults, something which has characterised previous discussions of female crime and misbehaviour.[35] Trespass pleas were dealt with in an apparently fair, even-handed and distinctly ungendered way by local courts.

Though women's actions in trespass and criminal suits were significantly fewer in number than men's, this should not be read as an indicator of passivity or dependency, or of women's invisible and insignificant roles in everyday life. These were offences that represented a broad range of urban interactions, tied to economic roles, household connections and personal relationships. As Walker has also argued, women's contribution to the household economy gave a sense of 'social identity and self-worth, as well as neighbourhood status, all of which have a relation to honour', connecting women's honour to their deeds (or misdeeds).[36] It makes sense, therefore, that women's honour was acted out, disputed, damaged and restored in ways that reflected their wide-ranging activities and contributions to both the household and the urban society and economy more broadly. Trespass pleas allow us to understand female behaviour and dispute beyond the model of sexual honour and 'feminine' crimes.

The numbers

One way to approach the study of women's involvement in trespass and misbehaviour is through quantitative analysis: how many women featured in litigation, whether they were victims (plaintiffs) or alleged perpetrators (defendants), what types of offences these pleas represented, and whether women acted on their own or alongside others, including men. This analysis does indicate some general features and patterns of women in trespass, and serves as a useful starting point for further examination. Yet, if we rely too closely on the numbers, two things can happen. First, as Garthine Walker has pointed out, the low proportions of women in trespass pleas can lead us to the conclusion that women's actions were insignificant or exceptional.[37] Second, focusing on numbers and statistics can obscure many of the nuances and complexities of women's interactions and litigation: who was assaulted, in what manner, what was stolen, where did this happen, who else was involved? In attempting to categorise these interactions in ways that can be easily counted, we lose sight of the individuals that were involved in these offences and the resulting court cases, and the unique nature of each of these interactions.

Nevertheless, the numbers do tell us some key facts about patterns of trespass litigation in general, and about women's involvement in these pleas. Trespass was always the second largest category of complaint across all three towns' courts, and in urban courts elsewhere too. This is illustrated in Figure 1.1 in Chapter 1. At Exeter's Mayor's Court during the 1380s, trespass accounted for 34 per cent of pleas.[38] Across the three towns, the proportion of pleas that concerned trespass declined from the fourteenth to fifteenth centuries, as debt pleas came to dominate the business of town courts. This was reflected in Colchester, where debt pleas rose tenfold while trespass pleas stayed at relatively stable levels, leading trespass to account for only 19 per cent of pleas by 1400.[39] The survival of each set of court rolls varies in fullness and quality, but the percentages of different types of suit are indicative of the balance between debt and trespass. This relative decline in trespass litigation was particularly notable in Nottingham and Winchester, as the graph illustrates. Whether this is indicative of less violent urban communities or a shift in litigious activity is impossible to judge, but several scholars have suggested an increase in indebtedness – and hence more debt pleas – after the Black Death and into the fifteenth century.[40] This is demonstrated in the relative proportions of these two main categories of suit when sampled across the period. Some of the decline in trespass pleas may be down to population loss following the Black Death, but the extent of the decline and shifting balance of debt litigation means that this cannot be the only explanatory factor.

Samples taken across the fourteenth and fifteenth century clearly indicate that women always accounted for a minority of trespass litigants, and the proportion of trespass suits that featured women was always less than half of the total. These figures varied between different towns, and over time, generally declining over the period. Women were less likely to act in trespass pleas at the end of the fifteenth century than they were at the beginning of the fourteenth century (Table 4.1).

Women acted as both plaintiffs (victims) and defendants (perpetrators), with no clear pattern or difference in how often women took on these roles. At Nottingham and Chester, the numbers of female plaintiffs and defendants were almost equal. However, in the Winchester samples, women featured more often as those accused of trespass (80 defendants to 57 plaintiffs). This contrasts with Karen Jones' study of Kent, where women were over twice as likely to be victims of non-fatal assaults than

Table 4.1 Women and trespass in Chester, Nottingham and Winchester.

Town	Year	All trespass litigants	Female trespass litigants	All trespass suits	Suits featuring women
Chester	1317–18	125	28 (22%)	64	21 (33%)
	1378	85	17 (20%)	42	15 (36%)
	1395	59	10 (17%)	31	10 (32%)
	1423	64	9 (14%)	32	8 (25%)
	1435	79	19 (24%)	36	15 (21%)
	1490	63	11 (17%)	39	11 (28%)
	Total	475	94 (20%)	244	80 (33%)
Nottingham	1323–4	240	72 (30%)	143	61 (43%)
	1375–6	146	25 (17%)	83	31 (37%)
	1394–5	88	18 (20%)	50	19 (38%)
	1433–4	100	22 (22%)	62	27 (44%)
	1446–7	151	13 (8%)	67	15 (22%)
	1491–2	146	11 (6%)	87	14 (16%)
	Total	871	161 (18%)	492	14 (16%)
Winchester	1299–1300	224	43 (19%)	136	33 (34%)
	1365–6	116	19 (16%)	49	12 (25%)
	1385–6	89	23 (26%)	50	25 (50%)
	1432–3	149	15 (10%)	114	18 (16%)
	1454–5	119	13 (6%)	79	15 (19%)
	1495–6	85	7 (8%)	55	10 (18%)
	Total	782	120 (15%)	483	113 (23%)

Source: CALS ZSR 21, 81–85, 109–112, 147–155, 201–210, 369–380; NA CA 1258B, CA 1279, CA 1294, CA 1324, CA 1325, CA 1336, CA 1374; HRO W/D1/3, W/D1/13, W/D1/27, W/D1/60, W/D1/61, W/D1/64.

assailants. The difference here may in part be accounted for by the wide remit of trespass pleas, which did not only represent supposedly 'non-feminine' physical assaults. Women complained and were accused of acts of unwanted entry to property (sometimes framed as housebreaking), theft and damage to property or goods. Some attacks also brought together a range of accusations, as shown by the example concerning Margery Dod and the Spondon family cited at the beginning of this chapter.

Women of all marital statuses acted in trespass pleas in all three towns across the fourteenth and fifteenth centuries. They litigated independently (usually) when widowed or never-married, and jointly with their husbands during marriage. In their misbehaviour they acted alone, as well as in collaboration with their husbands, children and other family members to commit violence, slander and damage or steal property. While many women were active litigants on both sides of these complaints, some women were simply the subject of a plea, with their husbands, fathers or employers complaining about attacks upon them without the women themselves being present or named as litigants. This was, however, an exception to the normal practice of trespass litigation, as the following sections of this chapter will illustrate. Stevens has similarly noted that husbands or guardians brought pleas on behalf of women in Ruthin in only a handful of instances, demonstrating that women's active involvement in litigation was a general factor across multiple places and jurisdictions.[41] The decline in women's actions in trespass pleas can in part be accounted for by the drop in the number of married couples acting together in trespass pleas in the fifteenth century. This was most notable in Nottingham, where spouses frequently litigated together during the fourteenth century. The nature of this joint litigation and the patterns that defined it will be explored in more detail in the following section.

Quantitative analysis tells us that women were involved in significantly fewer trespasses than their male relatives and neighbours. However, the lower numbers should not lead us to discount the experiences of women altogether. We need to pay attention to the women who *are* found in the records of trespass to attempt to understand their world, experiences and actions as well as attitudes to these incidents among the urban community. The numbers do not provide an insight into the *actual* nature of real, individual women's litigation in relation to interpersonal disputes and injury. While economic complaints offer an insight into patterns of trade, credit and debt within an urban community, trespass complaints reflect the more idiosyncratic nature of urban life – though of course some may have been linked to commercial disputes. By examining the details of women's trespass pleas, we not only illuminate their involvement in misbehaviour and the subsequent legal action, but also contribute to the re-entering of women into the histories of law, violence and misbehaviour. The remainder of this chapter will examine the differing nature of pleas of trespass, the types of misbehaviour they reveal and women's status within these actions.

Violent women and violence against women

Instances of physical assault were regularly brought to court as trespass complaints, including attacks both on and by women. They were involved in violence involving other women, as well as men, who apparently were not reluctant to publicise the fact that they had been attacked by a woman. Karen Jones noted that the proportion of female assailants in late medieval Kent was 'startlingly low' at less than 3 per cent, suggesting that women may have had less opportunity to engage in violence, but also that assaults by women were underreported except in more severe instances.[42] However, women in borough courts were almost equally likely to appear as plaintiffs and defendants – victims and assailants – in trespass pleas.

Perhaps unsurprisingly, there are numerous examples of fights and violence between women. In Chester in 1317, Leuka de Lysewis claimed that Alice le Gardener beat, wounded and mistreated her with force and arms, causing damages of 100s. An inquisition jury found that Alice was guilty of the attack but awarded only 6d. damages.[43] At Nottingham, Matilda, widow of John de Parys, complained that Lecia le Flecher had attacked and beaten her with a staff, breaking her tooth and making her bloody. She claimed damages of 20s for this violent attack, made more severe by the resulting bloodshed. Lecia was fined for the trespass, suggesting she was judged to be guilty, though we do not know the damages that were eventually awarded.[44] Married women typically litigated alongside their husbands even when it was clear that the alleged assaults had occurred between the two wives only. In Chester in 1318, William Holegheie and his wife Lucy brought a suit against Hugh Derby and his wife Adriana, complaining that Adriana had assaulted Lucy with force and arms and beaten her, resulting in William's loss of 100s. The jury reported that the 'evil' done to Lucy was by her own assault, and Hugh and Adriana were not guilty.[45] Alice, daughter of Christine Lichfeld, complained of Roger de Bichehill and his wife Cecilia in Nottingham in 1331, claiming that Cecilia had assaulted her, trampled on her and drawn blood. Cecilia was found to be guilty, and ordered to be imprisoned until she could pay the damages of 6d and the fine to the court (probably 3d).[46] While Cecilia could not answer the complaint alone, because she was married, the court recognised that she was individually responsible for the attack by ordering her to be imprisoned. In another comparable attack, where both John and Johanna Betesone attacked Matilda, daughter of John le Serjaunt, both husband and wife were ordered to be imprisoned until the various sums could be paid.[47] The use of imprisonment, itself unusual, was therefore meted out specifically to those responsible for assaults, illustrating that even joint litigation by spouses did not supersede the individual identities of husband and wife.

In some instances, both parties claimed to be the victims of trespass. In Nottingham, Thomas Beauchamp and his wife Margery claimed in December 1433 that Margaret Midilton had assaulted Margery using her fists, but Midilton also sued Thomas and Margery, alleging that in fact Margery had assaulted her with a wooden pottle. Both parties were later fined for not prosecuting their claims, suggesting the complaints were abandoned.[48] Whether these alleged instances of violence were the result of longstanding disputes, rivalries or animosity, or simply outbursts of anger, is impossible to ascertain without further details, but they demonstrate that women were ready to use their local court to punish the misbehaviour of others when they were wronged.

Women also attacked men. Several historians have suggested that female violence appeared less often in legal complaints as it was understood as unnatural or unfeminine, a departure from proper codes of gendered behaviour which could lead male victims of female violence to become subjects of ridicule.[49] Where women were assailants against men, the legal stories told about them often constructed their behaviour in ways that focused less on acts of direct violence and more on their abusive words, or the absurd nature of their actions.[50] But men were not ashamed to complain about the trespasses of women. If they were, we would not have seen men such as William Cancor of Nottingham choose to bring their complaints to public attention before the court. In 1376, William complained that Amya Hoxter had assaulted him, beat and wounded him causing bloodshed, and sought damages of 40d.[51] John Neuerk accused Agnes, wife of William Neuerk, of beating him and making 'grave violence' upon him with force and arms, emphasising the severity of the assault.[52] In Winchester in 1432, Agnes, servant of John Stone, was reported to be guilty of trespass against John Somerset, and ordered to pay 6d in damages.[53] In Chester in 1490, John Bower sued Elizabeth Knybbes, wife of Henry Knybbes, for assaulting and striking him, causing damages of 100s. There was no mention of her husband being involved in the plea, and the jury agreed that she was guilty and assessed damages at 6s 8d.[54] These cases were not exceptions, but representative of many instances in which men sued women for acts of violence and misbehaviour. Just as Elizabeth Ewan has argued for Scotland, urban women were not afraid or unable to assert themselves through violence or misbehaviour, but neither were their victims ashamed to publicise this misbehaviour in court.[55] Trespass litigation offered an opportunity for retribution and compensation, rather than shame, and it was the benefits of this potential outcome that informed the choice of complainants to air their cases.

The more stereotypical image of women's involvement in violence and misbehaviour is as victims. The patterns we have already seen demonstrate that women were almost equally likely to act out violence (or at least to be accused of doing so) as they were to be on the receiving end, and the examples discussed above provide plenty of evidence of women as violent or misbehaving trespassers. Where women were victims, the fact that they brought their complaints to court in order to seek retribution and compensation somewhat tempers the image of weak, defenceless women. Women were attacked by men, but were not cowed into avoiding legal action. Margaret Kaye sued Thomas Beauchamp for trespass in Nottingham in September 1433. The plea was repeatedly postponed over the course of the whole year to September 1434, and no outcome is known.[56] Johanna Burbache of Winchester's complaint against the chaplain William Crowk cited a long list of offences: coming armed to her house, breaking in, assaulting her and stealing a substantial sum of money. Her decision to bring her complaint to court eventually won her damages of £6 3s, along with the public declaration of Crowk's guilt.[57] Some women were victims of extreme violence: in Nottingham in 1398, Joan Brailsford sued John Nottingham and his wife Margaret, claiming that Margaret assaulted her at her house, dragged her and threw her down, breaking the bone in her thigh. The jury agreed that Margaret was guilty – a broken thigh would presumably be easily evidenced in court.[58]

Physical violence on and by women often involved weapons. Often these were tools and objects that were readily to hand, such as knives, sticks or fists.[59] Barbara Hanawalt found that in felony cases, women most commonly used knives and hatchets, but 'virtually never' used staffs, swords, bows and arrows or battle axes.[60] Though not every case recorded whether or not weapons were used, those that do typically detail the same types of weapon for both men and women, the most common being sticks, knives or daggers, and staffs. Patricia Turning observed a similar usage of weapons among the urban community of medieval Toulouse, noting how 'resourceful' both men and women were in using both illegal weapons and everyday objects in their attacks.[61] Henry le Cancur of Nottingham claimed that Alice, wife of John de Tumby, had called him a false man, a thief and drew a knife and struck him on the arm in July 1323.[62] Alice and her husband John answered the complaint together. The couple also brought a successful countersuit, demonstrating the use of violence and the law by both parties to damage the other and restore their own reputations.[63] At Chester, Margaret, servant of Ranulph de Clerk, complained in 1395 that John Man attacked her with force and arms, specifically with sticks or staffs (*baculis*).[64] John and

Elizabeth Hodyngs together were accused of using pick-axes and spades to tear down Edmund de Wheteley's wall in Nottingham in 1411.[65] When swords were used, this was generally in trespasses and assaults between men, such as John Mapurley's breaking and entering into the house of William Milis at Nottingham in 1492.[66] Perhaps women had less access to these military weapons, or perhaps litigants and court officials did not want to admit or believe that women could wield these more dangerous weapons. However, the low frequency with which these items appear among formulaic phrases recording force and arms and generic references to injury means that we should be wary of placing too much weight on the extent to which they actually depict the specific weapons used. At Winchester, the City Court rolls consistently record that trespasses were committed with sticks and knives, suggesting that this was in fact formulaic language referring to the use of some sort of unknown or unspecified weapon, or that its specific nature was not important.

Some physical attacks fell within the specific category of *hamsocn* (or *homsokin*), an Anglo Saxon offence of attacking someone within a house.[67] This offence featured regularly in Nottingham's court rolls though its appearance is limited to the first half of the fourteenth century. Pollock and Maitland suggest that this was a felony, reserved for pleas of the crown, and this may explain the shift away from *hamsocn* pleas under trespass in Nottingham and its general absence in Chester and Winchester, demonstrating the customary evolution of the borough court.[68] Women were the victims of these domestic attacks, and sometimes the perpetrators too, illustrating their actions in violence away from their own home. In December 1327, Serlo of Thorpe sued Henry le Meyreman, along with his wife and daughters. He alleged that Agnes, Henry's wife, and daughters Emma and Juliana, had entered his house in *homsokin*, beaten and maltreated him and made him bloody. He sought damages of 20s. The family members came to court together and denied the guilt of the three women.[69] The jury found that the women had not attacked Serlo, and he was amerced for a false suit.[70] The two sides were involved in numerous complaints against one another, and involving other family members, suggesting something of an ongoing family rivalry or feud. Another familial pair, Hawise of Cropwell and her daughter Cecilia, were accused of *homsokin* by Alice Slinge, who claimed they had beaten her with a staff, as well as attacking her in the market place opposite her house.[71] A rare reference to *homsokne* in Chester's Pentice Court appears in a 1318 trespass plea brought by Richard and Alice Runcorn against William le Wode, who was said to have attacked Alice as well as making *homsokne*.[72]

Women were also the subject of attacks within the home by male assailants. At Nottingham in October 1322, William de Wolde and his wife Matilda alleged that William le Barbur had entered their house after midnight in *homsokin*, called Matilda a perverse and false woman, and pulled out his knife to strike her. She fled into the street and raised the hue and cry, a means of raising the alarm to summon the assistance of other members of the community who heard it. The couple sought damages of 40s for this attack which combined an intrusion into their home with verbal assault and the threat of violence.[73] We know that both William and Matilda were present in court, as they were essoined by two different men.[74] Matilda had previously been wrongly accused by William le Barbur of a verbal attack, and this subsequent case might signal ongoing animosity between the pair.[75] Litigation could be used to air these grievances, but might also have been a strategic tool by which parties sought to damage the status of their rivals. In June 1323, William le Hatter and his wife Alice complained that Ralph de Cesterfeld had entered their house in *homsokin*, beaten Alice and made her bloody. We see an alternative strategy at play here, whereby Cesterfeld tried to get out of the case by producing a letter from York stating that William le Hatter had been excommunicated, though it appears that the mayor and bailiffs of Nottingham did not accept this as a reason to invalidate the case. William and Alice were awarded damages of one mark, and Ralph was taken to prison until he could satisfy the damages.[76] These acts of violence represented both an attack on the victim's home, via the act of unwanted entry, intensified by the purported intent of such an intrusion to also perform a physical attack on the victim's body. Where married women were the targets of these attacks, they also signified an attack on the symbolic status of the household, represented in court via husband and wife bringing their complaints together.

The tendency to frame these attacks as *hamsocn* declined over the course of the fourteenth century. Men and women still complained about assaults in the home under the plea of trespass, and with the facet of unpermitted entry into the home still being a central feature. In Nottingham in March 1395, Stephen Wade and his wife Isabella complained that John Sclatter had entered their house, without Stephen's permission. There, he violently touched or stroked Isabella 'in an adulterous manner', quarrelled with her and Stephen, and struck Stephen with a staff, to Stephen's shame, causing damages of £20.[77] Though no further details on the outcome of the case are known, the plea emphasises John's uninvited entry into the house, the site of his various attacks and the shame that this brought on Stephen as the head of the household.

Elsewhere, comparable complaints were brought to local courts, but were not categorised as *hamsocn*. The shift in the construction of these pleas, and the differences between towns, is indicative of the variability of local legal custom when it came to interpreting actions of a similar nature.

Beyond violence: verbal assault, property and goods

Women's involvement in trespass litigation was not limited to physical violence. They were also involved in legal actions concerning verbal assault as well as attacks on property. Sometimes pleas grouped together several offences, as seen in the physical and verbal assault that opened this chapter. In other cases, individual instances of non-violent misbehaviour were enough to cause victims to air their complaints in court. The construction of women's tongues as weapons of misrule is found widely in the historiography, dominated by the image of the female scold. Jones found that verbal offences constituted a substantial part of the prosecutions of women in late medieval Kent.[78] However, examples of this 'bad speech' are relatively rare in town court records compared to trespasses that involved violence or attacks on property. The best evidence of verbal offences comes from Nottingham, where the court rolls record the most detail on the nature of trespasses. Here we find some examples of women's bad speech. In September 1335, Ralph de Stanton and his wife Cecilia complained that Margery, widow of Robert de Esthull, had called them false and thieves in Nottingham's daily market – where presumably many people would have heard the allegations. The Stantons' daughter, Margaret, also complained that Margery had physically assaulted her on the same day, though Margery countered these complaints with her own, alleging that the Stantons had called her false, a whore and a thief.[79] Margery was later amerced in relation to all three complaints, suggesting that she acknowledged her own wrongdoing and dropped her complaint against the Stanton couple.[80]

Other complaints of verbal assault also drew in multiple family members, suggesting that trespass pleas could be rooted in entrenched interfamilial disputes that women played an active role in. In 1323, Richard, son of Richard de Grymeston, brought a suit against William Castelyn and his wife Alice, complaining that Alice had assaulted him, called him a false man and a thief, accusing him of stealing a cloak belonging to her husband and forging a key to her father's chest to steal his money. William and Alice argued that Alice was not guilty.[81] The fact that these were specific accusations that sat within a common formula attacking an individual's moral, social and economic fidelity may have made them all the more damaging, and it was this specific act of slander, rather than just formulaic accusations, which Richard sought to contest. One of the accusations made by Alice regarded an alleged wrong done to her husband in the theft of his cloak, blurring the lines of legal responsibility for individual property. Both husband and wife were required to respond to the suit brought by Richard, though it was clear that the accusations reflected only the actions of Alice rather than the couple together. As Garthine Walker has suggested, the legal context in which these complaints were heard helps to account for their nature: unlike defamation cases in church courts, which often centred on moral offences, many cases of verbal assault brought to town courts, by both women and men, were more 'secular' in nature, concerning economic accusations and allegations of criminal behaviour.[82] As forums where commercial relationships were negotiated, it made sense that assaults on an individual or household's credit would also be dealt with in the same courts.

Some cases did concern women's moral status and their sexual honour. These slurs were specifically used against women, by both other women and men, and had the power to damage women's reputations. Some cases explicitly recorded the damaging impact of this form of defamation. In 1307, Joan, widow of Matthew le Potter, complained that Robert le Potter and Isabella his wife had called her a thief and a whore, causing her to lose her good reputation (*bonam famam*) among her neighbours.[83] Others suggest the public nature of these verbal attacks. John, son of Laurence le Parmenter, and his wife Christiana complained in Nottingham in 1328 that Agnes Warsop had called Christiana a false woman and a whore, claiming damages of 20s. The incident was said to have occurred in Great Smith Gate, a central street that adjoined the town's large Saturday market. This may have made the allegation all the more damaging due to its public nature, and also added an extra incentive to publicly contest and seek retribution for the alleged offence in court. However, John was later amerced, suggesting the couple were deemed to have brought a false plea.[84] This insult fits readily within the discourse of female moral and sexual dishonour, which Christiana and her husband sought to publicly refute. In the same year, two other women (both married) complained of similar verbal assaults. Juliana, wife of Richard Saumon, alleged that Robert Doget had called her false, a whore and a receiver of thieves, which amounted to the larger sum of 40s being claimed as damages.[85] The outcome is unknown. A few years earlier, Margery de Byngham alleged that William, son of Matthew, called her both a false woman and a whore.[86]

Whether or not these alleged incidents of slander were really based on actual instances of sexual misconduct is impossible to know. The label of whore was often used alongside other insults or allegations, as many of these examples have shown. Laura Gowing and Elizabeth Ewan have both argued that 'whore' was the typical insulting label thrown at women, regardless of the issue that might have led to an altercation. These insults were not only about sex but 'absorbed and refracted every kind of female transgression'.[87] The fact that Juliana Saumon was also accused of hosting thieves suggests that the label of whore was intended to further discredit her character, along with the specific accusation of dealing with criminals. Diota, wife of Ralph le Peyntur, was accused of stealing fish but was also called false and a whore, though it was not her sexual behaviour that was at issue here.[88] We should therefore read 'whore' to represent more general allegations of a woman being dishonest, deceptive, malicious or dishonourable. Many instances of sexual defamation also involved physical violence, suggesting that the label of whore also stemmed from moments of intense personal and physical conflict, perhaps as the culmination of a disagreement or the breakdown of a relationship.

Defamation and verbal assault had the power to harm the status of even the most powerful local figures. In Winchester in March 1366, John and Matilda Byketoun complained that Agnes Halle had assaulted them both with malicious words, calling them false and faithless merchants causing damages of £20, the substantial amount reflecting the damage to their honour and reputation as good and honest people who could be trusted in economic transactions.[89] While the complaint may frame Agnes Halle as a troublesome, quarrelling woman, she was in fact tapping into the male discourse of honour, based on trust and economic fidelity, in her defamation of the Byketouns. John Byketoun was a member of the city's elite, a merchant who was also bailiff, MP, alderman, constable of the Staple, collector and mayor at various points throughout the 1350s and 1360s.[90] The high damages of £20 represented the high status of the couple, whose united marital reputation was performed publicly through this joint plea. Despite this, the court awarded only 40d damages upon agreeing that Halle was guilty, suggesting that it was the nature of the offence, not the status of litigants, that determined the assessment of damages.

We have already seen that married women were the victims of alleged verbal offences, including those that brought their sexual honour into question. Wives also had the power to harm the credit of their neighbours with their words. Though coverture meant that they were not sued on their own, they were not immune from litigation, but were sued alongside their husbands. These cases reflected their misrule onto their husband and the household, as well as having potential financial repercussions if adjudged to be guilty of the offence. In 1324, William Breton of Nottingham claimed that Albreda, wife of Walter le Pulter, had verbally assaulted him, calling him a false man, a thief and untrustworthy, accusing him of cutting purses. This defamation had a direct impact on his reputation, as he lost credit of 20s from John de Bredon.[91] The retributive power of trespass litigation meant that, like other plaintiffs, William had more to gain in airing his complaint than the potential damage of publicising the accusations about his fidelity and alleged criminality. Perhaps he was secure enough in his local reputation to be confident that this would not further damage his credit, and felt that there was more to gain in shaming Albreda and her husband for her misbehaviour.

These examples all demonstrate the power in women's voices to damage the social and financial status of others. They move us away from the framing of women's bad speech as something simply associated with quarrelling and sexual accusations to a wider form of damaging speech. Even Margery Dod (discussed at the opening of this chapter), who was called a whore, also had accusations of moral and economic infidelity thrown at her by the Spondon family. But these were not just female 'cat fights'; men also committed verbal trespasses and were the victims of defamation too. At Nottingham in 1323–4, 12 suits referred specifically to verbal assaults; men were accused in 10 of these cases, while women featured in only 4. In 1330–1, men were accused 7 times out of 11 suits, while women were accused in 5 instances. In 1308, Robert le Cotiller and his wife Isabella were both allegedly defamed by Astin Freeman and his wife Margery. They called Robert a thief and false man, and Margery a whore, thief and murderer of men, saying she procured her husband to kill men.[92] While making clear the involvement of both men and women in these assaults, this case clearly demonstrates a gendered divide in the way that women and men experienced verbal attacks and the sexual characteristics of the labels that were used against women. In medieval Bologna too, Trevor Dean has argued that recorded insults against women tended to focus on their sexual activity, while those against men attacked their roles as carriers of public trust.[93] Sandy Bardsley has argued that women's voices were increasingly associated with problematic speech, understood as gossipy and argumentative.[94] This may have been true, but it did not mean that only women were accused of verbal attacks. Integrating trespass pleas into the discussion of the gendering of 'bad speech' demonstrates that this was not a purely feminine form of disruption or misbehaviour. The historiographical focus on criminal presentments and church court records has centred 'bad speech' as a key facet of women's misbehaviour and experiences of justice.[95] But when we expand the analysis beyond the prosecution of criminal offences, or presentments by local juries or views of frankpledge, we are reminded that this was just one of many forms of misbehaviour enacted by women and men.

Women also had the capacity to cause physical damage to property, as well as forcibly enter and steal goods from the homes of their neighbours. The instances of *hamsocn* from Nottingham, discussed earlier, demonstrate that women could be the perpetrators as well as victims of attacks upon the home, in which violence was often involved. Even without violence, this was an unacceptable act. The essence of this misbehaviour lay in the perpetrator's unwanted or uninvited entry into the home, with many pleas specifically citing that the defendant entered 'without licence' or permission. This facet of trespass was common across all complaints that featured real property. Domestic space was not particularly private in late medieval towns, often functioning simultaneously as a site of production, trade, business, as well as family and domestic life. Various studies of medieval and early modern domestic space have emphasised the fluidity of so-called 'public' and 'private' spaces within the home, in which domestic living 'combined working and trading with the everyday routines of domestic family life'.[96] The presence of non-household members – neighbours, extended family, trading partners – was not unusual or problematic in itself, but their unwanted or unwarranted presence could be.

Trespass litigation reveals some of the misbehaviour that was associated with this unwanted domestic presence, including attacks on the fabric of property and the theft of goods and chattels, sometimes suggesting considerable force. At Nottingham in 1434, Margery Tapster was accused by Thomas Beauchamp of breaking the door of his house using a staff, causing damages of 6s 8d. Tapster denied the offence.[97] In a separate complaint, he said that she had blocked the latrine of his house using ashes and straw, as well as breaking the floors of his chamber and shop.[98] While we do not know the outcome of either of these complaints, they suggest that Margery Tapster had single-handedly attempted to destroy much of the fabric of Beauchamp's house. At Chester in 1317, Mabilla de Haurdin was accused by Richard le Bruin of causing similar damage. He alleged that she had entered his house in St John Lane and taken away shingles, palisades and other timbers, causing damages of half a mark. Haurdin initially denied the trespass, but later acknowledged the offence.⁹⁹ An attack on the fabric of the home such as this would obviously cause practical material damage, but the implication of a poorly maintained home might also damage the householder's credit and status. Jeremy Goldberg has highlighted the symbolic importance of the home in business, noting that 'a comfortable and attractively furnished home, where clients could be entertained and perhaps even dined, would help create a suitable space for negotiating contracts in a world where credit, creditworthiness, and trust were the very essence of commerce'.¹⁰⁰ The removal of doors, roofs, fences and timbers and the blocking of latrines could have a serious impact on the reputation of the householder and on the physical state of the house itself.

The theft of movable goods (via larceny, burglary or housebreaking) was also a common subject of trespass pleas, and women were accused of taking and carrying away a wide range of items. Perhaps the most significant accusation of theft from the three towns was that brought against Emmota Boston of Nottingham by Thomas Marmeon, a knight, in 1442. He said that Boston had, with force and arms (her fists), taken and carried away various goods that he had inherited from his mother to the value of 117s 4d. These included a bed and bedding, clothing and pots. He claimed damages of 10 marks (133s 4d) – more than the value of the goods stolen. Emmota Boston first denied the accusation, but later was amerced for a licence to agree.¹⁰¹ It is unlikely that the plea reflected the real nature of the alleged theft, as one person – male or female – would surely have been unable to carry out this act alone. However, the accusation was focused on Boston. Similar accusations, though concerning goods of lesser value, can be found elsewhere. In Chester in 1490, Johanna Hill was accused by Llewellyn Pardon of breaking and entering into his messuage and taking bedding, a candelabra, knife, 'choppyngknyf' and other household items worth 20s. He sought damages of 26s, the additional 6s presumably representing the detriment that the theft had on his personal status. Hill replied that she was not guilty, and had in fact received or purchased the goods from Howell ap Res, and the jury agreed that she was not guilty of trespass.¹⁰² Peter Mason of Nottingham accused Joan Bate, also of Nottingham, of using force and arms (a staff and knife) to take 20 stones worth 10s 4d, claiming damages of 6s 8d. Bate denied the theft.¹⁰³ The record does not detail what type of stones these were, but they were apparently of considerable size and value, again casting doubt as to whether Bate could have carried out the theft alone. In the same year, Joan Taneson was accused by Richard Paunton of breaking into his house and close, armed with a staff and knife, taking various metal and clothing items worth a total of 15d.¹⁰⁴

At the same time, Paunton sued Taneson for debt, indicating a wider antagonism between the pair or perhaps a two-pronged legal attack from Paunton. In December 1394, a jury found that Agnes Godesalve was guilty of taking 7s, a necklace worth 40d and three linen sheets worth 4s from the close of Robert Gudwyn. Robert won damages totalling 13d (despite the 40s claimed).[105] In 1491–2, Isabella Marshall, Isabella Tanley and Agnes March were all accused by various men of stealing different household goods from their homes in Nottingham, though none were found to be guilty.[106] Elizabeth Melburne was accused by Thomas Bult of stealing crops and fish worth 20s, though the outcome of the jury inquisition is not recorded.[107] Accusations of theft brought against women were varied in their nature and in the value of the goods stolen, and were certainly not all classed as petty thefts. As Trevor Dean also found for fifteenth-century Bologna, while the lesser involvement of women in suits of this nature demonstrates that they were less frequently accused of these offences than men, when they were, they did not accord to any gendered patterns of supposed 'female' theft.[108]

Trespass pleas were also brought against individuals accused of receiving stolen goods, indicative of networks of criminality and exchange. Richard Bluell, a corviser from Chester, sued Lewys le Baxter and his wife Johanna in 1423, claiming that Johanna had received goods belonging to him, including bedding worth 6s 8d and three pairs of shoes worth 12d. Johanna denied the accusation.[109] In Nottingham in January 1376, Richard Spondon accused Richard Webster and his wife (who was unnamed) of receiving goods and chattels worth 40d stolen from him. Webster and his wife denied this, and the jury found that they were not guilty.[110] This may well have been an offence that was frequently committed by wives, though the numbers of examples here are too low to read as a definitive trend. These women may have been drawn into crime and wrongdoing through their husbands, or it may have been the wives who were the instigators, but they were sued alongside their husbands because they were married. Garthine Walker has suggested that these cases may indicate women's own economic activities and interactions as expert household managers, and that some were dealing independently in particular types of stolen goods – whether they knew it or not.[111]

Attacks on property were not limited to domestic space. Some complaints allow us to situate the misbehaviour of women and men within other areas of the urban environment. John Samon senior, Mayor of Nottingham, accused John Fenel and his wife Christina, along with John their servant, of taking grain from his land in the town fields. The parties came to an agreement and John Fenel was fined 3d, suggesting the couple acknowledged the offence.[112] Joan Etwell and Margery, her servant, were accused by Richard Etwell of entering his curtilage, by day and night, and pulling up his plants and herbs that were growing there. He sought damages of 20s. Joan denied the plea on behalf of herself and Margery.[113] Both these pleas indicate the collusion of members of the household in the act of theft away from their own home and domestic space, offering a challenge to the notion of a sex-specific division of space and misbehaviour within the urban environment.[114]

Marriage, family and household in trespass pleas

Acts of trespass often bring ties of family and household to bear in the court records. We see glimpses of both the physical and material household, as well as some of the relationships that constructed the household as a social, domestic and political unit. Many of the instances already discussed in this chapter saw spouses, parents and children, or employers and servants, acting together in acts of misbehaviour and in litigation. Married women, though theoretically 'covered' by their husbands' legal eminence, could not avoid litigation when they were accused of misbehaviour. Nor did their coverture 'protect' (as Blackstone claimed in the eighteenth century) or shield them from sometimes being on the receiving end of violence, attacks on or within the home.[115] Jones' study of late medieval Kent suggested that married women could not be sued in civil complaints, though the town court records examined here involve numerous couples litigating jointly, serving as a means of negotiating wives' supposed legal subordination.[116] These pleas, which recognised the range of married women's interpersonal interactions and behaviours, exemplify the 'legal fiction' of coverture.[117] However, the way in which these offences were represented in litigation was neither straightforward nor consistent, and deserves focused attention. Other supposedly subordinate members of the household, such as servants, also featured in trespass pleas alongside their masters and mistresses, illustrating the implications of misbehaviour for the entire household, not just the individuals directly involved.

Married couples appeared most frequently in trespass pleas in Nottingham, though the number of these suits declined from the fourteenth to fifteenth centuries. These cases represented a range of complaints: some involved alleged attacks upon or by wives, while others involved both spouses committing trespasses together, or both being the victims of an offence. In 1323-4, 30 couples litigated in 38 different trespass suits. In contrast, in 1446-7, only three couples can be recovered from three suits. In 1491-2, there were no cases in which husband and wife acted jointly in a complaint of trespass. However, one apparently married woman, Agnes Gybson, wife of John Gybson, was the subject of a plea brought by William Guymer, though her husband was not named alongside her. He claimed that she had broken into his house with force and arms, taken and carried away bedding worth 3s, and he sought damages of 40d. Agnes denied the trespass, and a jury later agreed that she was not guilty.[118] It is hard to believe that married women somehow became less violent or disorderly, or less likely to be on the receiving end of trespasses, so it is likely that this change instead represents a shift in how married women participated in litigation. The decline helps to account for the overall fall in women's trespass litigation, if husbands came to account for their wives' misbehaviour, or complain about assaults upon their wives, without them being in court themselves. A number of couples litigated together in trespass suits in Winchester, at seemingly continuous levels across the period, though the lack of detail recorded makes it impossible to ascertain the type of offences that most of these pleas represented. Spouses also brought and answered trespass pleas together in Chester. However, following the general pattern for married women's litigation in Chester, the frequency of these suits also declined over the fourteenth century so that by c.1400 they were somewhat exceptional, rather than the norm.

Couples complained together when wives were attacked. Thomas Butcher and his wife Isabella accused William Schakemantel of beating Isabella in Winchester in 1299.[119] Some of these complaints were framed in terms of the damages or loss experienced by the woman's husband, even though both husband and wife were acting as co-litigants. In Chester in March 1318, Richard and Alice Runcorn brought a plea of trespass against William le Wode, saying that he had assaulted Alice in 'Cuppinslone' in Chester, beating and wounding her and (perhaps because William also committed *hamsocn*) causing damages to Richard of 100s.[120] When goods were stolen from the marital household, both husband and wife could come to court to seek retribution. In Winchester, Hugh Trevor and his wife Albreda complained that Alice Cappere had come to their house with sticks at the feast of Epiphany in 1386, and with her servant Margaret Dumond had stolen linen cloth worth 40d. They claimed damages to the value of 20s, and the jury later presented that Cappere was indeed guilty of trespass.[121] There was no mention of her servant's guilt, however; perhaps she was deemed to have been under her mistress's instruction.

Married women also had the power to harm others, and were brought to court alongside their husbands when they did so. Sara Butler has suggested that in some of these cases at least, husbands were sued alongside their wives because they had failed to control them, and a handful of Colchester cases refer to this specific failure of husbands, their wives acting 'for want of chastisement'.[122] None of the cases studied here spell out the husband's fault in this way, though the pattern of joint accountability is clear in numerous cases. Agnes, wife of Robert Benet, was the subject of two trespass complaints brought by Thomas Doo and Matilda, his wife, in 1446. She was accused of assaulting Matilda and beating and wounding her with a staff. However, when the jury was summoned, the plaintiffs did not appear in court, and so were fined. The second complaint alleged another assault by Agnes, again with a staff, when she took and carried off a craper (graper?) worth 4d and chemise worth 12s. Robert and Agnes settled this complaint, paying a fine to the court for a licence to agree with the plaintiffs, suggesting recognition of the offence.[123] At Nottingham in 1351, an alleged attack on Henry Hoppidust by Joan, wife of John Plumtree, with her servant, saw John Plumtree in court alongside Joan and her servant. It appears that John had nothing to do with the assault, but the misbehaviour of his wife and servant meant that he was also forced to answer the complaint.[124]

Some couples committed trespasses together. Elizabeth Ewan has suggested that, in Scotland, 'a woman's most common accomplice was her spouse'.[125] In Winchester in 1385, Alice Rolfs complained that John and Christina Beneyt had assaulted with her sticks and knives, wounded her and stolen a fur tunic worth 10s. The couple initially denied the assault, but later paid a fine for licence to agree with Rolfs, indicating that the parties settled.[126] Jones argued that in Kent, wives could not be sued for theft, yet this example indicates that, though wives were not sued independently, they nevertheless had to face the consequences of their actions alongside their husbands.[127] Similarly, Juliana Lavender complained that she had been assaulted by William Wyntur and his wife, Matilda, in the same year.[128] In Nottingham in July 1324, Agnes Bugge complained that Robert Lyfthand and Emma, his wife, had assaulted her, beaten and trampled upon her, which Robert and Emma denied. The jury reported that they were not guilty and Agnes was fined 4d.[129] Richard Webster and his wife were also accused of receiving goods worth 40d stolen from Robert Spondon.[130] William and Beatrice Pycheweyre of Chester were accused together of stealing goods and chattels worth 20s from Thomas Gernett in 1435.[131] Whether or not these were instances of (alleged) collusion and conspiracy to do harm, or simply outbursts of misbehaviour in which one spouse supported the other, these pleas reveal that joint spousal litigation was not simply a result of husbands being held accountable for their wives' misbehaviour, and Johnson has shown that a similar practice existed in civil complaints before the courts of Wales.[132] Instead, there existed a broader pattern of interpersonal litigation whereby married women were held jointly accountable alongside their husbands.

There were some exceptions to this rule of joint pleas by husband and wife, as some wives did appear to take independent legal action. In Chester in 1490, Agnes, wife of Gervase Bulber, was sued by Agnes Huett, also known as Agnes Filon, who claimed that she had assaulted her, beaten, wounded and maltreated her, causing damages of 10s. The jury reported that she was guilty of the assault, and awarded damages of 3s 4d.[133] There is no indication that Agnes Bulber's husband was involved in this plea, though he is found later in the same roll bringing a complaint against Elena Coider, so we know that he was still alive. Some widows were occasionally recorded as 'wife of', but this was not the case in this instance. Nor did Agnes Bulber claim immunity for failure to follow legal procedure because her husband was not named in the suit, as some women did.[134] It appears that both the litigants and the court were content to see through the case between the two women without any involvement of her husband. Similarly, in Nottingham in 1491, Agnes Gybson, wife of John Gybson, was accused of breaking and entering and taking bedding worth 2s from William's house. Agnes denied the trespass and the jury reported that she was not guilty.[135] Again, the complaint was able to progress without her husband's involvement, though she was specifically recorded as a married woman.

Women did not always act as litigants when they were the victims of trespasses. In some cases, men litigated on behalf of their wives or other female relatives for attacks upon their person without the woman acting as co-litigant. In these rare instances, we see how women could be conceptualised as a form of property, listed among other 'stolen' or damaged goods, with the male householder being the injured party. In October 1433, in Nottingham, William Lemeryng accused William Parwych of assaulting and affraying his wife, as well as breaking Lemeryng's mazer.[136] He claimed damages of 40s – the same sum as the reported value of the mazer – suggesting that the attack on his wife was not quantifiable, or that he chose not to convert this to additional damages. Likewise, Robert Ingelbright complained in Nottingham in 1441 that William, servant of Nicholas Bochre, had assaulted his wife using a staff, affrayed and maltreated her.[137] It is not clear why in these cases men brought their suits alone, while in other seemingly comparable suits (such as the attack on Matilda Doo by Agnes Benet) husbands and wives brought their complaints to court together. This may simply have been a choice on the part of the plaintiffs regarding the best or most appropriate way to achieve legal redress. However, the majority of these examples of husbands suing on behalf of, not with, their wives, occurred from the mid-fifteenth century onwards, though this was not an absolute shift in these patterns of litigation as some couples did continue to enter their pleas jointly. Nevertheless, this pattern fits in with the overall declining numbers of spouses pleading together in all types of plea, and suggests that husbands were increasingly taking action on behalf of their wives, indicating a stricter and perhaps more literal understanding of coverture as the fifteenth century progressed.

These pleas were not just limited to husbands acting on their wives' behalf, but could see men suing for attacks on their daughters or servants too. In 1397, Richard of Lindsey complained of John Herle and his wife Agnes, alleging that Agnes had twice entered his house and assaulted his daughters Agnes and Katherine both inside and outside the house.[138] The parties later came to an agreement, and John and Agnes were amerced for the offence. Lindsey's daughters may have been too young to bring their complaint in their own name or jointly with their father, or he may simply have chosen to complain on their behalf as an act of parental protection. Other women referred to as daughters did bring complaints in their own names, indicating that their youth or unmarried status did not automatically preclude legal action. The distinction may have been whether or not the young women were over the age of majority.

Men also complained about the 'theft' or abduction of women alongside the taking of other forms of property. In November 1446, John Abbot of Newark complained that Henry Monyassh of Nottingham, a barber, had broken into his house and close armed with a staff and knife, carried away and abducted his wife, plus two pots, two dishes, two coverlets and two pairs of linen sheets. The value of each of these goods was listed, and damages were claimed at £10. Monyassh replied that he was not guilty, but the outcome of the case is not known.[139] If this really was a case of abduction, this should have been a felony dealt with by the king's courts (such as the general eyre or assizes of gaol delivery), or alternatively a civil trespass case (in Chancery, King's Bench or Common Pleas), rather than the local borough court.[140] But there is no suggestion that the court or defendant challenged Abbot's right to bring his complaint under this jurisdiction. There is also no reference to the offence as *raptus*, which may have been key to it being constructed as trespass rather than abduction.[141] Sara Butler has suggested that husbands' pleas of ravishment in manorial courts could in fact relate to wives running away with their lovers, and these pleas were in fact aimed at gaining compensation for the goods taken away by or with the wife.[142] This was generally meant to be a plea reserved for common law jurisdiction, though a handful of cases did appear in manor and borough courts. There are also parallels here with cases of abduction brought before the courts of Dyffryn Clwyd, where cases also listed the husband's stolen goods.[143] Similarly, in Norwich's leet roll of 1299–1300, Richard de Berton was presented for the *raptus* of the wife of William Stedefast, as well as her husband's goods.[144] It appears that the framing of the wife being taken and carried away, alongside a list of household goods, enabled her to be conceptualised in this way as part of a collection of property unlawfully removed from Abbot's house. This may have been an act of legal strategy, in that the couple hoped this plea would achieve a more successful outcome, or it may have reflected the fact that Abbot's wife in fact chose to run away with Monyassh, so was not complicit in bringing the complaint to court.

It was not just wives who were the subject of this plea of trespass and/or abduction. At Chester in 1435, John ad Byche alleged that Bellyn Henster had broken into his house, taken and carried away his daughter and servant Johanna (it is unclear as to whether these are two separate individuals) as well as other goods and chattels, including bread and ale worth 20s. The defendant was accused of 'carnally knowing' Johanna against her will, causing damages of 20 marks. Henster denied the accusation, and a jury was summoned, though the outcome is not known.[145] Here, the loss of the daughter, her service and possibly her virginity, were grouped with a broader claim about the theft of goods. It is impossible to pass judgement on whether this was consensual abduction or non-consensual abduction and rape, but the courts did not appear to take issue with men bringing what should in fact have been criminal abduction cases as interpersonal complaints for which monetary damages could be sought. A number of other cases adhere to similar patterns. In Chester in 1490, Hugh ap Ithel Foueber sued Hugh Alens for trespass, claiming that he broke and entered into his messuage and abducted his servant Elizabeth against his will, seeking damages of 40s. The jury later reported that Alens was not guilty.[146] Similarly, in Winchester in December 1365, John Lacy complained that Richard Stoke had entered his house against his will, armed with sticks and knives, and taken John's servant Magota along with gold and silver worth 20 marks. Lacy claimed total damages of £20.[147] None of these women were parties to the complaints, though they concerned attacks on their persons specifically. Many other men complained about abduction of their maidservants, along with various household goods, but the nature of the records mask whether these were instances of sexual violence, attempts at forced marriage, elopement or rather the stealing of labour from the household.

In one case, the issue of the borough court's jurisdiction was brought into dispute through the suggestion that it was unable to determine a suit concerning a sexual assault. At Nottingham in May 1354, Adam Packer complained that Thomas, vicar of St Mary's Church, had crossed his fence and broken the door of his house, whereupon he violated Adam's wife Agnes against her will, and took 2s from Agnes's purse. Packer sought damages of £100. The defendant responded that this was effectively a rape or ravishment (*raptum*) case, which was outside the jurisdiction of the court.[148] Judgement was put in respite until the next court session, but no further record of the case survives, so we do not know whether the court agreed with the defendant's contestation or whether the case was simply discontinued. Like many other cases, the trespass against the woman was accompanied by references to stolen goods (or money, in this case). The only difference between this and other complaints cited above is the specific reference to Agnes's violation against her will, rather than abduction or the 'taking' of a woman. This may have been the root of the call to move the plea to another court.

While Caroline Dunn has shown that various uses of *rapuit* could relate to theft of property, seizure of (female) dependants and rape, these examples also suggest that offences of these differing natures could, under different jurisdiction, be constructed under the broad umbrella of trespass, with no reference to *rapuit* at all.[149] Apart from the case of Agnes Packer, it was the taking or stealing of these women, sometimes coupled with alleged sexual activity, that was central to complaints of trespass which listed this theft alongside that of moveable goods. Though many of these cases did not indicate rape, the act of abduction should still have left them outside the remit of these civil trespass pleas. It is probable that both courts and litigants had, in practice, some flexibility over how to define and where to bring their complaints, and that by conceptualising the abduction of women as part of a larger theft of property and resultant claim for damages, these issues were able to fit within the general understanding of trespass within urban communities. It might have been that litigants felt unable to bring suits for rape or ravishment if they were unable to comply with the required means of proof and prosecution, including the raising of the hue and cry and the presentation of the woman's wounds or torn and bloodstained clothes.[150] The language with which these pleas were recorded also reflected conventions in the documenting of trespass pleas using common formulae such as 'force and arms' and 'against the peace', rather than terms to reflect the felonious nature of the offences.[151] Likewise, complaints concerning only the taking of goods were also framed as abduction, indicating the comparable nature by which a person's wife, servant, daughter, or goods such as hay and cloth, could all be legally understood and represented in court.[152] The nature of the town courts and their key areas of jurisdiction and interest therefore shaped the way in which these narratives were constructed and recorded according to different litigation strategies.[153] In none of these complaints do we hear anything of the woman's voice: unlike other trespasses where wives often pleaded jointly with their husbands, they were neither litigants in cases concerning their own bodies, nor were their accounts documented by the court.[154]

These wide-ranging pleas demonstrate how the medieval urban household extended beyond material or business concerns to encompass a wide range of interpersonal relationships and actions, both between members of the household, and with those outside it. In reading these pleas, we might therefore think not just of the 'household economy', but the 'household community'. Spouses, family members and servants acted together in defence of the household, and sometimes colluded in acts of trespass and misbehaviour, in what Karen Jones interpreted as evidence of household solidarity.[155] Cordelia Beattie has described the household as a unit of government, which brought with it various civic ideals in relation to how urban governments expected householders to govern behaviour.[156] But this also extended to how the household perceived itself and was conceptualised by others, and many pleas of trespass illuminate this perspective. The household was not just a physical space or residential group, but an organising principle and social unit through which status and reputation was built and performed, meaning that the actions of individuals – including disputes and disorder – had repercussions for all members.[157] While most households were governed by men, the actions of and attacks on other members were also fundamental to the standing of the household. It is this which led so many to air their complaints in court – both with and without other household members – to achieve redress for misbehaviour that attacked the household. Beattie has also argued that, as head of this unit of government, there was increasing acceptance that householders should govern their own dependents, and many trespass pleas indicate that this role also extended to taking responsibility to defend the status of the household and its members via the local court.[158] Householders had responsibility over their dependents, but these subordinate members of the household were nevertheless able to access justice and play their part in its negotiation, bar a handful exceptions which saw men complain about their dependents as property.

Of course, women could be householders too, as widows or never-married single women. Women's complaints concerning attacks on other members of their household were rare, in part because there were fewer female householders. But this also suggests that the act of suing for trespass on another person's behalf was generally a patriarchal role adopted by male heads of households responsible for governing and providing for their dependents. There are some examples, however. In May 1328, Isolda le Orfevere complained that Thomas, son of Emma le Orfevere (possibly some relation?), had entered her stall in *homsokin* and struck her servant Richard on the head, causing damages of half a mark.[159] Earlier records reveal that Isolda was married to Henry le Orfevere, but by 1328 she was a widow and had taken over responsibility for her servants from her late husband. The records of litigation therefore provide an insight into the identities and actions of 'dependent' members of the household who at other times, and in other records, are obscured by the dominance of the householder. Acts of trespass and their resulting legal action therefore allow us to 'look within the household'.[160]

The broad spectrum of trespass offences meant that it was not just the actions of people that could bring complaints of misbehaviour. When animals wandered where they should not have gone, their owners were liable for any damage caused by the 'trespassing' creatures. Householders, male and female, were thus responsible for all residents, not just the human ones. Richard Etwall sued Joan Etwall for trespass in Nottingham in 1399, alleging that her cockerels and hens entered his close and house and ate grain and corn – something that had apparently been going on for six years![161] Elizabeth Longes of Nottingham complained of Thomas Wolmersty, who, with his cow, destroyed and wasted herbs, mallow, parsley and sage growing in her garden.[162] When animals were attacked, the complaints were also presented as trespasses. John Kent and his wife Agnes complained of John, a chaplain, alleging that he hit and beat their pig worth 12d with a staff, so that the pig ran away and later died.[163] Though there was an aspect of financial loss through the death of the pig, its value being included in the plea, the offence was framed and dealt with in the same way as an attack on a human member of the household.

Conclusion

Trespass pleas allow us to access urban life and its sometimes turbulent nature in vivid detail. They reveal the identities and actions of a broad cross-section of the urban population – women and men, young and old, rich and poor – and the way that they negotiated the frictions of urban life at the most everyday level. Women's frequent involvement in these pleas situates them at the heart of interpersonal and household relationships, as people who were capable of harming others through their misbehaviour, and who readily took action to complain about the wrongdoing of others via their local court. While they did not feature in these complaints in equal numbers to men, their behaviour and interactions spanned the entire range of actions that fell under the category of trespass. As Andrew Finch has argued in relation to the violence of women in medieval Cerisy, women could 'act like violent men when the need arose and they were accorded like treatment by the court when they did'.[164] This lack of gendered patterns is in contrast to the findings of Karen Jones, who identified a heavily gendered construction of misconduct that reflected contemporary perceptions of femininity and honourable female conduct.[165] The trespass evidence demonstrates that we should not limit our perception of women's misbehaviour to particularly 'female' types. Women were not simply victims of violent, out of control men, and nor were female perpetrators only those who could not control their tongues. Trespass litigation broadens the framework of female misbehaviour, honour and legal action as not simply limited to issues of sexual repute or marriage, but revealing women's integration into all aspects of urban life.

Evidence of misbehaviour abounds in town court rolls. But this does not mean that these were wild, lawless, violent places, in line with popular imaginings of the middle ages. The nature of the urban environment, with its close domestic and trading arrangements, was one in which dispute and misbehaviour could occur frequently. However, it is important to remember that the reason that we know about any of these trespasses is down to the pervasive nature of law and justice within urban communities, and the willingness of town residents to resort to the use of law to settle their disputes and complaints. Town governments sought to create harmonious communities, punish misbehaviour and provide residents with a forum through which to achieve redress for these more minor offences, and it is the resulting records that allow us to examine the individuals, relationships and actions that lay behind these offences. Trespass was not just about the control of misbehaviour by officials, but the choices of individuals to seek compensation for and to publicise the wrongful actions of others. Women of all statuses played key roles in this negotiation of urban life, as plaintiffs and defendants, able to account for their own (mis)behaviour and complain about the actions of others, even when supposedly 'covered' by marriage. There were a small number of exceptions to this rule, suggesting a degree of choice on the part of plaintiffs about how to bring their complaints, and in some instances an understanding that women were akin to goods rightfully possessed by male householders. But the fact that most spouses chose to take legal action together demonstrates a commonly held understanding that married women could and should act alongside their husbands in the legal resolution of issues of trespass.

However, as was true with other types of legal action, women's involvement in these pleas was not consistent between different towns or over time. There was a marked decline in married women's involvement in trespass pleas as co-litigants with their husbands, particularly in Nottingham where this was a regular occurrence in the fourteenth century, but was exceptional by the end of the fifteenth century. This shift contributed to an overall decline in the involvement of women in trespass pleas. At the same time, we find more examples of men litigating on behalf of their wives and other dependent women, demonstrating an increasing adherence to an understanding of coverture that rendered wives' litigation unnecessary or perhaps not possible in many situations.

Notes

1 NA CA1258b rot. 13.
2 HRO W/D1/37 rot. 8.
3 See Teresa Phipps, 'Misbehaving women: trespass and honor in late medieval English towns', *Historical Reflections/Réflexions Historique*, 43 (2017), 62–76.
4 Patricia Turning, 'Women on trial: piecing together women's intellectual worlds from courtroom testimony', *Medieval Feminist Forum*, 46 (2010), 66–67.
5 S.F.C. Milsom, *Historical Foundations of the Common Law*, second edn (London: Butterworth, 1981), p. 283; M.S. Arnold, *Select Cases of Trespass from the King's Courts, 1307–1399*, vol. 1, Selden Society vol. 100 (London: Selden Society, 1984), pp. ix–x.
6 Frederick Pollock and Frederic William Maitland, *The History of English Law before the Time of Edward I*, vol. 2 (Cambridge: Cambridge University Press, 1895), p. 470.
7 Milsom, *Historical Foundations of the Common Law*, pp. 285–286.
8 G.D.G. Hall (ed. and trans.), *The Treatise on the Laws and Customs of the Realm of England Commonly Called Glanvill* (London: Nelson, 1965), p. 4.
9 Phillipp Schofield, 'Trespass litigation in the manor court in the late thirteenth and early fourteenth centuries', in Richard Goddard, John Langdon and Miriam Müller

(eds), *Survival and Discord in Medieval Society. Essays in Honour of Christopher Dyer* (Turnhout: Brepols, 2010), pp. 145–160.

10   Matthew Frank Stevens, *Urban Assimilation in Post-Conquest Wales: Ethnicity, Gender and Economy in Ruthin, 1282–1350* (Cardiff: University of Wales Press, 2010), p. 131. Violence plus trespass accounted for 42 per cent of all women's appearances, with detention plus debt being only 19 per cent.

11   Hannah Robb, 'Reputation in the fifteenth century credit market; some tales from the ecclesiastical courts of York', *Cultural and Social History*, 15 (2018), 306.

12   This quantification and categorisation is difficult for a number of reasons: not all pleas include details on the nature of an alleged trespass, and many involved multiple 'types' of wrong.

13   Barbara Hanawalt, *Crime and Conflict in English Communities, 1300–1348* (Cambridge, MA: Harvard University Press, 1979), p. 65.

14   Karen Jones, *Gender and Petty Crime in Late Medieval England: The Local Courts in Kent, 1460–1560* (Woodbridge: Boydell and Brewer, 2006), p. 34.

15   On the legal status of rape and abduction, as both felony and trespass, see Caroline Dunn, *Stolen Women in Medieval England: Rape, Abduction, and Adultery, 1100–1500* (Cambridge: Cambridge University Press, 2013), pp. 36–37.

16   George E. Woodbine, 'The origins of the action of trespass', *Yale Law Journal*, 33 (1924), 802.

17   Statute of Gloucester 1278 in *Statutes of the Realm*, vol. 1, chapter 8 (London, 1810), p. 48.

18   Elizabeth Ewan, 'Disorderly damsels? Women and interpersonal violence in pre-reformation Scotland', *Scottish Historical Review*, 89 (2010), 167; Ewan, '"Many Injurious Word"': defamation and gender in late medieval Scotland', in R. Andrew McDonald (ed.), *History, Literature and Music in Scotland, 700–1560* (Toronto: University of Toronto Press, 2002), p. 172.

19   CALS ZSR 153.

20   NA CA1306 rot. 1.

21   NA CA1306 rot. 24d.

22   NA CA1259 rot. 2d, 11.

23   Thomas Kuehn, '*Fama* as legal status in Renaissance Florence', in Thelma Fenster and Daniel Lord Smail (eds), *Fama: The Politics of Talk and Reputation in Medieval Europe* (Ithaca: Cornell University Press, 2003), p. 27.

24   See Jeremy Goldberg, 'The priest of Nottingham and the holy household of Ousegate: telling tales in court', in Richard Goddard and Teresa Phipps (eds), *Town Courts and Urban Society in Late Medieval England* (Woodbridge: Boydell and Brewer, 2019), pp. 61–63.

25   Craig Muldrew, *The Economy of Obligation: The Culture of Credit and Social Relations in Early Modern England* (Basingstoke: Macmillan, 1998), p. 2.

26   Patricia Turning, *Municipal Officials, Their Public, and the Negotiation of Justice in Medieval Languedoc* (Leiden: Brill, 2013), pp. 73–88.

27   Keith Thomas 'The double standard', *Journal of the History of Ideas*, 20 (1959), 195. For a revision of these ideas, see Bernard Capp, 'The double standard revisited: plebeian women and male sexual reputation in early modern England', *Past and Present*, 162 (1999), 70–100.

28 Shannon McSheffrey, *Marriage, Sex and Civic Culture in Late Medieval London* (Philadelphia: University of Pennsylvania Press, 2006), pp. 164, 188.
29 McSheffrey, *Marriage, Sex and Civic Culture*, p. 175-176; McSheffrey, 'Men and masculinity in late medieval London civic culture: governance, patriarchy and reputation', in Jacqueline Murray (ed.), *Conflicted Identities and Multiple Masculinities: Men in the Medieval West* (New York: Garland, 1999), pp. 258-261.
30 Ewan, 'Women and interpersonal violence', 171.
31 Turning, 'Women on trial', 70-71.
32 Garthine Walker, *Crime, Gender and Social Order in Early Modern England* (Cambridge: Cambridge University Press, 2003), pp. 75-76.
33 Walker, *Crime, Gender and Social Order*, p. 75.
34 Barbara Hanawalt, 'The female felon in fourteenth-century England', *Viator*, 5 (1974), 257-261.
35 See, for example, Jones, *Gender and Petty Crime*, pp. 94-128; Sandy Bardsley, *Venomous Tongues: Speech and Gender in Late Medieval England* (Philadelphia: University of Pennsylvania Press, 2006), especially pp. 69-89.
36 Garthine Walker, 'Expanding the boundaries of female honour in early modern England', *Transactions of the Royal Historical Society*, 6 (1996), 235-236, 245.
37 Walker, *Crime, Gender and Social Order*, pp. 4, 159.
38 Maryanne Kowaleski, *Local Markets and Regional Trade in Medieval Exeter* (Cambridge: Cambridge University Press, 1995), pp. 337-338.
39 Richard H. Britnell, *Growth and Decline in Colchester, 1300-1525* (Cambridge: Cambridge University Press, 1986), p. 99.
40 Britnell, *Colchester*, pp. 99-100; Richard Goddard, 'Surviving recession: English borough courts and commercial contraction, 1350-1500', in Richard Goddard, John Langdon and Miriam Müller (eds), *Survival and Discord in Medieval Society: Essays in Honour of Christopher Dyer* (Turnhout: Brepols, 2010), p. 78.
41 Stevens, *Ruthin*, p. 131.
42 Jones, *Gender and Petty Crime*, pp. 70, 75.
43 CALS ZSR 21 rot. 5d.
44 NA CA1258b rots 9d, 10.
45 CALS ZSR 21 rot. 10.
46 NA CA1261 rot. 16d.
47 NA CA1261 rot. 20d.
48 NA CA1324 rots 5, 5d.
49 Karen Jones suggested that men could not cope with the concept of violent women: Jones, *Gender and Petty Crime*, pp. 92-93. See also Miriam Müller, 'Social control and the hue and cry in two fourteenth century villages', *Journal of Medieval History*, 31 (2005), 41-42; Walker, *Crime, Gender and Social Order*, pp. 74, 81.
50 Walker, *Crime, Gender and Social Order*, pp. 81-82.
51 NA CA1279 rot. 25.
52 NA CA1277a rot. 4.
53 HRO W/D1/60 rot. 1.
54 CALS ZSR 376d.
55 Ewan, 'Women and interpersonal violence', 171.
56 NA CA1324 rot. 1.

57 HRO W/D1/37 rot. 8.
58 NA CA1297 rots 3, 8, 10d.
59 Ewan, 'Women and interpersonal violence', 165. Janka Rodziewicz makes a similar argument, that women tended to use objects of opportunity such as sticks, fists and stones, while men used knives and staffs. See Janka Rodziewicz, 'Women and the hue and cry in late fourteenth-century Great Yarmouth', in Bronach Kane and Fiona Williamson (eds), *Women, Agency and the Law, 1300-1700* (London: Pickering and Chatto, 2013), p. 93.
60 Hanawalt, 'Female felon', 259.
61 Turning, *Municipal Officials*, p. 78.
62 NA CA1258a rot. 21. The couple were named together in the suit as Alice was married.
63 NA CA1258a rot. 18.
64 CALS ZSR 112 rot. 1d.
65 NA CA1306 rot. 24d.
66 NA CA1374 f. 41d. He was accused of using a sword, staff and other defensive arms to break and enter the close and house of William Milis, causing damages of £40.
67 Tom Lambert, *Law and Order in Anglo Saxon England* (Oxford: Oxford University Press, 2017), p. 184.
68 Pollock and Maitland, *English Law*, vol. 2, p. 493.
69 NA CA1260 rot. 8d.
70 NA CA1260 rot. 9.
71 NA CA1260 rot. 12.
72 CALS ZSR 21 rot. 6.
73 NA CA1258a rot. 7.
74 NA CA1258a rot. 8.
75 NA CA1258a rot. 7.
76 NA CA1258a rot. 22.
77 NA CA1294 rot. 12. 'violenter in modum adulterii palpavit ...'.
78 Jones, *Gender and Petty Crime*, pp. 105, 108, 127.
79 NA CA1262 rot. 1.
80 NA CA1262 rot. 3.
81 NA CA1258b rot. 9d. '... in villa Notingham apud le Cokestolrowe insultum fecit ei Ricardus filius Ricardus et ipsum vocavit falsum hominem et latronem et sub posute [sic] ipsam furasse clocam Willelmi Casteleyn mariti sui et fabricasse quedam clavem ad aperiend cistam patris sui ad furand argenti suum per quod per quod detiorate [sic] ei et dampnum hic ad valentiam xx s ...'.
82 Walker, *Crime, Gender and Social Order*, p. 100.
83 NA CA1251b.
84 NA CA1260 rot. 14.
85 NA CA1260 rot. 12.
86 NA CA1258a rot. 23.
87 Laura Gowing, *Domestic Dangers: Women, Words and Sex in Early Modern London* (Oxford: Clarendon Press, 1998), pp. 113-118; Ewan, 'Defamation and gender in late medieval Scotland', 169, argues that 'hure' was used as an insult even when cases had little to do with sex.
88 NA CA1251b.

89 HRO W/D1/13 rot. 7. '... *quod verbis maliciosis viz. vocando ipsos falsos et infidels per quod admiserunt credenciam de creditoribis suis cum quibus solebant mercandisari et contra pacem etc.*'
90 HRO W/D1/13 rot. 5d.
91 NA CA1258b rot. 19d.
92 NA CA1251b.
93 Trevor Dean, 'Gender and insult in an Italian city: Bologna in the later Middle Ages', *Social History*, 29 (2004), 218.
94 Bardsley, *Venomous Tongues*, p. 142.
95 J.A. Sharpe, *Defamation and Sexual Slander in Early Modern England: The Church Courts at York*, Borthwick Papers no. 58 (York, 1980), pp. 15–16.
96 P.J.P. Goldberg and Maryanne Kowaleski, 'Introduction: Medieval domesticity: home, housing and household', in Goldberg and Kowaleski (eds), *Medieval Domesticity: Home, Housing and Household in Medieval England* (Cambridge: Cambridge University Press, 2008), p. 4; Felicity Riddy, '"Burgeis" domesticity in late-medieval England', in Goldberg and Kowaleski (eds), *Medieval Domesticity*, p. 17. See also McSheffrey, *Marriage, Sex and Civic Culture*, p. 121; Vanessa Harding, 'Space, property, and propriety in urban England, *Journal of Interdisciplinary History*, 32 (2002), 550, 558.
97 NA CA1325 rot. 12.
98 NA CA1325 rot. 12.
99 CALS ZSR 21 rot. 9.
100 Jeremy Goldberg, 'Space and gender in the later medieval English house', *Viator*, 42 (2011), 226.
101 NA CA1332 rot. 7.
102 CALS ZSR 376.
103 NA CA1336 rot. 10.
104 NA CA1336 rot. 5.
105 NA CA1294 rots 3, 4.
106 NA CA1374 pp. 51b, 86, 96, 113.
107 NA CA1374 p. 51b.
108 Trevor Dean, 'Theft and gender in late medieval Bologna', *Gender and History*, 20 (2008), pp. 405–406.
109 CALS ZSR 154.
110 NA CA1297 rot. 9.
111 Walker, *Crime, Gender and Social Order*, pp. 166–167.
112 NA CA1279 rot. 24.
113 NA CA1297 rot. 10.
114 See Barbara A. Hanawalt, 'Medieval English women in rural and urban domestic space', *Dumbarton Oaks Papers*, 52 (1998), 19–26.
115 William Blackstone, *Commentaries on the Laws of England*, book 1 (Oxford: Clarendon Press, 1765–9), p. 442.
116 Jones, *Gender and Petty Crime*, p. 37.
117 Tim Stretton, 'Coverture and unity of persons in Blackstone's commentaries' in Wilfred Prest (ed.), *Blackstone and his Commentaries: Biography, Law, History* (Oxford: Oxford University Press, 2009), pp. 112, 115.

118 NA CA1374 p. 81.
119 HRO W/D1/3 rot. 7.
120 CALS ZSR 21 rot. 6.
121 HRO, W/D1/37 rot. 6d.
122 Sara M. Butler, *Marital Violence in Later Medieval England* (Leiden: Brill, 2007), p. 32.
123 NA CA1336 rot. 1d.
124 NA CA1263 rot. 6.
125 Ewan, 'Women and interpersonal violence', 154.
126 HRO W/D1/37 rots 6, 8.
127 Jones, *Gender and Petty Crime*, p. 40.
128 HRO W/D1/37 rot. 5.
129 NA CA1258b rot. 18, 4 July 1324.
130 NA CA1279 rot. 9.
131 CALS ZSR 202d.
132 Lizabeth Johnson, 'Married women, crime and the courts in late medieval Wales', in Cordelia Beattie and Matthew Frank Stevens (eds), *Married Women and the Law in Premodern Northwest Europe* (Woodbridge: Boydell and Brewer, 2013), pp. 77–78, 88.
133 CALS ZSR 376.
134 For examples, see Teresa Phipps, 'Female litigants and the borough court: status and strategy in the case of Agnes Halum of Nottingham' in Goddard and Phipps (eds), *Town Courts*, pp. 87–88.
135 NA CA1374 p. 81.
136 NA CA1325 rot. 3.
137 NA CA1332 rot. 4.
138 NA CA1296/I rots 16d, 17d.
139 NA CA1336 rot. 3.
140 Dunn outlines that cases of ravishment could be initiated in civil and criminal courts. Civil lawsuits were begun by purchasing a writ from Chancery. See Dunn, *Stolen Women*, pp. 5–6. See also Anthony Musson, 'Crossing boundaries: attitudes to rape in later medieval England', in Anthony Musson (ed.), *Boundaries of the Law: Geography, Gender and Jurisdiction in Medieval and Early Modern Europe* (Aldershot: Ashgate, 2005), pp. 90–91.
141 On the definitions of abduction and sexual assault, see Dunn, *Stolen Women*, pp. 18–51.
142 Butler, *Marital Violence*, p. 85.
143 Johnson, 'Married women, crime and the courts', pp. 74–77.
144 William Hudson (ed.), *Leet Jurisdiction in the City of Norwich during the XIIIth and XIVth Centuries* (London: Quaritch, 1892), p. 52. 'De Ricardo de Berton quia rapuit uxorem Willelmi Stedefast cum bonis mariti sui'.
145 CALS ZSR 201d (*carnalit' cognovit ... cepit et asportavit*).
146 CALS ZSR 374d (*abduxit*).
147 HRO W/D1/13 rot. 3d.
148 NA CA1265 rot. 11d.
149 Dunn, *Stolen Women*, p. 20.
150 Dunn, *Stolen Women*, p. 68.

151 Musson, 'Attitudes to rape', p. 91.
152 NA CA1272 William de Findern sued Henry de Gaddesby for abducting a haircloth worth 20s 6d in 1362; John del Wiche sued Richard Billing for abducting hay. Numerous other examples can be given, including bread, pots and pans, pigs, chickens, timbers and plants.
153 Musson, 'Attitudes to rape', pp. 86–90.
154 Dunn, *Stolen Women*, p. 6.
155 Jones, *Gender and Petty Crime*, p. 85.
156 Cordelia Beattie, 'Governing bodies: law courts, male householders, and single women in late medieval England' in Cordelia Beattie, Anna Maslakovic and Sarah Rees Jones (eds), *The Medieval Household in Christian Europe c.850–c.1550* (Turnhout: Brepols, 2003), pp. 199–200.
157 Walker, *Crime, Gender and Social Order*, p. 10.
158 Beattie, 'Governing bodies', p. 203.
159 NA CA1260 rot. 18.
160 This phrase is borrowed from Jeremy Goldberg's preface in Beattie, Maslakovic and Rees Jones (eds), *The Medieval Household in Christian Europe*, p. 226.
161 NA CA1297 rot. 10.
162 NA CA1329/II rot. 3d.
163 NA CA1329/II rot. 12.
164 Finch, 'Women and violence in the later middle ages: the evidence of the officiality of Cerisy', *Continuity and Change*, 7 (1992), 29.
165 Jones, *Gender and Petty Crime*, p. 196.

5

Public disorder, policing and misbehaving women

Between Michaelmas 1395 and Michaelmas 1396, Nottingham's decennaries – the pairs of residents responsible for reporting offences that took place within their street or neighbourhood – reported 100 affrays: 25 of these were serious, involving bloodshed; 34 involved women as either the victims or culprits. If medieval society is typically seen as one where violence was endemic, where disputes were frequent and settled physically, often using weapons, records such as these do little to challenge these images. Historians have, over past decades, characterised the medieval world as one where 'everything from the most trivial insults to serious questions of rights and property [was] settled by homicide'.[1] Certainly, the records of medieval law and order abound with examples of numerous felonies, including murder and assault, as well as disorder and misbehaviour at less severe levels. But these records in fact stem from the extensive efforts of governments and officials to punish and control misbehaviour. The resulting impression is that both law and violence were defining features of everyday life, as the reason we know so much about crime and disorder is due to the systems that were put in place to punish and control misbehaviour. As well as the personal pleas discussed previously in this book, urban court records document the policing and punishment of misbehaviour at the more banal, less dangerous level, offering a different focus to the traditional attention on felonies – though the dividing line between criminal and other offences was far from clear.[2] While town officials sought to create and maintain peaceful communities in order to promote their civic status, preserve respectability and foster economic prosperity, the reality of urban life did not live up to these ideals. The records of urban policing reveal the regular violent and disruptive interactions between individuals, as well as outbursts of 'bad speech' and actions which were deemed to cause nuisances and detriment to the urban community. We see how women and men used their voices, bodies and weapons to attack others and disturb the peace, and were required to pay monetary fines when reported by local officials.

As we have already seen, towns were sites of violence, theft, disruption, slander and many other eruptions of interpersonal strife. Derek Keene has suggested that the hundreds of presentments concerning breaches of the peace, bloodletting and the hue and cry among Winchester's city records 'are ample enough demonstration that violence was ingrained in medieval society'.[3] Through personal pleas, such as trespass, individuals who felt that they or their household had been harmed sought compensation and punishment for the offenders. But misbehaviour was not only conceptualised in its power to harm individuals, but also the entire urban community, and, by extension, the crown. Violence, 'malicious' speech and disruption that broke the peace or caused nuisance to urban inhabitants was prosecuted and punished on behalf of the town by urban governments via various local jurisdictions and policing – such as Nottingham's decennaries. The records of this policing therefore contextualise the evidence of litigation, and vice versa. These were different forms of law, with notable procedural differences, but they did not exist in isolation from each other, and both systems combined to create the experience of justice for urban women and men. This chapter considers the nature and policing of violence and disorder in medieval towns, and the way in which this was gendered in terms of both culpability and experience. The focus here is on the records from Nottingham and Winchester, which survive in far greater volume than those from Chester, though some supplementary material from Chester is included where possible.

Before turning to the records in detail, it is worth pointing out, as Hanawalt, Maddern and others have done before, that both the legal records and the context in which they arose do not allow us to access or reconstruct absolute levels of crime, violence or disorder.[4] The survival and quality of records is often poor, or varying over time and between places. On top of this, there were a great number of factors that determined how, why and if an incident came to the attention of the legal system, and thus entered into its records, including the attitudes and decisions of victims, the skill and knowledge of officials, and agreements to settle out of court. What we know about each incident is also influenced by the details that scribes wrote down, in accordance with local custom and legal culture regarding the documenting of violence and disorder. For example, if the custom was that only the presence or lack of bloodshed was to be recorded, we can make no further conclusions about the specific nature of a particular incident. In addition, how an act of violence or disorder might have been defined and dealt with could differ from one jurisdiction to another, despite attempts to define the nature of felonies and other offences. An increase in the number of presentments for affray or bloodshed over time does not, therefore, provide conclusive evidence of a more violent community. Thus, this chapter is not concerned with the absolute levels of female involvement in violence and other disorderly conduct, though some relative assessments and observations can be made. Instead, it explores how women's behaviour was understood, policed and recorded within urban jurisdictions.

Every town in England followed its own traditions and procedures for the presentment and punishment of violence and other instances of disorder. These were visible, disruptive instances of disorder that often took place in the public spaces and streets of towns. The punishment of these offences typically fell under towns' rights of leet jurisdiction, and offences were usually presented by juries or other local officials a few times each year, often at major feast days.[5] This chapter explores women's involvement in a range of types of disorder in turn. It examines how juries and officials presented affrays and violent incidents that disturbed the peace of their neighbourhoods, named women (and some men) whose scolding and public speech disturbed or affronted their neighbours, and policed prostitution and the running of brothels – and other disorderly, immoral or illegal behaviour, such as playing games and hosting thieves. Officials also reported immoral or undesirable behaviour and instances of social policing via the mechanism of raising the hue and cry. While personal pleas allowed for the response of the accused party, and the possibility for arbitration or settlement, leet presentments usually dictated the guilt of the offending individual and stipulated the punishment or fine to be exacted. While in theory an accused person could challenge the presentment, this happened very rarely in practice, so that 'the presentment functioned in effect as a conviction'. But the presentment of these offences, which Marjorie McIntosh defined as 'social' wrongdoing or misbehaviour, was only partly about illegality.[6] The decision to present and punish certain types of behaviour also reflected the attitudes and concerns of local juries and officials, offering an insight into perceptions of 'justice' (in the broadest sense) and misbehaviour at the community level. Many of these concerns were shared across different urban and rural communities, as we will see, but the varying practices recorded under leet jurisdiction also point to the importance of local custom, concerns and individuals.

In Nottingham, these offences fell under the jurisdiction of the Mayor's Court, a separate institution to the borough court that convened at fixed points throughout the year before the mayor. Offences were usually reported by pairs of men, called decennaries, charged with reporting wrongdoing in their street or neighbourhood. At Winchester, the policing of violence and bad speech came before the City Court and was recorded among the same rolls as pleas of debt and trespass, though it appears this also took place at set points throughout the year. The records of Nottingham's Mayor's Court survive in fragmentary fashion over the late fourteenth and fifteenth centuries, so the evidence discussed here is drawn from all the extant rolls of the Mayor's Court that record violence and disorder (1395–6, 1407–8, 1414–15), plus the 1459–60 Mayor's Court book. The 1395–6 rolls and 1459–60 book are the only complete sets. In contrast, the Winchester data is drawn from the same sample of City Court rolls used for the rest of this book's quantitative analysis. Here, the overall number of presentments recorded declined significantly over the fourteenth and into the fifteenth century, indicating a shifting focus of officials as well as reflecting population decline. For both towns, therefore, the quantitative evidence cannot be used to indicate the full extent of violence and its punishment in the town, and nor should the numbers of Nottingham presentments be directly compared with those of Winchester. However, those that do survive indicate the relative frequency with which women and men were presented for violence and disorder and how this may have changed over time.

There is something of a tendency within the popular imagination to conceptualise women as victims of male violence in the medieval period, encapsulated in the image of the 'damsel in distress'. But, though the policing and punishment of violence was an important part of women's legal experiences, it did not define their engagement with the law. As we will see throughout this chapter, women were always among the minority of perpetrators *and* victims of violence and other disorderly offences. The exception to this was in specifically 'female' offences such as scolding and prostitution. Whether this was because women actually engaged in less illegal or disorderly behaviour, or whether officials took a different attitude to women's misbehaviour, is impossible to ascertain. Barbara Hanawalt suggested that, in criminal indictments, women's roles were not taken as seriously, and that they deserved special consideration if caught, leading more women to be acquitted than men.[7] While it is impossible to verify this using the records of urban policing, comparison of the acts of women and men may shed some light on how this was perceived by officials and the communities they represented.

Violence and affray

The policing of violence took place through presentments reporting affrays, bloodshed or the illegal drawing of weapons. While the trespass pleas that were the focus of the previous chapter arose from the complaints of alleged victims, the attacks dealt with under leet jurisdiction were brought to light by the declarations of juries or officials who policed their neighbourhoods. The distinction between violent trespasses and the assaults and affrays presented by officials was in legal procedure (who reported or complained about the assault, and how it was punished), rather than the inherent nature of an offence. In Nottingham, there appears to be little or no overlap between the specific assaults that were the subject of personal trespass pleas and the violence presented as affrays by local officials, though they shared common characteristics, suggesting that these were prosecuted under one, but not both, jurisdictions.[8] In Winchester, however, some reports of bloodshed or the raising of the hue and cry preceded the entering of a trespass plea involving the same individuals, indicating that these offences could be the subject of double legal action. The recording of violence often gave limited detail on the precise nature of an assault, though in some instances the language of trespass (beat, wounded and maltreated, etc.) was applied, further demonstrating the linked nature of trespass and the presentment of violence. In Nottingham, an affray without bloodshed was fined at 6d and this doubled to 12d if bloodshed was involved. This may have been a common custom across local jurisdictions: Andrew Finch observed a similar doubling of fines for assaults involving bloodshed in the officiality of Cerisy (Normandy) and higher fines for bloodshed were also common in Scottish towns.[9] In Winchester, violence was normally defined as bloodshed, though other attacks may have been punished via the reporting of instances where the hue and cry was raised.

Men were the main perpetrators of violence in both towns, and they predominated among victims too, in line with other studies of medieval violence.[10] Male violence has been attributed to testosterone, as well as to social and cultural understandings of violence as an acceptable or normal part of life for men and a means of proving masculinity.[11] While it is impossible to prove from the records of medieval law that women had an inherently less violent 'essence', the numbers nevertheless depict women's less frequent involvement in the violent acts that were documented in official records. This does not mean that those incidents that women were found in should be disregarded. Both married and single women were involved in violence, as assailants and victims, though they

Table 5.1 Assailants and victims of affray in Nottingham.

Year	Men		Not married women		Married women	
	Assailants	Victims	Assailants	Victims	Assailants	Victims
1395–6	66	70	5	13	5	3
1407–8	48	48	5	9	1	4
1414–15	20	19	5	4	0	1
1459–60	29	32	6	2	1	2
Total	163	169	21	28	7	10

Source: NA CA 3942, CA 3943, CA3944, CA4478.

were more likely to be victims than perpetrators of violent acts, a fact also observed by Matthew Stevens for Ruthin and Finch for Cerisy.[12] Women recorded with no reference to their marital status were more prevalent than married women. Nottingham women were 15 per cent of those identified as perpetrators of violence, and 18 per cent of victims. In Winchester, women only accounted for 7 per cent of those committing violent bloodshed. This lower proportion of female assailants may be partly explained by the fact that the Winchester presentments were only for bloodshed, so less severe acts of violence, which women may have been involved in, were not documented. As in Nottingham, Winchester women were more likely to be victims of violence, accounting for 16 per cent of victims, with married women notably being more likely to experience violence than to be punished for being violent themselves (also true in Ruthin). These figures, displayed in Tables 5.1 and 5.2, are not surprising, and are replicated in towns elsewhere, indicating a common pattern by which women were more likely to experience violence than to mete it out themselves. In Wakefield, more women suffered wounds than drew blood themselves.[13] Norwich's published leet records feature very few women, and a particular absence of women in presentments for violence and bloodshed.[14]

As the number of Winchester presentments declined, the gap between men's and women's violence and bloodshed decreased. By the fifteenth century, women's presentments for violence had declined further, with more women being fined for theft than violence. In 1454, only two women, Agnes Frankeleyn and Margery Coombe, were fined for bloodshed in one single act of violence: both were reported to have used daggers to assault the other in Goldestreet.[15] Margery Combe was also presented for breaking and entering the house of Nicholas Salesonrye and stealing 12s worth of goods, though there was no indication that

Table 5.2 Assailants and victims of violence in Winchester.

Year	Men		Not married women		Married women	
	Assailants	Victims	Assailants	Victims	Assailants	Victims
1299–1300	40	34	2	4	0	2
1365–6	45	43	1	2	2	3
1385–6	11	11	4	5	0	0
1432–3	20	16	0	1	0	3
1454–5	19	13	2	2	0	2
1494–5			*No presentments for violence*			
Total	135	117	10	13	2	10

Source: HRO W/D1/3, W/D1/13, W/D1/27, W/D1/60, W/D1/61, W/D1/64.

this involved personal violence.[16] It is hard to imagine that these were the only two violent women across the whole year. Rather, this suggests that officials were choosing not to record violence, perhaps focusing on only the most serious altercations (such as those involving weapons), in which women were less often involved. All of the instances of violence recorded in this year involved bloodshed and the use of weapons, such as daggers and knives. In 1495, Winchester's City Court rolls included no presentments for violence, nuisance or any other forms of disorder, only punishing trading offences alongside hearing personal pleas.

The overall number of presentments for affray also declined in Nottingham in the two complete sets of documents, the 1395–6 rolls and 1459–60 book. This is most notable in the numbers of men recorded as both assailants and victims, which fell by more than half across the 65-year period. The number of female victims also declined significantly, from 13 to 2, perhaps as a reflection of the lower numbers of affrays perpetrated and reported by men. As in Winchester, this shift indicates a reflection in the changing priorities of officials, and in the numbers of people living in the town, and should not simply be read as an absolute decline in levels of violence.

Looking beyond the statistics gives further insight into the nature of women's violence. There were certain characteristics to 'female' violence, though there were no consistent or persistent gendered patterns of violence. We have already seen that, statistically, women were less violent than men. When they were, they usually attacked other women and they rarely acted with accomplices or in support of others. For example, of the 11 affrays committed by women in Nottingham in 1395–6, 7 of the victims were women. Johanna de Bawtry of Nottingham was presented for throwing Maud Donne down on the ground in Moothallgate, and was imprisoned until she could pay the 6d fine.[17] This may be a typical image of female violence, resulting from a quarrel or rivalry that got out of hand. Magota Swepton assaulted her sister, Joan, in Bridlesmithgate in Nottingham in 1414, revealing the violence that could arise from familial disputes.[18] This prevalence of violence between women suggests that their lives brought them more regularly into contact, and thus dispute, with other women. Alternatively, officials may have chosen mainly to prosecute violence in accordance with gendered cultural associations about the behaviour and misbehaviour of women, creating distinct patterns in the nature and prevalence of violence.

When married women committed affrays, they were presented and fined independently. Several wives were involved in assaults against other married women, such as Margaret, wife of Hugh Spicer, who threw stones and drew her knife against the wife of William Spicer at Nottingham in 1395.[19] Unlike the trespass pleas discussed in the previous chapter, wives' violent actions as presented by local officials did not directly implicate their husbands in legal action, though the fact that married women were generally recorded as 'wife of' served to emphasise the marital ties of these disorderly or dangerous women, a potential source of humiliation for their husbands who were expected to govern their wives' behaviour. It is not always easy to identify women's marital status, as some wives were only referred to by first and surname, and their marital status only becomes apparent through cross-referencing with other complaints. Isabella, wife of John le Cras, raised the hue and cry against Agnes Beaupris in Winchester in 1365, who was recorded with no reference to her husband or marital status, despite the fact that in trespass suits in the same year she was recorded as the wife of Thomas Beaupris.[20] In 1386, Robert, servant of Adam Jonnyng, was fined 6d for causing the bloodshed of Alice Norman.[21] However, Alice was in fact married, and can be found litigating jointly with her husband John.[22] Because this type of legal action did not involve any form of response, but instead simply listed and fined offenders, there is no evidence that the husbands of married offenders were held jointly accountable.[23] In practice, the fines assigned for each offence would be drawn from the finances of the marital household, but the legal responsibility for the offence sat with the individual responsible for carrying out the act of violence or disorder.

As we have seen from the trespass evidence, spouses could join together in committing acts of violence. These actions blur the lines of gendered violence. However, because spouses were dealt with as independent legal actors under leet jurisdiction, they were recorded separately. In Winchester Emma Strokhose and William Strokhose were separately presented and fined for a hue raised and blood issued between themselves and Edith, wife of John le French.[24] It is likely here that William and Emma attacked Edith, causing her to raise the hue, for which they were subsequently fined. However, they were named and fined separately. Two weeks later, John and Edith le French also brought a trespass complaint against William Strokhose. Though Emma was not mentioned, it is possible that this trespass may have been related to the same instance of violence.[25]

Some instances of disorder reveal in detail the interlinked actions of husband and wife and the ties of the marital partnership in defending the honour of one's spouse. This did not always come in the form of a husband defending his wife. The decennaries of Middle Pavement in Nottingham, sometime in 1395 or 1396, presented an affray between Thomas Benton, a barber, and Hugh Wymondeslawe. They said that Thomas had seized Hugh by his breast in the Common Hall, drawn his knife and said malicious words, so that Hugh feared for his life. Thomas was attached and came to court to pay his 12d fine.[26] The entry that follows reveals what happened next. Joan, wife of Hugh Wymondslawe, came into the Common Hall and there spoke malicious words to the same Thomas Benton and slapped his face. As a result, she also paid a fine of 12d.[27] Though not explicitly stated, it is likely that the second affray was a result of the first. Joan appears to have been angry at the attack on her husband, perhaps feeling it to be an affront to his (and therefore her own) honour, and decided to let Thomas know how she felt. As Elizabeth Ewan has argued, wives could and did act in defence of their husbands and other family members.[28] Joan's retaliation would have served to damage Thomas Benton's own reputation, particularly by being slapped in the face by a woman in such a public place. The 'malicious words' used, a common phrase referring to verbal attacks and defamation, may also have contained attacks on his character or honour for all to hear. Despite being married, however, she acted alone in her retaliation, and was therefore presented alone. Both parties were fined at the higher level of 12d, usually reserved for attacks that caused bloodshed, but in this case it may have reflected the disruption caused within the important civic space of the Common Hall.

Not all evidence of marital relationships depicts this supportive union, however. Husbands could sometimes harm their wives in ways that were deemed unacceptable by the community and court. John le Tappetor of Winchester was presented and fined 6d for drawing the blood of his (unnamed) wife in 1366.[29] This is the only case of marital violence that has been found among any of the town court records, which does not mean that it did not occur within these towns, but that it was not generally recorded in the records of local justice. The common law stated that a husband should 'treat and govern her [his wife] well and honestly, and to do no injury or ill to her body other than that permitted lawfully and reasonably to a husband for the purpose of control and punishment of his wife'.[30] The limits to this 'lawful and reasonable' castigation are not clear, though the case of John le Tappetor suggests that he had overstepped this mark.[31] As Sara Butler has noted, the ecclesiastical courts were the 'obvious venue' for cases of excessive force within marriage, explaining the relative absence of similar cases from town court rolls.[32] Manorial and borough courts were generally reluctant to intervene in marital issues, but sometimes stepped in when marital strife was deemed to impact on the wellbeing of the community, in a manner that Butler interprets as assuming the role of 'marriage counsellor', an extension of informal familial supervision.[33] As a result, it was the local officials who raised the issue of Tappetor's violent behaviour, not his wife. His actions may have represented an extreme instance of marital violence, perhaps reflected in the fact that the assault had caused bloodshed, leading local officials to intervene.

As perpetrators of violence, women's involvement was not just restricted to members of the same sex. We have seen in Chapter 4 that men sued women for violence through trespass pleas, and the records of policing also reveal women's violence against men. Margaret Gay of Nottingham threw William Leadenham against a post, causing bloodshed, in 1395.[34] In the same year, an unnamed maidservant of Joan de Crophill slapped Thomas Briddam, a tinker, in the face.[35] In 1414, Isabella Flecher assaulted John Frauncys with a stick.[36] Winchester presentments for the raising of the hue and cry, discussed below, also indicate that women attacked men. Conversely, some women experienced violence and bloodshed at the hands of men. We have already seen that Robert, servant of Adam Jonnyng, drew the blood of Alice Norman at Winchester in 1386, and John Wynhale drew the blood of Amice Grymes in 1365.[37] Isabella, wife of Richard Sherman, was assaulted by William Byngley with a stick in Houndgate in Nottingham in 1407 or 1408.[38] In 1395, Henry Webster raised his club and struck Katherine Kempster in Frenchgate in Nottingham. Stephen Wade beat Alice de Swetenham with a stick and Agnes Irish using his fists.[39] These examples fit more with the stereotype of female victims being abused by men, though we do not know the context surrounding any of these events.

Both women and men were clearly capable of causing bloodshed, and the higher fines awarded at Nottingham reflect the severity with which courts viewed this. But while women and men committed the same types of violent offences, it is noteworthy that the language used to report male violence depicts it as more extreme and harmful than the cases where women attacked others, particularly in the Nottingham records. Male violence involved force, malice and the frequent use of weapons, and the 1395–6 records from Nottingham featured particularly detailed accounts of violence. Some attacks were reported to have been carefully plotted: Thomas Beddefford attempted to kill Adam de Newton and John Utterby, servant of William Prentice, laying in wait to attack them using a club.[40] Henry Hikkelyng was reported to have drawn his knife and stabbed John Pulter, drawing blood.[41] In contrast, typical female affrays involved more generic references to beating and mistreating, or being thrown down into the street. In Winchester, the same language that was used in trespass pleas featured in jury presentments for bloodshed. The court rolls from November 1432 record that Henry Cosewyke came with force and arms, namely sticks and knives, at night-time to assault Hugh Sawiere and Johanna, his wife, beating and wounding them so that they despaired for their lives, a case which again indicates a form of pre-planned, intentional violence.[42] The couple raised the hue and cry, and Cosewyke was ordered to come before the court.

As these examples demonstrate, male violence regularly cited the use of weapons, including knives, axes and clubs. Though these were not assaults that resulted in death, the types of weapons used certainly had the potential to kill.[43] Many of these items would have been carried or used by men (and some women) regularly, rather than being sought out specifically for the purpose of a violent assault. John Frenssheman drew the blood of Alice, wife of John Summer, skinner, using a knife worth 1d in December 1432. The court rolls also show that Alice raised the hue and cry on John, and it was probably this that meant he ended up in court.[44] In crown cases relating to murder, it was common for the value of weapons used to be assessed and recorded, as they were to be forfeited to the crown.[45] This convention filtered down to the types of assault recorded by various towns' leet courts, even though the incidents were less serious. The use of weapons was not exclusively male, and women (such as Winchester's Agnes Frankeleyn and Margery Coombe) were reported for armed attacks too. Nottingham's Margaret Spicer drew her knife against the wife of William Spicer, and also threw stones at her, making the most of the weapons that were easily to hand.[46] These examples extend the significance of women's assaults beyond simply petty female 'cat fights', or 'bitchy fisticuffs', as described by Helen Jewell.[47] But women more frequently used their bodies as weapons to beat or slap their victims, and were subject to this type of violence themselves, giving the impression of unruly and disorderly behaviour, rather than dangerous or life-threatening violence. For example, Maud, wife of John Boyn, threw Agnes Lenton down upon the ground and beat her with her fists in Nottingham's Moothallgate in 1395.[48] Domestic items could sometimes be turned into weapons, like the firebrand that Matilda Latham used to beat the servant of Nicholas Lambley, also in Moothallgate in 1395.[49] Janka Rodziewicz has suggested that women were less likely to be carrying weapons that might lead to escalated violence or bloodshed, and that they instead used 'objects of opportunity', such as sticks, stones, their fists – or in this case, a firebrand – more often than men.[50]

The difference in the volume of male and female violence depicts women's violence as somewhat exceptional. However, female violence was not necessarily less serious or dangerous: the majority (two thirds) of Nottingham affrays did not involve bloodshed, and this was true whether women or men were the perpetrators. The shedding of blood in assaults by both male and female attackers in Ewan's study of sixteenth-century Glasgow was equally rare, and these various records suggest, as Finch has argued for medieval Normandy, that most assaults were minor affairs and 'far from life-threatening'.[51] We should not, therefore, imagine a gendered binary of extreme (male) and petty (female) violence.

As well as violence, local juries and officials presented instances of theft and breaking and entering. Though the numbers of presentments were low, women were more predominant among those fined for stealing and distributing stolen goods than men. Of 17 individuals fined for stealing or receiving stolen goods at Winchester in 1433, 10 were women. They stole assorted goods and chattels from men and women, and received and distributed these goods too. Women have been found elsewhere to have been disproportionately active in receiving and disposing of stolen goods. Their role in household management and provisioning may have given easier access to networks through which to dispose of stolen goods.[52] In Kent, 14 women and 11 men were charged as accessories or receivers.[53] In 1454, Margery Coombe was the only person fined for theft in Winchester, when she broke and entered into the house of Nicholas Salesonrye, stealing silver worth 12s.[54] Chester's sheriff's books also note women being fined for their involvement with stolen goods. In 1508, a woman called Agnes was reported for receiving servants and apprentices into her house with goods unjustly taken from their masters.[55] While it is unlikely that men did not also deal in stolen goods, this was an offence that was characterised and presented as being particularly female.

Policing and the hue and cry

The raising of the hue and cry was also presented by local officials and offers an additional perspective on the extent, nature and gendering of violence and its legal repercussions. The hue was a means of raising the alarm upon experiencing or witnessing crime, and was often a precursor or prerequisite to prosecution and punishment of the assailant. Individuals shouted to those nearby when offences were committed and witnesses were obliged to pursue the offender. London's *Liber Albus* reports that every witness to a felony was expected to raise the hue, with those hearing it to pursue the transgressors, in order 'to preserve peace in the city'.[56] In Norwich, and probably other towns too, the hue was most often raised when a person felt an immediate threat to their person or property. The mechanism of the hue and cry provided an alternative means of seeking retribution for attacks on property or person, 'a means of short-circuiting the justice system that required neither money nor political clout'.[57] Samantha Sagui has observed that borough custumals rarely mention the hue specifically, but that this was indicative of the practice's establishment and embedding into town custom.[58] Following the raising of the hue, local courts considered the legitimacy of each hue raised, and their records sometimes detail whether the hue was deemed to have been raised justly or unjustly. The permissible raising of the hue was limited to instances of assault, *hamsokn*, theft and discovery of a dead body.[59] Here, the majority of evidence for the raising of the hue comes from Winchester, though some instances are found in the Nottingham records too.

While many legal actions were circumscribed by gender or status, it has been argued that the hue and cry offered a more accessible form of legal engagement for women: 'the only requirement for raising the hue and cry seems to have been proximity to, or victimization by, an act of violence or felony – plus a good, strong pair of lungs. Women were as qualified as men on both scores.'[60] Janka Rodziewicz has argued that the use of the hue and cry offered women a positive means of becoming involved in regulating their community in the context of a legal system that was generally coded masculine and which subordinated women.[61] Samantha Sagui has also argued that the hue and cry in Norwich became increasingly feminised over the fourteenth century, with women more frequently being justified in their raising of the hue, which served to

Table 5.3 Individuals against whom the hue and cry was raised at Winchester.

Year	Men	Not married women	Married women	Total
1299–1300	79	32	14	125
1365–6	12	4	1	17
1385–6	2	5	0	7
1432–3	4	0	0	4
1454–5	1	0	0	1
1494–5	0	0	0	0
Total	98	41	15	154

Source: HRO W/D1/3, W/D1/13, W/D1/27, W/D1/60, W/D1/61, W/D1/64.

sanction women's involvement in the public sphere.[62] Sagui suggests that this was a result of their inability to access justice in any other way, rather than a sign of empowerment.[63] When set in the context of the full spectrum of women's legal actions in towns, these arguments appear to overplay the significance of the hue for women. It was not the only legal option for women who were attacked or wronged, as the evidence of trespass litigation has already shown, so should not be interpreted as the only 'female' option for legal recourse. Furthermore, the nature of recording the raising of the hue was often brief, formulaic, giving little detail on the nature of an offence, meaning that any attempts to characterise the use of this tool as 'positive' are somewhat problematic. We can, however, assess women's involvement in this system as further evidence of their participation in the legal system of their local community.

Presentments for raising the hue and cry were the most numerous at Winchester, particularly in the early fourteenth century, as Tables 5.3 and 5.4 show. This should not automatically be read as indicative of a more violent society: it may have been that the Winchester court took a more thorough approach to recording the raising of the hue, or that the city's residents more readily used their voices to draw attention to illegal behaviour in this earlier period. The rolls of 1299–1300 include a particularly high number of incidences of hue-raising, though many of these reports were of the unjust raising of the hue by both women and men.[64] The recording of the hue often preceded the entry of a plea of trespass, demonstrating that it was often raised in relation to these offences. Women accounted for approximately a third of those who raised the hue (56 of 154), and of those whose actions caused the hue to be raised by others (34 of 103). Though the sample size is smaller than that available for litigation and other presentments, this nevertheless indicates that raising of the hue and cry was less divided according to gendered lines

Table 5.4 Raisers of the hue and cry at Winchester.

Year	Men	Not married women	Married women	Total
1299–1300	52	13	8	73
1365–6	10	4	3	17
1385–6	4	3	0	7
1432–3	2	1	2	5
1454–5	1	0	0	1
1494–5	0	0	0	0
Total	69	21	13	103

Source: HRO W/D1/3, W/D1/13, W/D1/27, W/D1/60, W/D1/61, W/D1/64.

than any other form of legal action. Women feature in greater numbers in relation to the hue than other types of presentment or litigation, and if we exclude the exceptionally high number of presentments from 1299–1300, we see that men only slightly outnumbered women in raising the hue (17 men and 13 women across the 5 remaining samples). This is comparable to Rodziewicz's study of Great Yarmouth, where women raised the hue only marginally less than men (15 to 18 times).[65] Sagui found that women raised the hue in 44 per cent of instances in Norwich, 45 per cent in Colchester, 54 per cent in Ramsey (Cambridgeshire), but only 30 per cent in London.[66]

The recording of the hue and cry declined significantly over the fourteenth century in Winchester, further demonstrating that this was not a defining feature of women's legal experience over much of the period studied here. The tables clearly show how presentments fell by half over the first 60 years of the fourteenth century. In 1432–3, only three instances of hue-raising were recorded, all of which involved women raising the alarm when they were attacked.[67] Alongside these entries, we find more detailed recording of incidences of violence and bloodshed, revealing a shift away from communal to more official policing. Sandy Bardsley has suggested that the decline of hue-raising as a form of communal policing was linked to the demographic upheaval of the Black Death and the resulting mobility that changed community dynamics. The gap in the Winchester records from 1300 to 1361 means that we cannot ascertain the immediate impact of the plague, though there was clearly a significant shift in the use of the hue over this 60-year period. This shift may help to explain the relative absence of the hue from the Nottingham Mayor's Court rolls, as there are no pre-plague rolls extant. According to Bardsley, people became less likely to pursue a hue raised by neighbours they did not know or trust, meaning that victims were less likely to use this form of law if it was deemed to be less effective.[68] The result for women was a curtailment of their legitimate opportunities to raise their voices – though not an intentional or misogynist move, it certainly functioned to silence women.[69] However, in Winchester, the decline in hue-raising clearly effected both men and women's use of this legal tool. Demographic decline, and the overall declining status of the city, should also be considered in the falling number of hues reported, reflected in the decline in the number of trespass suits heard as civil pleas at the City Court too. Fewer people meant fewer potential perpetrators and victims of crime and misbehaviour. However, this does not account for the extent of the decline in reporting the hue at Winchester, indicating a real change in legal and policing practice within the city, as Bardsley has suggested.

Beyond the numbers, there are a number of issues involved in examining the recording of the hue in the Winchester records. The focus of Winchester's officials was on recording the instance of the hue being raised as a means of reporting violence, meaning that it was often recorded alongside bloodshed. The brevity of the records means that it is sometimes difficult to verify why a hue was recorded and how the accompanying amercements were apportioned. In some instances, the recording of a hue is used as a shorthand for violence or bloodshed, rather than indicating the individual who raised a hue. For example, an entry in Winchester's 1299 records simply reads that Walter le Roppere and Christina, his wife, were attached for a hue.[70] Many of these instances, particularly from the largest sample in 1299–1300, do not report who the victim of violence was, meaning that the numbers of assailants recorded is larger than the number of hue-raisers. Details on the nature of the incident rarely accompany this reporting, and many instances do not record an outcome, but just that the parties involved were ordered to come to court or that an individual was fined. Where the hue was unjustly raised, this was specifically noted and the individual amerced. Some of these unjust hues included instances where the assailant had raised the hue in an attempt to implicate their victim.[71] Juliana Gog3e was presented and fined for raising the hue unjustly against Juliana le Northerner in 1299, and a subsequent entry records that she was also amerced for committing a trespass against the same Juliana le Northerner.[72] Similarly, the wife of Thomas Reddhed was fined for raising the hue unjustly against Matilda la Frie, when in fact she and her husband had committed trespass against Matilda.[73]

The coupling of the hue and cry with reports of bloodshed demonstrates how Winchester women raised the hue when they either experienced or felt the threat of personal violence. Sometimes the recording of jury presentments also reveals more detail about the raising of the hue and cry, and again, we see a preponderance of incidents between women. For example, the 1410–11 Winchester rolls record how Matilda, wife of Henry Bac, unjustly came to the house of John Dy, broke and entered against his will and assaulted Alice, wife of John Dy, beating and mistreating her, causing Alice to raise the hue upon Matilda.[74] Seven instances of hue-raising from 1299–1300 involved women only, though three of these were deemed to be unjust. Alice de Ros raised the hue and cry against the wife of Richard de Saundone, the sister of John de Bedeford did so against Margaret de Hampton, and Lucy Viman and Matilda le Vag' both raised the hue against each other.[75] However, women were also the victims of attacks by men. Margery Yenan raised the hue when John Chepman assaulted her and drew blood in February 1433.[76] Men also raised the hue and cry upon female assailants, drawing attention to these attacks despite any connotations of weakness or attacks upon their masculinity that this may have had. Edith Smale of Winchester was fined twice following the raising of the hue by two of the city's bailiffs, and though we do not know why the hue was raised, this suggests that she had attacked the officials, perhaps simultaneously, as the reports sit together in the record.[77] Robert Colfre raised the hue against William Swetecross and his wife in 1300, and an unknown 'outsider' raised the hue against Johanna Mity.[78] Many other men raised the hue against women, including wives and widows, though most of these were deemed to be unjust.

Spouses could join together in raising the hue when they were attacked. Hugh Sawiere and his wife, Johanna, raised the hue together when they were attacked by Henry Cosewyke. The couple were attached, ordered to come to court, and their attacker was also presented and attached for his offence.[79] There may have been an expectation that the husband protect his wife, but because the attack was upon both spouses, they both raised the alarm together. Other married women acted alone in raising the hue. Alice, wife of John Summer, raised the hue when John Frenssheman drew her blood with a knife in January 1433.[80] Though she was married, she took an active role in raising the alarm, and thus initiating prosecution. Married women were not only victims in need of protection by either their husbands or the local community. Their violent actions also caused others to raise the alarm. The wife of John Pope was fined for a hue, indicating that she had committed some form of violent misbehaviour, though the victim and hue-raiser's identities were not documented. The court rolls recorded that her husband came to court to pay the fine, representing the financial limits to married women's legal accountability for their misbehaviour.[81] In this way, the identities of husband and wife – and thus the household – were tied through his financial responsibility for her misbehaviour.

Occasionally, the active role of women using the hue extended to married women raising the alarm against their husbands, presumably when they had been unjustly castigated. Like the instance of a man assaulting his wife, these examples are rare, but they provide further evidence that there was an enforced limit to a husband's power of correction over his wife. The wife of John Coterel raised the hue and cry against her husband in 1300.[82] In 1366, the jury presented a hue raised between John Goulde and his wife, for which John was amerced. Though there are no other details of the event, this suggests that he was deemed to have behaved wrongly, perhaps having beaten his wife and caused her to raise the alarm.[83] Though small in number, these examples show that the City Court could deem it acceptable for women to raise the hue against their husbands, in common with Sara Butler's findings for Wakefield's manor court.[84]

Evidence for the use of hue and cry in Nottingham is rarer than in Winchester. As discussed above, this may be a reflection of the declining use of the hue after the Black Death, in the period for which there are extant rolls of the Mayor's Court. In the complete rolls of 1395–6, only two instances of the hue and cry being justifiably raised were recorded. In both cases, it was lone women who had raised the hue in response to the actions of men.[85] In addition, Margaret Gay was fined for attacking William Leadenham, and then raising the hue against William, perhaps to make out that he had attacked her.[86] In 1414–15, the hue was only recorded when deemed to have been unjustly raised, and three of these five instances involved women.[87] While these instances are small in number, they add to the suggestion that the hue and cry was a tool that was particularly used by women.

The records of the raising of the hue and cry, though problematic and patchy in their survival, thus provide an additional perspective on the existence, reporting and policing of violence within urban communities. Women are more visible among the records of this form of social policing, as other studies have shown, confirming that the mechanism of the hue and cry could offer women a means of direct access to justice. This was borne out of a desire to root the policing of misbehaviour firmly within the community, building mutual obligations and expectations among members of the community – both male and female. However, this mechanism could also be used to report and punish women's misbehaviour, and nor was it the only option available to women, so it should not simply be understood as an exceptional tool of female resistance in the context of a patriarchal legal system.

Scolding and verbal offences

If bodily violence was generally gendered male, less often meted out and experienced by women, verbal offences were more commonly associated with women. This pattern is clearly displayed through statistical comparison of male and female offences. The construction of 'bad speech' as a feminine offence has been documented by various historians, most notably Sandy Bardsley who argued that while the offence was not solely reserved for women, they dominated among the individuals fined for disruptive use of their voices. The label of the scold was attached to those who engaged in troublesome, disruptive speech of various means, including malicious gossip, nagging, swearing and quarrelling.[88] Scolds were often constructed as being persistently disorderly and disruptive to the community at large, hence why many complaints concerned 'common scolds'.[89] A large majority of scolds were female – 80 to 95 per cent according to Bardsley – though on occasion men were also branded with this label.[90]

In Nottingham and Winchester, the vast majority of scolds were female, as Table 5.5 shows. Because the Nottingham records only survive sporadically, and the Winchester records have been sampled, the figures presented here do not represent all scolds. However, the figures clearly indicate the dominance of women in scolding presentments, and specifically of women recorded with no marital status, who are likely to have been either never-married or widows. The naming of married scolds was particularly rare in Winchester. This suggests that this was a label largely attached to independent women who were perhaps perceived to be more disruptive as they were not governed over by a husband.

Nottingham's female scolds were labelled '*communes objurgatrices*', with the presentment sometimes including details of where they

Table 5.5 Scolds in Nottingham and Winchester.

	Man	Not married woman	Married woman
Nottingham	6	27	13
Winchester	1	23	3

Source: NA CA 3942, CA 3943, CA3944, CA4478; HRO W/D1/3, W/D1/13, W/D1/27, W/D1/60, W/D1/61, W/D1/64.

committed the offence. For example, Alice Slater, wife of John Slater, and Joan, wife of John Layburn, were fined 6d each for being common scolds in Goosegate where they lived.[91] Alice de Swetenham received the same fine for being a common scold, though was forgiven because she was poor.[92] In 1407, Cicilia Molde was presented for being a common scold, her bad speech being particularly targeted at Helen Mylner, demonstrating that scolding could also be a product or source of interpersonal attacks or disputes.[93] The majority of Winchester scolds, here called '*communis rixatrix*', were documented by just their full name, such as Agnes Prat, Isabella Sleymakyare and Johanna Capmakyare, who were all attached for scolding in 1385.[94] Seven Winchester women were labelled scolds in 1432–3, their bad speech said to disturb the peace of the town and of the king. Margaret Batte was accused of scolding John Reson against the peace, as well as being labelled a common scold two weeks earlier, suggesting her repeated verbal misbehaviour.[95] Scolding fines could also represent troublesome quarrelling between women, none of whom were necessarily 'victims', but whose behaviour was disruptive to the community more generally. The Nottingham records feature a number of women fined for scolding one another, sometimes recorded in sequence in the court records suggesting a concerted effort to police and document this form of female disturbance. In 1459, Agnes Boland was fined for scolding Alice Adamson, who was herself presented for scolding Agnes. In addition, Margaret Hulton was also fined for scolding Alice Adamson. Later in the same mayor's book, eight women were all fined for scolding offences against each other, the majority being recorded as 'the wife of' with no forename.[96] In contrast to the women recorded by their full name, suggesting their independent (and ungoverned) status, the central facet of these married women's identities was their relationship to their husband. Their scolding reflected badly on their husbands who were apparently unable to control their wives, causing them to disrupt the peace of the local community.

As Bardsley identified, and as Table 5.5 shows, scolding was not an offence reserved only for women. In Nottingham in 1415, John Aldyrche, William Smalley and John Cathorp were all fined 6d each for being common scolds, accounting for 3 of the 14 scolds fined in that year.[97] Alice Smalley was named as a scold directly after William Smalley, suggesting that the two may have been related, perhaps by marriage. By this point, the term used to refer to the offence had changed to '*litigator/litigatrix*' suggesting a shift in the understanding of the offence pertaining more to quarrelling than scolding or chastising.[98] The inclusion of men under this category reveals that this was an action and characteristic that could be applied to men as well as women. Thomas Lokwod and his wife Alice were both presented together for scolding against the mayor and other men of Nottingham in 1459, causing harm through their contentious words.[99] At Winchester in 1454, when ten women were fined for scolding, Thomas Bartelot, a weaver, was also labelled alongside them as a common scold and disturber of the peace.[100] All were called '*objurgator et perturbator pacis*'. This was something of an exception in Winchester, however, where there was generally a distinction in the way that men's and women's disruptive voices were constructed and recorded.

The gendering of 'bad speech' is demonstrated in the way that the malicious words of one Winchester couple were dealt with in 1366. John le Schetare and his wife Synnota were both presented for malicious words spoken by them to their neighbours. The couple were presented separately, and while Synnota was labelled a common scold and agitator of the peace, using malicious words against her neighbours, the complaint about her husband's behaviour only recorded his use of malicious words against the collectors of the city.[101] Though the behaviour was apparently the same and perhaps committed together, in the eyes of the court the label of scold was gendered female and thus only attached to Synnota. Bardsley has identified a similar distinction between the disruptive voices of men and women, with the abusers of officials typically being men, and similar behaviours of men and women being labelled differently.[102] Jones and Zell similarly found that in Fordwich in Kent, scolding was an overwhelmingly female offence, even though men were also guilty of using 'bad words'.[103] Garthine Walker has also suggested that men's and women's scolding behaviour was labelled differently along gendered lines, with men being presented for barratry and women for scolding.[104] We know that men's speech could be the cause of contention from numerous trespass pleas that centred on allegations of name-calling and slander, and from defamation cases recorded in numerous church courts. However, the construction of the offence of scolding was largely as a specifically female type of speech, perceived as something that urban officials sought to govern or control, and to punish when deemed unacceptable or disruptive. This extended to women's unjust raising of the hue and cry, demonstrating the conflagration of women's troublesome speech with their involvement in social policing.[105] Agnes Lister of Nottingham was named a common scold after being presented for raising the hue and cry, suggesting that her proclamations were deemed to be frequently troublesome.[106] Helen Milner was scolded by Cecily Mold, but was also fined for raising the hue and being a scold herself.[107]

Scolds were therefore disruptive, troublesome and typically women, whose behaviour damaged the urban community in a number of different ways. As Bardsley has shown, the imprecise definition of scolding meant it was a label applied to anyone who seemed disruptive or problematic in a way that threatened local peace and order.[108] Garthine Walker has suggested that this was an attribution that developed by the late sixteenth century, but this association of scolding with physical and sexual misbehaviour is found in the fourteenth and fifteenth centuries too.[109] Several of Nottingham's scolds, such as Joan Pynner and Isolda Hunt, were also fined for assault, indicating that the violent use of women's voices often went alongside physical violence.[110] This follows the pattern identified from the trespass evidence, wherein we see women using or experiencing physical violence along with acts of defamation, so it is not surprising to find similar evidence of physical and verbal attacks among the records of policing too. Agnes Frankeleyn and Margery Coombe of Winchester were both named as common scolds in 1454, as well as being fined for violent assault.[111] Margery Coombe was also fined for breaking and entering.[112] Alice Pynne of Winchester was labelled a common scold, and was also presented for stealing clothing and receiving or selling stolen goods.[113] Though she was named and attached in all of these offences in her own name, she was in fact married to Robert Pynne, as the couple were falsely accused of trespass in the same year.[114] Her marital status may have been known within the urban community, but for the purposes of policing and punishing her misdemeanours, her marriage appears to have been irrelevant.

In Winchester, there was also a particular association between scolding and prostitution (discussed in detail in the following section). In 1366, Isabelle Bolle, Alice Pykot, Alice Kembestre and Isabelle Scheppestre were presented for holding a common bordel (brothel), receiving a priest and men of ill-fame, as well as being common scolds.[115] Alice Hertyng was named a scold and a prostitute in 1433.[116] In Chester's sheriff's books, common scolds were recorded alongside other women deemed to cause nuisances to the town community. Joan More (also known as Joan Skotte) and Joan Oveot, both labourers, were each fined 4d for being common scolds in 1502 or 1503.[117] These were all disorderly women whose behaviour defied the codes of proper behaviour within the town in multiple ways. Their frequent legal punishment may have garnered them reputations for dishonourable behaviour, bringing them more closely to the attention of officials and perhaps making them more likely to be presented for various offences than other women. Presentments for scolding were gendered punishments related to the image of disorderly, ungoverned women, concerning breaches of particularly gendered codes of behaviour, and the application of this label to female disorder and misbehaviour clearly reveals the different codes of behaviour for men and women.

Prostitution and immoral activities

Jurisdiction over sexual misconduct theoretically sat with the church courts. However, this did not stop other local courts presenting and punishing it, though the focus was on prostitution and brothel keeping, probably because this was deemed to be the most detrimental to the community and thus in need of regulation.[118] This regulatory aspect of the policing of prostitution has been identified by Ruth Karras and others, suggesting that fines relating to prostitution were akin to licensing fees, particularly where these fines were issued regularly to the same individuals.[119] A small number of individuals fined for prostitution and related offences feature in the records of all three towns. Though statistically this is a very small sample, close examination of the nature of the offences that were punished and the identities of those named offers an insight into the way that systems of local justice perceived and policed sexual activity within their communities.

A handful of Winchester women were fined for prostitution offences from the time of the earliest City Court records onwards, and we have already seen how some of these women were also named for other 'female' offences such as scolding. Though McIntosh has argued that concern about sexual misconduct was found more from the later fifteenth century onwards, Winchester's court took steps to punish prostitution from its earliest days.[120] The majority of these women were not categorised under any marital status, though in other towns, married women have been found to have engaged in prostitution.[121] In 1299–1300, two women were fined for being prostitutes, while a man called Baldewyn was fined 6d for receiving the 'wife of le Dine', a woman called Johanna, and Lucy le Bakyster. William Alis and William Swift were also fined 3d each for the same offence, and one of the women involved was called Johanna Meretricis, who may also have been the same Johanna. Another of the women presented as a prostitute was Lucy Pistori (baker), suggesting that this was in fact the same woman said to have been 'received' by Baldewyn.[122] Isabella Brasyer, wife of John Brasyer, was also accused of running a brothel.[123] These presentments continued over the fourteenth and fifteenth centuries. Four women were presented for running brothels and receiving priests and men of ill-fame in Winchester in 1366.[124] In 1432–3, four women were fined for prostitution, while five were reported to be running brothels. Two men, John Frensshman, a carpenter, and William Sequens, were also listed as brothel holders.[125] Twenty years later, John Frenshman was still (or again) running a brothel, and was named alongside two other men.[126] Johanna Myldene was presented for prostitution, and for also running a common brothel.[127] These later presentments were recorded using formulaic language to describe the detriment to the community, indicating a general attitude and discomfort towards prostitution – particularly that which took place within brothels – whereby it was perceived as damaging to the peace of the community, a form of nuisance, rather than offering specific details concerning the actual behaviour of individual women.

In Chester too, both women and men were named as common keepers of brothels, each being fined different amounts from 40d to 6s 8d.[128] Agnes Felenes was ordered to pay this higher sum in 1510 for keeping in her house 'persons of bad conduct committing adultery'.[129] In February 1505, Henry Chalner was fined 3s 4d for keeping in his house 'diverse persons of bad conduct, namely in keeping a common brothel'.[130] A few years later in 1509, Giles Romour, Elena Stephanson, Geoffrey Lloid drover, Agnes Pantre and Alice Mon' were all fined 6s 8d for keeping common brothels.[131] Agnes Robynson and Joan Mascy were also fined for keeping brothels in their houses and allowing diverse ill-conducted persons to frequent their homes.[132] These individuals cropped up frequently in the presentments of the Chester sheriffs for various misdeeds, demonstrating how running a brothel was also associated with other forms of rule-breaking and disorder. In March 1510, Elizabeth Rosengreve was fined 6s 8d for constantly keeping a brothel as well as selling bread and ale while not in the franchise of the city.[133] Other women (and some men) were fined for adultery, though these fines were presented individually, not as couples. These presentments represent further policing of the sexual activity of both women and men, even if this did not specifically concern the sale of sex.[134] Women could be imprisoned while seeking sureties for their conduct, demonstrating the threat that their sexual activity was perceived to pose. For women engaging in prostitution and the individuals charged with running brothels, these presentments constituted a comment on their moral character, which was often intensified through their involvement in other immoral and illegal activities, and the resulting detriment that this conduct had on the wider urban community.

For some women, the penalty for prostitution was more severe. In 1366, Isabella Bolle of Winchester was attached to respond to the presentment that she was a 'common wife' and held a brothel in the city.

Though she disputed the allegation, the city's 12 jurors reported that she was indeed guilty, and the mayor and court adjudged that Isabella should no longer live within the city of Winchester, and that she would be punished by the pillory if she did so.[135] This expulsion, probably requiring that she reside outside the city walls, was a common means of dealing with prostitution across many medieval towns and cities.[136] The reference to corporal punishment was rare, however, as the vast majority of punishments for sexual and other offences in these courts were monetary. This further suggests that those subjected to monetary fines were in fact part of a system of regulation, not dissimilar to other commercial regulation, rather than simply a system of punishment and prohibition.

Prostitution and illicit sex were not the only issues of morality that urban governments sought to police, though they may have been the most obvious. Though many of these offences took place within individuals' homes, they were not 'private' activities but instead deemed to be harmful to the community of the town in general. One such concern was the playing of unlawful games, prohibited by various statutes across the late medieval period. A 1388 act required all servants and labourers to cease from playing football, tennis and other games, and instead to practise with bows and arrows on Sundays. The military focus of this act demonstrates that it was concerned with the activities of men. A century later, in 1477, games were prohibited for all, and harsh penalties were also set out for those allowing games to be played inside their houses. However, 20 years later, legislation reverted to having a narrower focus, banning games for servants, apprentices and labourers.[137] This regulation is certainly evident among the urban records, though the penalties consisted of varying monetary fines rather than the imprisonment and heavy fines that were set out in the various statutes. Karen Jones found that prosecutions for unlawful games fluctuated throughout the period 1460–1560, and bore only limited relation to statutory prohibitions against game-playing.[138] Playing unlawful games was a 'male' offence, representing the 'male culture' of young men who gathered in alehouses and inns, and one in which women were not involved.[139] Of 216 presentments for illegal gaming, Jones found only 3 women accused of permitting games on their premises, and none who actually played themselves.

Similar patterns are found among the records studied here. In Winchester, only men were presented for playing games, some of whom were said to have played for money, as a form of gambling.[140] The Chester sheriff's books also list men presented for playing unlawful games, gambling and hosting gamblers in their homes, at the start of the sixteenth century. In 1504, Thomas Fenton and John Fenton, both butchers, were called common gamblers and each fined 2s, while Richard Legh and John Wrone, wrights, were termed 'common receivers of diverse persons into their houses, namely common gamblers'. Legh was fined 12d while Wrone was fined 3s.[141] The common occupations of these two pairs of men suggest that occupational ties provided men with the networks through which to engage in games and gambling. One woman, Elena Stevenson, was also said to keep servants playing at unlawful games by night and day, and was fined 3s 4d.[142] In Nottingham, the playing of games such as tennis and quoits led numerous men to be punished.[143] Many others were said to keep disorders in their houses at night, receiving servants who had stolen goods of their masters to play unlawful games.[144] Gambling and the playing of games was therefore a particularly male form of misrule and disorder, which represented a disruption to the expected roles for men of work of good household governance. Furthermore, these gaming and gambling networks and groups were male, with activities taking place illicitly within individuals' homes, spaces of male householder authority, to the exclusion of women. Rather than ensuring the good conduct of the members of their household, these men were inviting others in to engage in prohibited activities. And if, as seems to have often been the case, playing games also involved gambling, this may have been something from which women were excluded due to their limited access to cash with which to gamble. These factors combined to make gaming a concern that centred on the activities of men, while the policing of women's moral conduct, in contrast, related to the disruption caused by their sexual activity and their public voices.

Conclusion

As the survey of various forms of violence and misbehaviour in this chapter has shown, no type of disorder was uniquely male or female. Men and women generally committed the same types of offence, having the capacity to harm others and the urban community more widely through their unlawful and immoral behaviour, and they were punished accordingly. Punishment was linked to the nature and severity of the offence, rather than the identity of the offender. Nevertheless, the records of urban policing reveal how officials constructed images of disorderly behaviour and sought to control and punish this in ways which conformed to stereotypes of disorderly women who were violent and disruptive and were labelled as scolds and prostitutes. This meant that certain offences were more 'female' than others, most notably scolding as a form of harmful speech that came largely from the mouths of women.

Women's involvement in prostitution was also judged to be particularly undesirable and in need of regulation, but this could also impact upon men who orchestrated the sale of sex within brothels. But women also had the power to harm in other ways, including through their bodies and the violent use of weapons, and they were punished for doing so.

Urban communities and officials did not seek to obscure women's misdemeanours. Nor were married women covered or protected by their marital status: they also broke the rules and were reported independently when they did so. While assumed ideas about gender and violence might lead us to expect that women did not act out violence or harm others, especially men, or that officials paid less attention to this than to the violence of men, the records show that the preservation of order was more important than enforcing gender roles or ideologies. Garthine Walker has discredited many of these ideas in the context of early modern law and order, but the evidence presented in this chapter demonstrates that these stereotypes about medieval women and misbehaviour must also be re-examined.[145] When set alongside the evidence of trespass pleas, we see that both individuals and officials perceived of women's misbehaviour often in similar terms to men's, and sought to punish this as part of their overarching attempts to preserve the social order and enforce proper rules of behaviour.

Notes

1 Barbara Hanawalt, 'Violent death in fourteenth- and early fifteenth-century England', *Comparative Studies in Society and History*, 18 (1976), 317. See also Barbara Hanawalt and David Wallace (eds), *Medieval Crime and Social Control* (Minneapolis: University of Minnesota Press, 1999), p. ix.

2 Andrew Finch, 'The nature of violence in the middle ages: an alternative perspective', *Historical Research*, 70 (1997), 266.

3 Derek Keene, *Survey of Medieval Winchester*, vol. 1 (Oxford: Clarendon Press, 1985), p. 395.

4 Philippa C. Maddern, *Violence and Social Order: East Anglia 1422–1442* (Oxford: Clarendon Press, 1992), p. 9; Barbara Hanawalt, *Crime and Conflict in English Communities, 1300–1348* (Cambridge, MA: Harvard University Press, 1979), pp. 13–17. See also Sara M. Butler, *The Language of Abuse: Marital Violence in Later Medieval England* (Leiden: Brill, 2007), p. 6.

5 Maryanne Kowaleski, 'An introduction to town courts in medieval England', in Richard Goddard and Teresa Phipps (eds), *Town Courts and Urban Society in Late Medieval England* (Woodbridge: Boydell and Brewer, 2019), 29–32; Marjorie Keniston McIntosh, *Controlling Misbehavior in England, 1370–1600* (Cambridge: Cambridge University Press, 1998), pp. 35–37.

6 McIntosh, *Controlling Misbehavior*, pp. 36–37.

7 Hanawalt, *Crime and Conflict*, p. 54.
8 There is no overlap between the complete Mayor's Court roll of 1395-6 and the trespasses pursued in the borough court in the same year, suggesting that these were separate actions and represented different instances of misbehaviour.
9 Andrew Finch, 'Women and violence in the later middle ages: the evidence of the officiality of Cerisy', *Continuity and Change*, 7 (1992), 26; Elizabeth Ewan, 'Disorderly damsels? Women and interpersonal violence in pre-reformation Scotland', *Scottish Historical Review*, 89 (2010), 165.
10 For example, Barbara Hanawalt has found that the vast majority of homicides were committed by men: 'Violent death', 305. See also Karen Jones, *Gender and Petty Crime in Late Medieval England: The Local Courts in Kent, 1460-1560* (Woodbridge: Boydell and Brewer, 2006), pp. 63-64; Finch, 'Women and violence', 29.
11 Jones, *Gender and Petty Crime*, pp. 64-65.
12 Women appeared more often as plaintiffs than defendants in violence cases in Ruthin 1312-21. Matthew Frank Stevens, *Urban Assimilation in Post-Conquest Wales: Ethnicity, Gender and Economy in Ruthin, 1282-1350* (Cardiff: University of Wales Press, 2010), p. 132; Finch 'Women and violence', 27.
13 Helen Jewell, 'Women at the courts of the manor of Wakefield, 1348-1350', *Northern History*, 26 (1990), 64.
14 See William Hudson (ed.), *Leet Jurisdiction in the City of Norwich during the XIIIth and XIVth Centuries* (London: Quaritch, 1892).
15 HRO W/D1/61 rot. 10.
16 HRO W/D1/61 rot. 10.
17 NA CA3942 rot. 2.
18 NA CA3944 rot. 3d.
19 NA CA3942 rots 2, 2d.
20 HRO W/D1/13, rot. 3d.
21 HRO W/D1/37, rot. 9d.
22 HRO W/D1/37, rot. 5.
23 Lizabeth Johnson has similarly identified the different ways in which marital identity informed women's legal actions in Wales, and the joint accountability of husbands. Criminal presentments for assaults and the breaking of the king's peace saw married women prosecuted independently of their husbands, and the same was true of violent offences within urban jurisdictions. Lizabeth Johnson, 'Married women, crime and the courts in late medieval Wales', in Cordelia Beattie and Matthew Frank Stevens (eds), *Married Women and the Law in Premodern Northwest Europe* (Woodbridge: Boydell and Brewer, 2013), pp. 77-78, 81-82.
24 HRO W/D1/13, rot. 3d.
25 HRO W/D1/13, rot. 3.
26 'Robertus Ostiler et Willelmus Boteler butcher decenarii de Midilpament presentant unam affraiam sine sanguine super Thomam Benton berbour versus Hugonem Wymondeslawe pro eo quod predictus Thomas in Communi Aula cepit predictum Hugonem cum pectore suo cum una manu et in alia manu cepit cultellum suum proprium tractatum et dicebat ei verba malitosia contra pacem Domini Regis unde predictus Hugo fuerat indesperatus vitae suae unde predictus Thomas attachiatus est etc. Et inde idem Thomas venit et ponit se in gratia majores et solvit xii d.' NA CA3942 rot.

2d; W.H. Stevenson, *Records of the Borough of Nottingham*, vol. 1 (London: Quaritch, 1882), pp. 306-307.

27 'Robertus Ostiler et Willelmus Boteler butcher decenarii de Midilpament presentant unam affraiam sine sanguine super Johannam uxorem Hugonis Wymondeslawe versus Thomam Benton berbour pro eo quod predicta Johanna venit in Communem Aulam et ibi locuta fuerunt [sic] verba malitiosa predicto Thomae et ibi eum alapizavit contra pacem Domini Regis etc. unde attachiatus est etc. Et inde eadem [sic] Thomas venit et ponit se in gratia majores et solvit xii d.' NA CA3942 rot. 2d; Stevenson, *Nottingham*, vol. 1, pp. 306-307. The reference to face-slapping comes from the use of '*alapizavit*' which may be one of a few rare uses of this term.

28 Ewan, 'Women and interpersonal violence', 161.
29 HRO W/D1/13 rot. 10d.
30 Butler, *Marital Violence*, p. 31.
31 Butler, *Marital Violence*, pp. 33-49 for discussion of the limits of castigation in church and secular law.
32 Butler, *Marital Violence*, p. 70.
33 Butler, *Marital Violence*, pp. 81, 83, 86.
34 NA CA3942 rot. 2.
35 NA CA3942 rot. 2.
36 NA CA3944 rot. 3.
37 HRO W/D1/37 rot. 9d; HRO W/D1/13 rot. 1.
38 NA CA3943 rot. 3.
39 NA CA3942 rots 2, 2d.
40 NA CA3942 rot. 2.
41 NA CA3942 rot. 2.
42 HRO W/D1/60 rot. 4d.
43 Hanawalt, 'Violent death', 310-311.
44 HRO W/D1/60 rot. 5d.
45 Sara M. Butler, *Forensic Medicine and Death Investigation in Medieval England* (London: Routledge, 2014), p. 136.
46 NA CA3942 rot. 2.
47 Jewell, 'Women at the courts of the manor of Wakefield', 64.
48 NA CA3942 rot. 2.
49 NA CA3942 rot. 2d.
50 Janka Rodziewicz, 'Women and the hue and cry in late fourteenth-century Great Yarmouth', in Bronach Kane and Fiona Williamson (eds), *Women, Agency and the Law, 1300-1700* (London: Pickering and Chatto, 2013), p. 93.
51 Elizabeth Ewan, 'Impatient Griseldas: women and the perpetration of violence in sixteenth-century Glasgow', *Florilegium*, 28 (2011), 164; Finch, 'The nature of violence', 266; Andrew Finch, 'Women and violence in the later middle ages: the evidence of the officiality of Cerisy', *Continuity and Change*, 7 (1992), 25.
52 Garthine Walker, *Crime, Gender and Social Order in Early Modern England* (Cambridge: Cambridge University Press, 2003), pp. 165-167.
53 Jones, *Gender and Petty Crime*, p. 54.
54 HRO W/D1/61 rot. 10.
55 CALS ZS/B5d f.61v.

56 *Liber Albus: The White Book of the City of London*, ed. H.T. Riley (London, 1861), pp. 44–45, quoted in Samantha Sagui, 'The hue and cry in medieval English towns', *Historical Research*, 87 (2014), 181.
57 Sandy Bardsley, *Venomous Tongues: Speech and Gender in Late Medieval England* (Philadelphia: University of Pennsylvania Press, 2006), p. 38. See also Miriam Müller, 'Social control and the hue and cry in two fourteenth century villages', *Journal of Medieval History*, 31 (2005), 33; Rodziewicz, 'Women and the hue and cry', pp. 87–97.
58 Sagui, 'Hue and cry', 180.
59 Sagui, 'Hue and cry', 183–184.
60 Anne Reiber DeWindt and Edwin Brezette DeWindt, *Ramsey: The Lives of an English Fenland Town, 1200–1600* (Washington, DC: Catholic University of America Press, 2006), p. 75.
61 Rodziewicz, 'Women and the hue and cry', p. 88.
62 Sagui, 'Hue and cry', 192.
63 Sagui, 'Hue and cry', 187.
64 In 1299–1300, 10 women and 32 men unjustly raised the hue; 14 unjust hues were raised against women in the same year, while 28 unjust hues were raised against men.
65 Rodziewicz, 'Women and the hue and cry', p. 93.
66 Sagui, 'Hue and cry', 186.
67 HRO W/D1/60 rot. 4d, 5d, 6d.
68 Bardsley, *Venomous Tongues*, pp. 38–40.
69 Bardsley, *Venomous Tongues*, p. 77.
70 HRO W/D1/3 rot. 1d. '*Walterus le Roppere et Cristina uxor eius pro hutesis preceptum est attachiatus*'.
71 This also happened in Great Yarmouth: see Rodziewicz, 'Women and the hue and cry', pp. 92–93.
72 HRO W/D1/3 rot. 3d.
73 HRO W/D1/3 rot. 2d.
74 HRO W/D1/45 rot. 2d.
75 HRO W/D1/3 rots 2, 3d, 9.
76 HRO W/D1/60 rot. 6d.
77 HRO W/D1/37 rot. 2.
78 HRO W/D1/3 rots 5, 10.
79 HRO W/D1/60 rot. 4d.
80 HRO W/D1/60 rot. 5d.
81 HRO W/D1/3 rot. 2d.
82 HRO W/D1/3 rot. 9.
83 HRO W/D1/13 rot. 10d.
84 Butler, *Marital Violence*, pp. 82–83.
85 NA CA3942 rot. 2d.
86 NA CA3942 rot. 2.
87 NA CA3944 rots 3, 3d.
88 Bardsley, *Venomous Tongues*, p. 6. Terms for female scolds included *litigatrix*, *objurgatrix*, *garulatrix*, *rixatrix*, the latter two being the most frequently used in Winchester.

89 Bardsley, *Venomous Tongues*, p. 109. Bardsley goes into more depth on this subject in chapter 5: 'Communities and scolding' and chapter 6: 'Who was a scold?', pp. 106–140.
90 Bardsley, *Venomous Tongues*, p. 85. See also McIntosh, *Controlling Misbehaviour*, pp. 58–65.
91 NA CA3942 rot. 2d.
92 NA CA3492 rot. 2.
93 NA CA3943 rot. 3.
94 HRO W/D1/27 rots 1d, 7d, 8.
95 W/D1/60 rots 15d, 16d.
96 NA CA4478 pp. 12–13.
97 NA CA3944 rot. 3.
98 Stevenson translates both '*communes objurgatur*' and '*communis litigator*' as referring to scolding. See *Nottingham*, vols 1–2. See also Sandy Bardsley, 'Sin, speech and scolding in late medieval England', in Thelma Fenster and Daniel Lord Smail (eds), *Fama: The Politics of Talk and Reputation in Medieval Europe* (Ithaca: Cornell University Press, 2003), p. 159.
99 NA CA4478 p. 12.
100 HRO W/D1/61.
101 HRO W/D1/13 rot. 8. Synnota is described as '*communia garulatrix et perturbatrix pacis cum verbis maliciosis inter vicinos suos*' while the account of her husband's behaviour only noted the type of words spoken: '*est culpabilis de verbis maliciosis dictis Ricardo Wamberghe, Radulof Foude, Waltero le Bolour et Ricardo Curry collectoribus ...*'.
102 Bardsley, *Venomous Tongues*, pp. 100–102.
103 Karen Jones and Michael Zell, 'Bad conversation? Gender and social control in a Kentish borough, c.1450–c.1570', *Continuity and Change*, 13 (1998), 22–23.
104 Walker, *Crime, Gender and Social Order*, p. 105.
105 Bardsley, *Venomous Tongues*, p. 76.
106 NA CA3942 rot. 2d.
107 NA CA3943 rot. 3.
108 Bardsley, *Venomous Tongues*, p. 139.
109 Walker, *Crime, Gender and Social Order*, p. 101.
110 NA CA3944 rot. 3.
111 HRO W/D1/61 rot. 4, 7.
112 HRO W/D1/61 rot. 10.
113 HRO W/D1/60 rots 17d, 18.
114 John Hertyng v Robert Pynne and Alice his wife. HRO W/D1/60 rot. 18d.
115 HRO W/D1/13, rot. 10. '*Item predicti jurati presentant quod Isabella Bolle Alicia Pykot Alicia Kembestre et Isabella Scheppestre non sunt abiles ad comorandum in Civitate Wyntonia eo quod ipsi [sic] tenant communiam bordel et receptant persbiteri [sic] et alii homines non boni [sic] fame et quod ipsi [sic] sunt communes garulatrices ideo preceptum est serviente attachiare predictos [sic] Isabellam Aliciam Aliciam Kembestre et Isabella Scheppestret citra proximam etc.*'
116 HRO W/D1/60 rot. 19.
117 CALS ZSB/5a.

118 McIntosh, *Controlling Misbehavior*, pp. 69-70.
119 Ruth Karras, 'The regulation of brothels in later medieval England', *Signs*, 14 (1989), 407; P.J.P. Goldberg, *Women, Work and Life Cycle in a Medieval Economy: Women in York and Yorkshire c.1300-1520* (Oxford: Clarendon Press, 1992), pp. 150-151.
120 McIntosh, *Controlling Misbehavior*, pp. 69-70.
121 Of the Canterbury women described as harlots, 26 of 56 were married, while 4 inmates of Sandwich's 'Galley' brothel were married. Jones, *Gender and Petty Crime*, pp. 161, 163.
122 HRO W/D1/3 rot. 5.
123 HRO W/D1/60 rot. 15.
124 Isabella Bolle, Alice Pykot, Alice Kembestre and Isabella Scheppestre. HRO W/D1/13 rot. 10.
125 HRO W/D1/60 rot. 15.
126 W/D1/61 rot. 4, 7.
127 HRO W/D1/60 rot. 14, 15.
128 Giles Romour, Elena Stephanson, Geoffrey Lloid, Agnes Pantre and Alice Mon' were all fined 6s 8d for keeping brothels in 1508. Alice Robynson was fined 40d for keeping a brothel in her house. Joan Mascy and Marion del Cornell were reported to run brothels, but were fined for offences against the assizes. CALS ZSB/5d.
129 CALS ZSB/5e.
130 CALS ZS/B/5 b f. 34v.
131 CALS ZS/B/5 d f. 61v.
132 CALS ZS/B/5 d f. 63v.
133 CALS ZS/B/5 e f. 85.
134 For example, Agnes [no surname], Katherine Irisshe, Agnes Haslyngton, Petronilla Tuder, Agnes Kanner, Margaret Fissher and Thomas Eccles. CASL ZS/B/5 e f. 92v.
135 HRO W/D1/13 rot. 10d.
136 Richard Holt and Nigel Baker, 'Towards a geography of sexual encounter: prostitution in English medieval towns', in Lynne Bevan (ed.), *Indecent Exposure: Sexuality, Society and the Archaeological Record* (Glasgow: Cruithne Press, 2001), p. 205; Jones, *Gender and Petty Crime*, pp. 164-165.
137 McIntosh, *Controlling Misbehavior*, pp. 98-99.
138 Jones, *Gender and Petty Crime*, p. 186.
139 Jones, *Gender and Petty Crime*, p. 187.
140 Three men in the 1432-3 sample: HRO W/D1/60 rot. 19.
141 CALS ZS/B/5 b f. 35.
142 CALS ZS/B/5 g f. 138v.
143 For example, John Mold, Richard Colman, Thomas Tall, William Mall, William Conington, John Brierly, John Watson and John Colman. Stevenson, *Nottingham*, vol. 2, p. 265.
144 Stevenson, *Nottingham*, vol. 2, p. 331.
145 Walker, *Crime, Gender and Social Order*.

Conclusion

This study has examined the wide-ranging means by which women engaged with and were defined by the legal system within their local urban community. In doing so, it has offered glimpses and fragments of the lives of hundreds of ordinary women who lived in different English towns through the details that were recorded within the court rolls, revealing individuals, actions and relationships that would otherwise go undocumented. The comparative nature of this study, drawing on evidence from multiple English towns and a wide range of legal disputes and offences, enhances our understanding of urban women's engagement with the law at the local level, revealing the multiple reasons for which they were drawn into contact with the law throughout the course of their everyday lives. Women were always a minority among litigants and individuals who came under the purview of local justice, but this does not mean that their legal experiences were insignificant or should be dismissed as exceptional. Some of the instances in which we have found these women may have been defining moments of their lives or points of crisis, but most of the cases and actions included here were more quotidian, representing the inordinate negotiations that made up everyday life and work. The negotiation of justice was therefore a normal part of urban life. Women and men living within England's hundreds of medieval towns actively used their local courts to manage their interpersonal relationships, enforce business obligations and seek restitution for attacks that brought harm to their persons, property or honour. They were also subject to the demands and regulations that the law imposed upon them. Women who were not married litigated independently, without need for a male guardian, suing others and being sued for a wide range of offences involving other women and men, indicating their integration within urban society and its legal system. Married women exercised less independent legal agency, though they did often answer the complaints of their peers, neighbours and officials, or bring complaints of their own to court, though the extent to which they did so varied according to different types of plea, as well as across time and place.

Much of what has been discussed here represents the idiosyncratic, messy nature of everyday life and so does not fit into neat patterns, but there are three key points that cut across the many hundreds of varied individuals, disputes and offences that have provided the material for this study, and it is these three findings that this conclusion addresses. First, the richness of these sources for examining women's legal lives, and enriching our understanding of urban justice in general, through the telling of stories that would not otherwise be told. This is perhaps the most significant issue for the ongoing project of recovering and writing women's history. Second, the fact that much of women's legal action was not defined primarily or solely by gender, as they were involved in largely the same types of legal action and processes as their male relatives and neighbours. Finally, and perhaps most importantly, this study has highlighted that the way that women litigated was unique to each woman and circumstance and was influenced by a number of intersecting variables: the type of plea or offence, a woman's marital status, and the customs and practices of the town in which she lived. These second and third conclusions join together to demonstrate that there was, therefore, no singular type of urban woman litigant, and no definitive legal experience for urban women.

Illuminating women's legal lives

By foregrounding the active nature of women's experiences of and engagement with the law – not just their subjection to it – this study has populated the history of medieval borough courts with the stories and identities of those who used them. As a result, it has also enhanced and added colour to our understanding of the workings of medieval town courts, and the nature of the urban societies that they governed over. The focus on the legal actions of urban women has revealed aspects of women's lives and experiences that we would not otherwise know about. It is these stories that have been pieced together to provide a new, detailed, often complex picture of women's engagement with the law within the three English towns that lie at the heart of this study: Nottingham, Chester and Winchester. Through the court rolls, we can access details of women's work and business connections, what they bought and sold and from whom, and what action was taken when obligations and agreements were not met. We find women operating at various levels within the urban economy, through debt pleas that record transactions of a few pence for the purchase of household necessities such as bread or milk, and others that indicate individual business activities – like those of Nottingham's Agnes Halum – or involvement in higher value, mercantile trade, such as that of William and Alice de Ellehale of Chester.[1] Women actively used their local courts to complain about other women and men who owed them money or goods, and they were also subject to the complaints of others with whom they had done business. Local records documenting the enforcement of trading regulations also demonstrate that women were expected to adhere to rules concerning quality, prices, weights and measures, as well as the proper times, places and manner in which to buy and sell at local markets, and they were penalised when they failed to do so. Some aspects of married women's work were obscured through patriarchal traditions in the enforcement of these regulations, for instance when women's brewing was attributed to their husbands, but other aspects of their marketing away from the home and involvement in the victualling trades saw women of all marital statuses being subject to legal regulation. This was particularly true of women whose commercial dealing undermined the status of the local market, such as Elizabeth Fissher of Nottingham who was accused of inflating prices by taking malt from Nottingham to sell in Derby.[2]

While women's work is relatively well established within the historiography of medieval women, much less is known about women's interpersonal relationships and particularly the way that relationship breakdown could lead to legal action. This is despite the wealth of information contained within trespass pleas that illuminate how a wide range of misbehaviours played out within urban communities. Detailed examination of women's roles within these pleas has identified the wide range of wrongdoing that women experienced and acted out themselves, revealing interpersonal disputes, clashes between neighbours or illegal behaviour such as theft and damage to property. Without these records, we would not know about incidents like that between Johanna Burbache of Winchester and the chaplain William Crowk, who broke into her house, assaulted her and stole her money.[3] Women, like men, were the perpetrators of violence and misbehaviour, including women such as Margaret, wife of John Nottingham, who was found guilty of breaking Joan Brailsford's leg.[4] They also defamed other members of the community, attacked property and stole personal and household items, sometimes using weapons to help carry out their attacks. The evidence contained within these pleas opens up the personal, human aspects of medieval women's lives, their identities and their deeds, and the legal options for redress that were available within communities.

The court records also reveal women's ties of marriage and family, through instances where family members acted together in seeking dispute resolution, or where they were accused of illegal activity together. Through these pleas we are able to reconstruct family networks and relationships, including the ties or disputes that could develop between families, such as the families of Serlo of Thorpe and Henry le Meyreman of Nottingham, who accused each other of various trespasses.[5] Women acted as co-litigants with their husbands, but also with their siblings, parents and children. We occasionally glimpse other household ties, such as those between servants and employers – sometimes acting in support of one another, and at other times in moments of discord, such as the failure to pay wages or fulfil the terms of service. All of these details reveal otherwise unknown aspects of urban women's lives, as well as the extent to which the law permeated everyday life.

But while these records are invaluable for the light they shed on ordinary urban lives, particularly those of the women who are so often hidden from history, they also bring with them various questions and unknown factors. We often cannot recover the outcomes of many suits, and even when we do, the formulaic nature of the records leaves many unanswered questions about why a dispute came to a particular conclusion. We will never know if or why Robert, Hawise and/or Alice de Spondon really did call Margery Dod a whore in Nottingham's market place.[6] We do not know what was said when a complaint was brought to court, how individual women were treated by officials and other litigants, or what prejudices and barriers they faced in accessing justice. Some of these barriers are of course implied through the presence or lack of certain individuals or groups in the court record, such as the fact that married women did not (typically) bring their complaints independently of their husbands, but there may have existed other more subtle barriers to women's litigation that simply cannot be recovered. Did they feel confident in bringing their complaints to court, or were some women intimidated or discouraged by the all-male patriarchal legal system that they faced? And for all our attempts to pin down and classify the identities and status of women according to their marital or life cycle status, much of this must inevitably be based on guesses or assumptions. While the historiography of medieval women has repeatedly constructed female status around the classification of women according to their marital status, this was not a model that was consistently applied in the creation of town court records, where large numbers of women were recorded in the court rolls by just their full names. In most instances this probably reflected their unmarried status, but this system of naming reveals nothing about the age or ever-married status of women. Furthermore, we have seen that there were certainly some married women who were documented with no reference to their husband and so on first examination appear to be single. The piecing together of Nottingham's Agnes Halum's legal 'career' and identity exemplifies this. This presents problems in assessing the legal actions of women across the life cycle, as we simply do not know the life cycle stage of many women. But the fact that these details were so frequently undocumented is also telling of contemporary attitudes, suggesting that the specific details of a woman's marital or life cycle status were often irrelevant for the workings and documentation of these local courts. These details were recorded in relation to cases where they were specifically pertinent, such as debt suits relating to a widow's role as executor, or the youth of young women defined as their father's daughters. But in many other cases, these details of identity were simply not necessary.

The status of women in urban justice

The stories and disputes captured in the court records have, throughout the various chapters of this book, shed new light on the status of women within the justice systems that governed their towns. We have seen how they brought debt complaints when commercial obligations were not met, and how they complained when they were harmed by the actions of others. We have also seen how women were held to account for their actions by other members of their communities and by urban officials, through their appearances as defendants. But the wide scope of individuals, legal actions, places and chronology that this study encompasses has not provided a neat or well-ordered model of women's legal roles and actions within urban jurisdictions. Furthermore, the majority of women's legal experiences and actions were not specifically gendered female; their legal actions were not defined solely or primarily by their sex. The actions, pleas and presentments in which they featured were largely comparable to those of men, and were generally dealt with in the same way by the courts. Women's (and men's) experiences as litigants were defined by many factors: the nature of the plea they were involved in, their role as plaintiff or defendant, the decisions and personality of the opposing party, their status and connections within the urban community, as well as their sex and marital status.

Both sexes were involved in commercial networks of credit and debt that sometimes led to pleas of debt and detinue, though those in which women were involved frequently related to typical areas of women's work that were often marginal, unspecialised and low-status, or activities located in the home, such as brewing. There were no clear gender markers in the nature of women's misbehaviour aside from the fact that they were less frequently involved in litigation relating to trespass, but when they were, it was for the full range of offences. Women were not passive victims of violence or misbehaviour, and they regularly used their local courts to complain when they had been wronged, including when they were victims of physical assault. Their neighbours took advantage of the local justice system by publicly complaining about the violent or illegal behaviour of women too, including their male victims. Women's behaviour was not just subject to the complaints of their neighbours and peers, but to the policing and punishment meted out by local juries and officials too. It is in these presentments that there appears more of a gendered division in women's and men's misbehaviour: the majority of individuals punished for 'bad speech' were women, demonstrating that their disruptive speech was construed and punished as particularly damaging to the peace of the community. But these records, along with those recounting trespass pleas, also demonstrate that women were not cloistered or hidden away in a private, domestic world, but were living public lives in the streets and market places of their towns, which sometimes brought them into conflict with others. The nature and extent of women's legal actions were, nevertheless, underpinned by gendered structures under which, for example, women as a group were of lower economic status than men, and often experienced limits on their ability to litigate independently. The gendering of women's legal actions and experiences thus lay in the numbers of litigants and offenders who came before the courts, which represented their differing opportunities and need to engage in legal action, rather than in its inherent nature. But by looking beyond the numbers and statistical patterns for women's legal actions, this study has been able to construct a more nuanced picture that situates women's legal engagement within the broader system of urban justice and highlights the many continuities between the actions of women and men, rather than depicting women as exceptional litigants.

While the lack of gendered patterns in the nature of litigation and law enforcement means that there were no notably 'female' types of litigation, nor did urban women inhabit a singular female legal identity, status or experience. There was, therefore, no essence of 'the female litigant' within late medieval towns. The way in which a woman engaged with the law depended upon a number of variables: the nature of the case or issue in question, her marital status and the customs and practices of the court(s) in the town in which she lived, which evolved over time. These factors intersected in unique ways to produce the legal identities and experiences of the hundreds of ordinary women who have featured in this book. It is here that the advantages of a comparative, wide-reaching study of women's legal action in a range of towns and legal contexts, based on the records of legal practice, rather than theory or ideals, come to the fore.

Histories of women and the law in medieval and early modern periods once defined women's legal status in relatively straightforward terms, usually by listing the legal actions that women could not take part in with a small number of exceptions, an approach that essentialised women as one category – or perhaps two: married and not married – and perceived of women as an opposite category to men, defined by their disabilities. However, the findings of this study situate it within a growing body of scholarship that reveals differences in women's legal statuses and their ability to litigate, thereby breaking down the category of women in relation to their legal status. By examining women's engagement with the law in a range of contexts and forms, and comparing this across different courts and places, it has been possible here to create a more rounded picture of women's 'legal lives' than previous studies that have focused on one type of litigation or legal action. This wide scope has resulted in the creation of a composite image of women's legal status that more accurately represents the nuances of individual experience and the variables that helped to define these experiences.

The most significant force in determining a woman's legal actions was the nature of her marital status. This is something that has been acknowledged in numerous other studies, but the specific and varying way in which this was manifested in women's different legal actions has not previously been explored or problematised. The theme of coverture has been a dominant one throughout this study, reflecting both its historiographical prominence and the undeniable role that marriage played in defining if and how women engaged with local justice and acted out their legal status. Because marriage was such a common experience for adult women, the differing levels of wives' participation in legal action is essential to the understanding of broader patterns in women's legal action. While there has been something of a gradual evolution in the historiography to recognise the capabilities that married women could exercise despite the supposed limits of their 'covered' status, the evidence examined here allows us to go further in assessing and understanding the influence of coverture across multiple jurisdictions and legal situations, highlighting the ambiguous and flexible nature of coverture as it was applied in everyday legal practice.

Despite sitting outside the formal limits of the common law, urban jurisdictions clearly displayed the force and influence of coverture. Married women did not litigate (as either plaintiffs or defendants) independently of their husbands (though a handful of exceptions to this rule have been identified), and they were often defined and identified by their status as 'wife of' their husband. Yet each town and its court(s) interpreted and applied the limits of coverture in unique ways when it came to the litigation and legal presentment of married women, so that coverture was a fluid and malleable concept, rather than a monolithic force that was constantly and consistently invoked. As Shennan Hutton has argued for Ghent, unwritten customary law was intrinsically mutable, allowing it to be interpreted in different ways at different times, and though the customary law of English towns drew on the more formal doctrines of the common law, we nevertheless see this mutability in action across the late medieval period.[7] While coverture was not a fiction, as it certainly impacted upon married women's experiences of the law, it did so in markedly different ways across different legal contexts. This is something that has been alluded to in other discussions of coverture, particularly in the work of Tim Stretton and Krista Kesselring, but this study has provided considerable tangible evidence for this in practice.[8]

By paying attention to the instances where spouses pleaded together, as well as the situations in which wives did not or could not appear in court, we are able to gain an enhanced understanding of the practical implications of coverture. There have been many components to this analysis throughout this study. First, the comparison of wives' involvement in the two main types of civil plea – debt and trespass – reveals significant differences in their ability to bring their complaints and in the ways that they were held accountable via the pleas of others. Furthermore, the application of coverture in relation to these different forms of plea was specific to the jurisdiction, customs and legal practice of individual towns. In Winchester, for example, married women rarely acted alongside their husbands in debt suits, but they were able to litigate jointly in relation to trespasses, both as complainants and when they themselves were accused as perpetrators. The same general rule was found in the Chester records from the mid-fourteenth century onwards. In both towns, this meant that wives were unable to bring or answer complaints in relation to commercial agreements, presumably because it was not recognised that they possessed any capital of their own and were thus always trading on behalf of their husbands (apart from the small number of Chester *femme sole* women). However, there was a legal recognition of married women's interpersonal (mis)behaviour which meant that they were able to use the law to negotiate instances of violence, theft or defamation. These actions and interactions could not so easily be rendered to their husband, and thus required married women to represent themselves personally in court, yet always with the support of their husbands. While there were deviations from these general patterns, this clear difference in wives' status in economic and interpersonal pleas demonstrates that married women's legal actions could hinge upon the specific nature of a complaint, not just general proscriptions that were tied solely to their marital status. It is therefore not sufficient to claim that married women were denied a legal status and prevented from legal action due to coverture, as their 'covered' status manifested itself in specific ways in different situations.

In addition, the comparison of multiple towns in this study has also made it clear that we cannot conceptualise urban women's legal experiences on a 'national' scale, but instead need to pay attention to the variations in custom and practice that existed at the local level. The pattern described above for Winchester and Chester is not applicable to Nottingham. Here, the joint litigation of spouses was common in both debt *and* trespass pleas. In fact, married women's joint pleas with their husbands accounted for a significant proportion of all women's litigation, and spanned a broad range of actions, interactions and obligations. While Nottingham's married women did not (typically) litigate independently, the borough court offered them greater possibilities to represent themselves and their disputes as both plaintiffs and defendants than the other courts included in this study. This included pleas arising from wives' work and trade. Married women like Isabella, wife of Laurence Tyryngton, and Magota, wife of Richard Grantham, did not become legally invisible upon marriage, but were able to use the court alongside their husbands to negotiate and settle disputes that probably arose from the two wives' roles in the production and sale of ale.[9] This practice also allowed married women to take an active part in the resolution of violent interpersonal disputes that they were part of, such as Agnes, wife of Robert Carter, and Joan, wife of Hugh Kynder, who came to court with their husbands when Joan was accused of assaulting Agnes.[10] This less restrictive version of coverture allowed married women to take a more active role in the settlement of a wide range of disputes, despite the theoretical limitations of their marital status.

The position of Nottingham women should not, however, be overemphasised as some sort of 'golden' age or jurisdiction. While they may not have been rendered legally invisible upon marriage, married women's participation in local justice was still dependent on the cooperation of their husbands. Instead, the situation at Nottingham appears to more accurately reflect the nature of the marital partnership and the way in which this extended from the household economy into the negotiation of justice, with wives often playing a significant – not just symbolic – role in litigation. Most importantly, wives were not only present in name but were also required to be present in court and to take part in the negotiation of disputes. Furthermore, these pleas reveal the underlying aspects of the marital partnership and of married women's individual agency, particularly in relation to their economic activities, that led to their involvement in disputes over debt and detinue. The influence of coverture in urban justice did not simply result in a binary for women of either independence or invisibility: it also offered a middle ground representative of partnership between husband and wife in commercial, household, interpersonal and legal issues. Nottingham's borough court operated according to a practical application of coverture that did not simply require men to take absolute responsibility for the negotiations and interactions of their wives, but permitted spouses to do so jointly in a way that was surely far more reflective of the reality of the marital partnership. It was this recognition that led to the joint pleas of spouses becoming a recognised practice in Nottingham during the fourteenth century. But despite this, there were undoubtedly an innumerable number of pleas in which husbands did act on behalf of their wives, rather than in cooperation with them, for reasons which cannot be identified.[11]

The specific and malleable nature of coverture within and across jurisdictions is further revealed by the examination of women's legal actions beyond litigation. The presentments made by urban juries and officials shared much in common with the offences that were the subject of pleas of debt and trespass, yet these 'policing' regulations saw different forms of legal engagement for women, particularly those who were married. In all three towns, presentments concerning illegal trading behaviour could see wives who might have been 'covered' by their husbands in civil debt pleas being independently named and punished for their failure to adhere to regulations. This included women such as Margery, wife of John Clyffe, fined for forestalling in Winchester, or the wives of various Nottingham men, whose forenames were not documented when they were fined for the same offence.[12] Yet in other presentments, the productive activities of married women were concealed behind the legal representation of their husbands, and this was particularly prominent in fines relating to the regulation and licensing of brewing. When women's misbehaviour, including violence and disruptive speech, was presented by juries under systems of local policing, they tended to be held independently accountable for their actions even if they were married – and sometimes their status as 'wife of' was not even documented. Ultimately, of course, the responsibility for payment of fines would have fallen on the husband as head of the household, but legally, many married women were recognised as independent legal actors and required to take responsibility for their transgressions. The customs of multiple jurisdictions that existed even within the same town therefore played a fundamental role in determining women's engagement with multiple arms of the law and the manner in which this was documented.

Finally, the picture is further complicated by the fact that these were not static, fixed patterns. When considered as a whole, the evidence of litigation reveals a tightening up of coverture in its impact on married women's involvement in civil pleas, most notably in relation to wives' involvement in debt pleas as part of the negotiation of commercial life. In both Nottingham and Chester, the figures for wives' involvement in joint debt suits alongside their husbands were significantly different at the end of the fifteenth century compared to the beginning of the fourteenth century. Nottingham's borough court heard numerous debt suits where spouses acted jointly as plaintiffs during the fourteenth century, but by the mid-fifteenth century these cases were much more exceptional. Chester's married women all but disappeared from debt suits after the first quarter of the fourteenth century, reflecting the shift identified in Nottingham but occurring perhaps a century earlier. Non-married women continued to litigate, though the decline in married women's litigation had a notable impact on the overall numbers of female litigants. Though the scale and chronology of this change was unique to each town, there was nevertheless a clear trajectory towards a more 'orthodox' version of married women's legal identity, which saw them generally excluded from litigation in relation to their commercial activities, or those of their household.

This pattern adds weight to the suggestion of Matthew Stevens that there was tightening up of patriarchy within the legal environment by the fifteenth century – represented in London by the disappearance of women acting as co-litigants with their husbands – and bringing further doubt as to the existence of a 'golden age' for medieval women after the Black Death.[13] This clear change over time presents a notably different picture of women's legal experiences across the late medieval period, particularly in Nottingham where the decline in married women's pleas was the most notable. Craig Muldrew's suggestion that married women were barred from litigation in their own names in early modern borough courts may slightly overplay the legal invisibility of married women, though his assessment holds much more in common with the picture we have of the borough courts here by the end of the fifteenth century.[14] In other areas of the law, it has also been proposed that married women were losing independence, suggesting an increasingly 'covered' status in line with more absolute interpretations of coverture. Richard Helmholz, for example, argued that married women's wills almost disappeared over the course of the fifteenth century, and that by the late sixteenth century, the issue of husband's consent for their wives' wills had become increasingly important.[15] Helmholz suggested that this shift was due to changing ideas about married women's property, specifically the idea that married women had no separate property.[16] More recently, however, Cordelia Beattie has found considerable regional variation in married women's will-making, as well as highlighting the need to think about *why* some married women made wills, which requires looking at contextual information regarding their families, communities and the impact of different legal jurisdictions on how their legal position was interpreted. As with the records of litigation, these are details that cannot be understood through quantitative analysis alone. Beattie's study therefore brings into question the notion of a widespread and coherent trajectory or pattern in married women's legal capabilities.[17]

There are echoes of both of these arguments – Helmholz's and Beattie's – in the changing role of married women in litigation, particularly that relating to commercial issues. Where wives' litigation declined, this can also be interpreted as evidence of changing ideas about their legal capability and the nature of coverture: if married women had no property, they also had no ability to contract – to buy and sell – independently, and so their involvement in litigation relating to commercial issues was not necessary, or perhaps even impossible. But Beattie's call for caution and the need to pay attention to the context surrounding wives' legal roles and actions has also been a recurrent issue that the town court evidence, and comparison across places, time and different legal issues, has brought to centre stage. In the individual agency of husbands, under common law, to decide whether to permit their wives to make a will, there are also echoes of the inevitable decisions between husbands and wives concerning the best way to approach litigation in their local courts, and whether to proceed jointly or for the husband to act on his wife's behalf. What we may be seeing in the borough court evidence, therefore, is a glimpse of a wider, longer term trajectory of decline in women's legal status, particularly that of married women, over several centuries, but one that was always tempered by the unique practices, interpretations and contexts of different jurisdictions and individuals. Though coverture did not change in its formal, theoretical definition, the way in which it was interpreted and applied in practice did undergo a shift, from a flexible principle to a stricter, patriarchal recognition of married women's inability to contract. This is something that warrants further attention, both in extended studies that span the medieval/early modern divide, and in research that encompasses and compares a variety of women's legal actions.

The varying and changing nature of coverture highlights the dangers of an overreliance on the seemingly neat, tripartite categorisation of women and their status under the law. Instead, the findings of this study, contextualised by other existing research, serve to refocus our emphasis away from 'types' of women onto the individual and individual experience, situated within a specific context of jurisdiction, time and place. The legal experiences of urban women were not defined by a simple binary of freedom while single or widowed, and restrictions or invisibility under coverture during marriage. This binary model rests on assessments of women's status that compare them to men and male status as the embodiment of legal freedom and opportunity, which itself is an inaccurate benchmark that is of limited use, for not all men were able to access the law on equal terms, and the simple comparison of women to men masks many of the intricacies of women's individual experiences. But while attempts to identify patterns and trends in women's legal actions can be illustrative and valuable in thinking about the big picture and long-term assessments of women's legal status, this should not detract from the individual stories and lives that form the building blocks for these large-scale narratives of continuity and change. The women who used their local courts did so in order to negotiate their own relationships and business interests and to settle disputes as they navigated their way through the daily pressures of urban life. They would not have perceived of their lives in relation to 'golden ages', nor progress or patriarchy, and it is equally important for women's history that we remember the importance of these individuals and their stories as we try to piece together the long history of women's oppression and opportunities under the patriarchal legal systems that governed their lives.

Notes

1. CALS ZSR 21 rot. 9; NA CA1279; Teresa Phipps, 'Female litigants in medieval borough courts: status and strategy in the case of Agnes Halum of Nottingham', in Richard Goddard and Teresa Phipps (eds), *Courts and Urban Society in England, 1250–1550* (Woodbridge: Boydell and Brewer, 2019), pp. 77–92.
2. W.H. Stevenson, *Records of the Borough of Nottingham*, vol. 3 (London: Quaritch, 1885), p. 79.
3. HRO W/D1/37 rot. 8.
4. NA CA1297 rots 3, 8, 10d.
5. NA CA1260.
6. NA CA1258b rot. 13.
7. Shennan Hutton, 'Property, family and partnership: married women and legal capability in late medieval Ghent', in Cordelia Beattie and Matthew Frank Stevens (eds),

Married Women and the Law in Premodern Northwest Europe (Woodbridge: Boydell and Brewer, 2013), pp. 156–157.

8   Tim Stretton and Krista J. Kesselring, 'Coverture and continuity' in Stretton and Kesselring (eds), *Married Women and the Law: Coverture in England and the Common Law World* (London: McGill-Queen's University Press, 2013), p. 8.
9   NA CA1279 rot. 9.
10 NA CA1278 rot. 11.
11 For more on this and examples, see Teresa Phipps, 'Coverture and the marital partnership in late medieval Nottingham: women's litigation at the borough court c.1300–c.1500, *Journal of British Studies*, 58 (2019), p. 782.
12 HRO W/D1/60 rot. 12d; NA CA3942 rot. 3.
13 Matthew Frank Stevens, 'London women, the courts and the "golden age": a quantitative analysis of female litigants in the fourteenth and fifteenth centuries', *The London Journal*, 37 (2012), 74, 79.
14 Craig Muldrew, 'A mutual assent of her mind? Women, debt, litigation and contract in early modern England' *History Workshop Journal*, 55 (2003), 54–57.
15 Richard Helmholz, 'Married women's wills in later medieval England', in Sue Sheridan Walker (ed.), *Wife and Widow in Medieval England* (Ann Arbor: University of Michigan Press, 1993), pp. 167, 169–170.
16 Helmholz, 'Married women's wills', p. 172.
17 Cordelia Beattie, 'Married women's wills: probate, property and piety in late medieval England', *Law and History Review*, 37 (2019), 43, 53, 60.

Bibliography

Archival sources

Cheshire Archives and Local Studies (CALS)
Chester Pentice Court rolls:
ZSR 21 (1317–18)
ZSR 27 (1320)
ZSR 35 (1325)
ZSR 62 (1350)
ZSR 81–85 (1378)
ZSR 109–112 (1395)
ZSR 147–155 (1423)
ZSR 201–210 (1435)
ZSR 369–380 (1490)

Chester Crownmote rolls:
ZQCR1–11 (extracts, 1316–1406)

Chester sheriffs' books:
ZS/B 5a–g

Hampshire Archives (HRO)
Winchester City Court rolls:
W/D1/3 (1299–1300)
W/D1/10 (1361–2)
W/D1/13 (1365–6)
W/D1/27 (1385–6)
W/D1/60 (1432–3)
W/D1/61 (1454–5)
W/D1/64 (1494–5)

J.S. Furley transcription of Winchester City Court rolls:
11M92W/24–37

Nottinghamshire Archives (NA)
Nottingham borough court rolls/books:
CA 1258a (1322–3)
CA 1258b (1323–4)
CA 1261 (1330–1)
CA 1262 (1335–6)
CA 1263 (1351–2)
CA 1265 (1353–4)

CA 1277a (1371-2)
CA 1279 (1375-6)
CA 1280a (extracts 1378×1379)
CA 1287 (extracts 1386×1387)
CA 1291 (1390-1)
CA 1294 (1395-6)
CA 1296/I (1396-7)
CA 1297 (1398-9)
CA 1306 (1410-11)
CA 1323 (1432-3)
CA 1324, CA 1325 (1433-4)
CA 1329/II (1437-8)
CA 1332 (1441-2)
CA 1336 (1446-7)
CA 1374 (1491-2)

Nottingham mayoralty rolls/books:
CA 4811 (1369-70)
CA 3942 (1395)
CA 3943 (1407-8)
CA 3944 (1414-15)
CA 4478 (1459-60)

Published primary sources

Arnold, M.S., *Select Cases of Trespass from the King's Courts, 1307-1399*, vol. 1, Selden Society, vol. 100 (Selden Society: London, 1984).
Bateson, Mary (ed.), *Borough Customs*, 2 vols, Selden Society, vols 18 and 21 (Selden Society: London, 1904 and 1906).
Bickley, Francis. B. (ed.), *The Little Red Book of Bristol* (London: Hemmons, 1900).
Blackstone, William, *Commentaries on the Laws of England* (Oxford: Clarendon Press, 1765-9).
Bracton, Henry de, *De Legibus et Consuetudinibus Angliae*, trans. Samuel E. Thorne, vol. 2 (Cambridge, MA.: Belknap Press, 1968-77).
Furley, J.S. (ed.), *City Government of Winchester from the Records of XIV and XV Centuries* (Oxford: Clarendon Press, 1923).
—— *Town Life in the XIV Century as seen in the Court Rolls of Winchester City* (Winchester: Warren, 1946).
Hall, G.D.G. (ed.), *The Treatise on the Laws and Customs of the Realm of England Commonly Called Glanvill* (London: Nelson, 1965).
Hopkins, A. (ed.), *Selected Rolls of the Chester City Courts* (Manchester: Chetham Society, 1950).
Hudson, Willam (ed.), *Leet Jurisdiction in the City of Norwich during the Xiiith and Xivth Centuries*, Selden Society, vol. 5. (London: Quaritch, 1892).

Morris, R.H. (ed.), *Chester in the Plantagenet and Tudor Reigns* (Chester, 1893).
Nichols, F.M. (ed. and trans.), *Britton: an English translation and notes* (Washington, DC: Byrne and Co., 1901).
Richardson, William H. (ed.), *The Annalls of Ipswche: the lawes customes and governmt of the same, collected out of ye records books and writings of that towne by Nathll Bacon serving as recorder and town clark in that towne. Anno. Dom. 1654* (Ipswich: Cowell, 1884).
Riley, H.T. (ed.), *Liber Albus: The White Book of the City of London* (London: R. Griffin, 1861).
Rothwell, Harry (ed.), *English Historical Documents: 1189–1327* (London: Eyre and Spottiswoode, 1996).
Statutes of the Realm, vol. 1 (London: Dawsons, 1963 reprint).
Stevenson, W.H. (ed.), *Records of the Borough of Nottingham*, vols. 1–3 (London: Quaritch 1882–9).
T.E., *The Lawes Resolutions of Womens Rights* (London, 1632).
Wilson, K.P. (ed.), *Chester Customs Accounts 1301–1556*, Record Society of Lancashire and Cheshire, vol. 111 (1969).

Secondary sources

Abram, Annie, 'Women traders in medieval London', *The Economic Journal*, 26 (1916), 276–285.
Alexander, J.W., 'New evidence on the Palatinate of Chester', *English Historical Review*, 85 (1970), 715–729.
Anton, A.E., 'The effect of marriage upon property in Scots Law', *The Modern Law Review*, 19 (1956), 653–668.
Attreed, Lorraine, 'Urban identity in medieval English towns', *Journal of Interdisciplinary History*, 32 (2002), 571–592.
Bailey, Joanne, 'Voices in court: lawyers' or litigants'?', *Historical Research*, 74 (2001), 392–408.
—— 'Favoured or oppressed? Married women, property and "coverture" in England, 1660–1800', *Continuity and Change*, 17 (2002), 351–372.
Barclay, Katie and Rosalind Carr, 'Rewriting the Scottish canon: the contribution of women's and gender history to a redefinition of social classes', *Études écossaises*, 16 (2013), 11–28.
Bardsley, Sandy, 'Women's work reconsidered: gender and wage differentiation in late medieval England', *Past and Present*, 165 (1999), 3–29.
—— 'Sin, speech and scolding in late medieval England', in Thelma Fenster and Daniel Lord Smail (eds), *Fama: The Politics of Talk and Reputation in Medieval Europe* (Ithaca: Cornell University Press, 2003), pp. 145–164.
—— *Venomous Tongues: Speech and Gender in Late Medieval England* (Philadelphia: University of Pennsylvania Press, 2006).
Barron, Caroline M., 'The "golden age" of women in medieval London', *Reading Medieval Studies*, 15 (1989), 35–58.

Barron, Caroline M. and Anne F. Sutton (eds), *Medieval London Widows 1300–1500* (London: Hambledon Press, 1994).

Barton, J.L., 'The mystery of Bracton', *The Journal of Legal History*, 14 (1993), 1–142.

Beattie, Cordelia, 'The problem of women's work identities in post Black Death England', in James Bothwell, P.J.P. Goldberg and W. Mark Ormrod (eds), *The Problem of Labour in Fourteenth-Century England* (Woodbridge: Boydell and Brewer, 2000), pp. 1–19.

—— 'Governing bodies: law courts, male householders, and single women in late medieval England', in Cordelia Beattie, Anna Maslakovic and Sara Rees Jones (eds), *The Medieval Household in Christian Europe c.850–c.1550* (Turnhout: Brepols, 2003), pp. 199–220.

—— 'Gender and femininity in medieval England', in Nancy Partner (ed.), *Writing Medieval History* (London: Hodder and Arnold 2005), pp. 153–170.

—— 'Single women, work and family: the Chancery dispute of Jane Wynde and Margaret Clerk', in Michael Goodich (ed.), *Voices from the Bench: The Narratives of Lesser Folk in Medieval Trials* (Basingstoke: Palgrave, 2006), pp. 177–202.

—— *Medieval Single Women: The Politics of Social Classification in Late Medieval England* (Oxford: Oxford University Press, 2007).

—— 'Married women, contracts and coverture in late medieval England', in Cordelia Beattie and Matthew Frank Stevens (eds), *Married Women and the Law in Premodern Northwest Europe* (Woodbridge: Boydell and Brewer, 2013), pp. 133–154.

—— 'Your oratrice: women's petitions to the late medieval court of Chancery', in Bronach Kane and Fiona Williamson (eds), *Women, Agency and the Law 1300–1700* (London: Pickering and Chatto, 2013), pp. 17–29.

—— 'Married women's wills: probate, property and piety in late medieval England', *Law and History Review*, 37 (2019), 29–60.

Beattie, Cordelia, Anna Maslakovic and Sara Rees Jones (eds), *The Medieval Household in Christian Europe c.850–c.1550* (Turnhout: Brepols, 2003).

Beattie, Cordelia and Matthew Frank Stevens (eds), *Married Women and the Law in Premodern Northwest Europe* (Woodbridge: Boydell and Brewer, 2013).

Beckerman, John S. 'The forty shilling jurisdictional limit in medieval English personal actions', in Dafydd Jenkins (ed.), *Legal History Studies 1972* (Cardiff: University of Wales Press, 1975), pp. 110–117.

Beckett, John (ed.), *A Centenary History of Nottingham* (Manchester: Manchester University Press, 1997).

Bennett, Judith M., 'Spouses, siblings and surnames: reconstructing families from medieval village court rolls', *Journal of British Studies*, 23 (1983), 26–46.

—— 'The village ale-wife: women and brewing in fourteenth-century England', in Barbara A. Hanawalt (ed.), *Women and Work in Preindustrial England* (Bloomington: Indiana University Press, 1986), pp. 20–36.

—— *Women in the Medieval English Countryside: Gender and Household in Brigstock Before the Plague* (Oxford: Oxford University Press, 1987).

—— '"History that stands still": women's work in the European past', *Feminist Studies*, 14 (1988), 269–283.

—— 'Medieval women, modern women: across the great divide', in David Aers (ed.), *Culture and History 1350–1600* (Detroit: Wayne State University Press, 1992), pp. 147–175.

—— *Ale, Beer, and Brewsters in England: Women's Work in a Changing World, 1300 to 1600* (Oxford: Oxford University Press, 1996).

—— 'Confronting continuity', *Journal of Women's History*, 9 (1997), 73–94.

—— 'Medieval women in modern perspective', in Bonnie G. Smith (ed.), *Women's History in Global Perspective*, vol. 2 (Urbana: University of Illinois Press, 2005), pp. 139–186.

—— *History Matters: Patriarchy and the Challenge of Feminism* (Manchester: Manchester University Press, 2006).

—— 'Forgetting the past', *Gender and History*, 20 (2008), 669–677.

Bennett, Judith M. and Amy Froide (eds), *Singlewomen in the European Past, 1250–1800* (Philadelphia: University of Pennsylvania Press, 1999).

Bennett, Judith M. and Ruth Mazo Karras, 'Women, gender and medieval historians', in Judith M. Bennett and Ruth Mazo Karras (eds), *The Oxford Handbook of Women and Gender in Medieval Europe* (Oxford: Oxford University Press, 2013), pp. 1–17.

Biddle, Martin (ed.), *Winchester in the Early Middle Ages: An Edition and Discussion of the Winton Domesday* (Oxford: Clarendon Press, 1976).

Bolton, J.L., 'What is money? What is a money economy? When did a money economy emerge in medieval England?', in Diana Wood (ed.) *Medieval Money Matters* (Oxford: Oxbow, 2004), pp. 1–15.

—— *Money in the Medieval English Economy: 973–1489* (Manchester: Manchester University Press, 2012).

Bonfield, Lloyd, 'What did English villagers mean by "customary law"?' in Zvi Razi and Richard Smith (eds), *Medieval Society and the Manor Court* (Oxford: Clarendon Press, 1996), pp. 103–116.

Brand, Paul, 'The origins of the English legal profession', *Law and History Review*, 5 (1987), 31–50.

—— *The Making of the Common Law* (London: Hambledon Press, 1992).

—— 'Local custom in the early common law', in Pauline Stafford, Janet L. Nelson and Jane Martindale (eds), *Law, Laity and Solidarities: Essays in Honour of Susan Reynolds* (Manchester: Manchester University Press, 2001), pp. 150–159.

—— 'Aspects of the law of debt, 1189–1307', in Phillipp R. Schofield and Nicholas J. Mayhew (eds), *Credit and Debt in Medieval England, c.1180–c.1350* (Oxford: Oxbow, 2002), pp. 19–41.

Briggs, Chris, 'Empowered or marginalized? Rural women and credit in later thirteenth- and fourteenth-century England', *Continuity and Change*, 19 (2004), 13–43.

—— 'Manor court procedures, debt litigation levels, and rural credit provision in England, c.1290–c.1380', *Law and History Review*, 24 (2006), 519–558.

—— 'The availability of credit in the English countryside, 1400–1480', *Agricultural History Review*, 56 (2008), 1–24.

—— *Credit and Village Society in Fourteenth-century England* (Oxford: Oxford University Press, 2009).

Britnell, Richard H., 'Colchester courts and court records, 1310–1525', *Essex Archaeology and History*, 28 (1986), 133–40.

—— *Growth and Decline in Colchester, 1300–1525* (Cambridge: Cambridge University Press, 1986).

—— 'Forestall, forestalling and the Statute of Forestallers', *English Historical Review*, 102 (1987), 89–102.

Butler, Sara M., *The Language of Abuse: Marital Violence in Later Medieval England* (Leiden: Brill, 2007).

—— *Divorce in Medieval England: From One to Two Persons in Law* (Abingdon: Routledge, 2013).

—— 'Discourse on the nature of coverture in the later medieval courtroom', in Tim Stretton and Krista J. Kesselring (eds), *Married Women and the Law: Coverture in England and the Common Law World* (London: McGill-Queen's University Press, 2013), pp. 24–44.

—— *Forensic Medicine and Death Investigation in Medieval England* (London: Routledge, 2014).

—— 'Medieval singlewomen in law and practice', in Andrew Spicer and Jane L. Stevens Crawshaw (eds), *The Place of the Social Margins, 1350–1750* (London: Routledge, 2017), pp. 59–78.

Cannon, Christopher, 'The rights of medieval English women: crime and the issue of representation', in Barbara A. Hanawalt and David Wallace (eds), *Medieval Crime and Social Control* (Minneapolis: University of Minnesota Press, 1998), pp. 156–185.

Capp, Bernard, 'The double standard revisited: plebeian women and male sexual reputation in early modern England', *Past and Present*, 162 (1999), 70–100.

Casson, Catherine, 'Reputation and responsibility in medieval English towns: civic concerns with the regulation of trade', *Urban History*, 39 (2012), 387–408.

Clanchy, Michael T., *From Memory to Written Record: England 1066–1307* (London: Edward Arnold, 1979).

—— 'Medieval mentalities and primitive legal practice', in Pauline Stafford, Janet L. Nelson and Jane Martindale (eds), *Law, Laity and Solidarities: Essays in Honour of Susan Reynolds* (Manchester: Manchester University Press, 2001), pp. 83–94.

Clark, Elaine, 'Debt litigation in a late medieval English vill', in J.A. Raftis (ed.), *Pathways to Medieval Peasants* (Toronto: Pontifical Institute of Medieval Studies, 1981), pp. 247–279.

Clarke, Catherine A.M. (ed.), *Mapping the Medieval City: Space, Place and Identity in Chester c.1200–1600* (Cardiff: University of Wales Press, 2011).

Clayton, Dorothy J., *The Administration of the County Palatine of Chester 1442–1485* (Manchester: Chetham Society, 1990).

Cohen, Elizabeth S., 'Honor and gender in the streets of early modern Rome', *Journal of Interdisciplinary History*, 22 (1992), 597–625.

Cohn Jr., Samuel K., *Women in the Streets: Essays on Sex and Power in Renaissance Italy* (Baltimore: Johns Hopkins University Press, 1996).

Colman, R.V., 'Domestic peace and public order in Anglo-Saxon law', in J. Douglas Woods and David A.E. Pelteret (eds), *The Anglo-Saxons: Synthesis and Achievement* (Waterloo, Ontario: Wilfred Laurier University Press, 1985), pp. 49–61.

Davies, R.R., 'The peoples of Britain and Ireland 1100–1400 I: Identities', *Transactions of the Royal Historical Society*, 4 (1994), 1–20.

Davis, Isabel, Miriam Müller and Sara Rees Jones (eds), *Love, Marriage and Family Ties in the Later Middle Ages* (Turnhout: Brepols, 2003).

Davis, James, *Medieval Market Morality: Life, Law and Ethics in the English Marketplace* (Cambridge: Cambridge University Press, 2011).

Dean, Trevor, 'Theft and gender in late medieval Bologna', *Gender and History*, 20 (2008), 399–415.

────── 'Gender and insult in an Italian city: Bologna in the later middle ages', *Social History*, 29 (2010), 217–231.

DesBrisay, Gordon, and Karen Sander Thomson, 'Crediting wives: married women and debt litigation in the seventeenth century', in Elizabeth Ewan and Janay Nugent (eds), *Finding the Family in Medieval and Early Modern Scotland* (Aldershot: Ashgate, 2008), pp. 85–98.

DeWindt, Anne Reiber and Edwin Brezette DeWindt, *Ramsey: The Lives of an English Fenland Town, 1200–1600* (Washington, DC: Catholic University of America Press, 2006).

Dincer, Aysu, 'Wills, marriage and business contracts: urban women in late-medieval Cyprus', *Gender and History*, 24 (2012), 310–332.

Doubleday, Herbert Arthur and William Page (eds), *A History of the County of Hampshire*, vol. 2 (London: Archibald Constable, 1903).

Dunn, Caroline, *Stolen Women in Medieval England: Rape, Abduction, and Adultery, 1100–1500* (Cambridge: Cambridge University Press, 2012).

Dyer, Alan, 'Ranking lists of English medieval towns', in D.M. Palliser (ed.), *The Cambridge Urban History of Britain*, vol. 1 600–1540 (Cambridge: Cambridge University Press, 2000), pp. 747–770.

Dyer, Christopher, 'The consumer and the market in the later middle ages', *Economic History Review*, 42 (1989), 305–327.

—— *Everyday Life in Medieval England* (London: Hambledon Press, 1994).
Erickson, Amy Louise, 'Coverture and capitalism', *History Workshop Journal*, 59 (2005), 1–16.
—— 'Marital status and economic activity: interpreting spinsters, wives and widows in pre-census population listings', *Cambridge Working Papers in Economic and Social History*, 7 (2012).
Erler, Mary C. and Maryanne Kowaleski (eds), *Gendering the Master Narrative: Women and Power in the Middle Ages* (Ithaca: Cornell University Press, 2003).
—— 'A new economy of power relations: female agency in the middle ages', in Mary C. Erler and Maryanne Kowaleski (eds), *Gendering the Master Narrative: Women and Power in the Middle Ages* (Ithaca: Cornell University Press, 2003), pp. 1–16.
Ewan, Elizabeth, 'Scottish Portias: women in the courts in mediaeval Scottish towns', *Journal of the Canadian Historical Association*, 3 (1992), 27–43.
—— '"Many injurious words"': defamation and gender in late medieval Scotland', in R.A. McDonald (ed.), *History, Literature and Music in Scotland, 700–1560* (Toronto: University of Toronto Press, 2002), pp. 163–186.
—— 'Disorderly damsels? Women and interpersonal violence in pre-Reformation Scotland', *Scottish Historical Review*, 89 (2010), 153–171.
—— 'Impatient Griseldas: women and the perpetration of violence in sixteenth-century Glasgow', *Florilegium*, 28 (2011), 149–168.
Fenster, Thelma and Daniel Lord Smail (eds), *Fama: The Politics of Talk and Reputation in Medieval Europe* (Ithaca: Cornell University Press, 2003).
Finch, Andrew, 'Women and violence in the later middle ages: the evidence of the officiality of Cerisy', *Continuity and Change*, 7 (1992), 23–45.
—— 'The nature of violence in the middle ages: an alternative perspective', *Historical Research*, 70 (1997), 249–268.
Finn, Margot, 'Women, consumption and coverture in England, c. 1760–1860', *The Historical Journal*, 39 (1996), 703–722.
Fleming, Peter, *Women in Late Medieval Bristol*, Bristol Branch of the Historical Association Local History Pamphlets, 103 (2001).
Flather, Amanda, *Gender and Space in Early Modern England* (Woodbridge: Boydell and Brewer, 2007).
Foulds, Trevor, 'The medieval town', in John Beckett (ed.), *A Centenary History of Nottingham* (Manchester: Manchester University Press, 1997), pp. 56–71.
—— 'Trade and manufacture', in John Beckett (ed.), *A Centenary History of Nottingham* (Manchester: Manchester University Press, 1997), pp. 72–83.
Foulds, Trevor, Jill Hughes and Michael Jones, 'The Nottingham borough court rolls: the reign of Henry VI (1422–57)', *Transactions of the Thoroton Society*, 97 (1993), 74–87.

Galloway, J.A., 'Driven by drink? Ale consumption and the agrarian economy of the London region, c.1300–1400', in Martha Carlin and Joel T. Rosenthal (eds) *Food and Eating in Medieval Europe* (London: Hambledon Press, 1998), pp. 87–100.

Gastle, Brian, '"As if she were single": working wives and the late medieval English Femme Sole', in Kellie Robertson and Michael Uebel (eds), *The Middle Ages at Work: Practising Labor in Late Medieval England* (Basingstoke: Palgrave, 2004), pp. 41–64.

Gilchrist, Roberta, *Medieval Life: Archaeology and the Life Course* (Woodbridge: Boydell and Brewer, 2012).

Goddard, Richard, 'Nottingham's borough court rolls: a user's guide', Nottingham Urban Culture Network, https://www.nottingham.ac.uk/ucn/documents/online-sources/nottinghamsboroughcourtrolls-usersguide2.pdf (accessed 23 November 2018).

—— 'Surviving recession: English borough courts and commercial contraction, 1350–1500', in Richard Goddard, John Langdon and Miriam Müller (eds), *Survival and Discord in Medieval Society: Essays in Honour of Christopher Dyer* (Turnhout: Brepols, 2010), pp. 69–87.

—— 'Coal mining in medieval Nottinghamshire: consumers and producers in a nascent industry', *Transactions of the Thoroton Society*, 116 (2012), 95–115.

—— 'Medieval business networks: St Mary's Guild and the borough court in later medieval Nottingham', *Urban History*, 40 (2013), 3–27.

—— *Credit and Trade in Later Medieval England, 1353–1532* (London: Palgrave, 2016).

—— 'Trust: business networks and the borough court', in Richard Goddard and Teresa Phipps (eds), *Town Courts and Urban Society in Late Medieval England* (Woodbridge: Boydell and Brewer, 2019), pp. 176–199.

Goddard, Richard and Teresa Phipps (eds), *Town Courts and Urban Society in Late Medieval England* (Woodbridge: Boydell and Brewer, 2019).

Goldberg, P.J.P., *Women, Work and Life Cycle in a Medieval Economy: Women in York and Yorkshire c.1300–1520* (Oxford: Clarendon Press, 1992).

—— 'For better, for worse': marriage and economic opportunity for women in town and country', in P.J.P. Goldberg (ed.), *Women in Medieval English Society* (Stroud: Alan Sutton, 1997), pp. 108–125.

—— 'Gender and matrimonial litigation in the church courts in the later middle ages: the evidence of the court of York', *Gender and History*, 19 (2007), 43–59.

—— 'Space and gender in the later medieval English house', *Viator*, 42 (2011), 205–232.

—— 'Echoes, whispers, ventriloquisms: on recovering women's voices from the court of York in the later middle ages', in Bronach Kane and Fiona Williamson (eds), *Women, Agency and the Law 1300–1700* (London: Pickering and Chatto, 2013), pp. 31–41.

—— 'Some reflections on women, work and the family in the later medieval English town', in Jesús Ángel Solórzano Telechea, Beatriz Arízaga Bolumburu and Amélia Aguiar Andrade (eds), *Ser Mujer en la Ciudad Medieval Europea* (Logroño: Instituto de Estudios Riojanos, 2013), pp. 191–214.

—— 'The priest of Nottingham and the holy household of Ousegate: telling tales in court', in Richard Goddard and Teresa Phipps (eds), *Town Courts and Urban Society in Late Medieval England* (Woodbridge: Boydell and Brewer, 2019), pp. 60–76.

Goldberg, P.J.P. and Maryanne Kowaleski (eds), *Medieval Domesticity: Home, Housing and Household in Medieval England* (Cambridge: Cambridge University Press, 2008).

Gowing, Laura, 'Women, status and the popular culture of dishonour', *Transactions of the Royal Historical Society*, sixth series, 6 (1996), 225–234.

—— *Domestic Dangers: Women, Words and Sex in Early Modern London* (Oxford: Clarendon Press, 1998).

Gross, Charles, 'Modes of trial in the mediaeval boroughs of England', *Harvard Law Review*, 15 (1902), 691–706.

Hanawalt, Barbara A., 'The female felon in fourteenth-century England', *Viator*, 5 (1974), 253–268.

—— 'Violent death in fourteenth- and early fifteenth-century England', *Comparative Studies in Society and History*, 18 (1976), 297–320.

—— *Crime and Conflict in English Communities, 1300–1348* (Cambridge, MA: Harvard University Press, 1979).

—— *The Ties that Bound: Peasant Families in Medieval England* (Oxford: Oxford University Press 1986).

—— (ed.), *Women and Work in Preindustrial Europe* (Bloomington: Indiana University Press, 1986).

—— 'Peasant women's contribution to the home economy in late medieval England', in Barbara A. Hanawalt (ed.), *Women and Work in Preindustrial Europe* (Bloomington: Indiana University Press, 1986), pp. 3–19.

—— 'Medieval English women in rural and urban domestic space' *Dumbarton Oaks Papers*, 52 (1998), 19–26.

—— *'Of Good and Ill Repute': Gender and Social Control in Medieval England* (Oxford: Oxford University Press, 1998).

—— *The Wealth of Wives: Women, Law, and Economy in Late Medieval London* (Oxford: Oxford University Press, 2007).

Hanawalt, Barbara A. and David Wallace (eds), *Medieval Crime and Social Control* (Minneapolis: University of Minnesota Press, 1999).

Harding, Alan, *The Law Courts of Medieval England* (London: Allen and Unwin, 1973).

Harding, Vanessa, 'Space, property, and propriety in urban England, *Journal of Interdisciplinary History*, 32 (2002), 549–569.

Hatcher, John, *Plague, Population and the English Economy 1348–1530* (London: Macmillan, 1977).
────── 'Women's work reconsidered: gender and wage differentiation in late medieval England', *Past and Present*, 173 (2001), 191–198.
Hatcher, John and Mark Bailey, *Modelling the Middle Ages: the History and Theory of England's Economic Development* (Oxford: Oxford University Press, 2001).
Hawkes, Emma, '"[S]he will ... protect and defend her rights boldly by law and reason ..."': Women's knowledge of common law and equity courts in late-medieval England', in Noel J. Menuge (ed.), *Medieval Women and the Law* (Woodbridge: Boydell and Brewer, 2003), pp. 145–161.
Helmholz, Richard H., 'Married women's wills in later medieval England', in Sue Sheridan Walker (ed.), *Wife and Widow in Medieval England* (Ann Arbor: University of Michigan Press, 1993), 165–182.
Herlihy, David, *Opera Muliebria: Women and Work in Medieval Europe* (New York: McGraw-Hill, 1990).
Hilton, Rodney, 'Lords, burgesses and hucksters', *Past and Present*, 97 (1982), 3–15.
────── 'Small town society in England before the Black Death', in Rodney Hilton, *Class Conflict and the Crisis of Feudalism*, revised edition (London: Verso, 1990), 19–40.
────── 'Towns in English feudal society', in Rodney Hilton, *Class Conflict and the Crisis of Feudalism*, revised edition (London: Verso, 1990), pp. 102–113.
────── 'Women traders in medieval England', in Rodney Hilton, *Class Conflict and the Crisis of Feudalism*, revised edition (London: Verso, 1990), pp. 132–142.
Holt, Richard and Nigel Baker, 'Towards a geography of sexual encounter: prostitution in English medieval towns', in Lynne Bevan (ed.), *Indecent Exposure: Sexuality, Society and the Archaeological Record* (Glasgow: Cruithne Press, 2001), pp. 201–215.
Howell, Martha, 'The gender of Europe's commercial economy, 1200–1700', *Gender and History*, 20 (2008), 519–538.
────── *Commerce before Capitalism in Europe, 1300–1600* (Cambridge: Cambridge University Press, 2010).
Hurl-Eamon, Jennine, 'Female criminality in the British courts from the middle ages to the nineteenth century', *Journal of Women's History*, 21 (2009), 161–169.
Hutton, Diane, 'Women in fourteenth-century Shrewsbury', in Lindsey Charles and Lorna Duffin (eds), *Women and Work in Pre-Industrial England* (London: Croom Helm, 1985), pp. 83–99.
Hutton, Shennan, '"On herself and all her property": women's economic activities in late-medieval Ghent', *Continuity and Change*, 20 (2005), 325–349.
────── *Women and Economic Activities in Late Medieval Ghent* (Basingstoke: Palgrave, 2011).

—— 'Property, family and partnership: married women and legal capacity in late medieval Ghent', in Cordelia Beattie and Matthew Frank Stevens (ed.), *Married Women and the Law in Premodern Northwest Europe* (Woodbridge: Boydell and Brewer, 2013), pp. 155–172.

Hyams, Paul R., 'What did Edwardian villagers understand by law?', in Zvi Razi and Richard Smith (eds), *Medieval Society and the Manor Court* (Oxford: Clarendon Press, 1996), pp. 69–102.

Ibbetson, David J., *A Historical Introduction to the Law of Obligations* (Oxford: Oxford University Press, 1999).

Ingram, Martin, 'Law, litigants and the construction of "honour": slander suits in early modern England', in Peter Coss (ed.), *The Moral World of the Law* (Cambridge: Cambridge University Press, 2000), pp. 134–160.

—— *Carnal Knowledge: Regulating Sex in England, 1470–1600* (Cambridge: Cambridge University Press, 2017).

Jewell, Helen M., 'Women at the courts of the manor of Wakefield, 1348–1350', *Northern History*, 26 (1990), 59–81.

Johnson, Lizabeth, '*Amobr* and *Amobrwyr*: the collection of marriage fees and sexual fines in late medieval Wales', *Transactions of the Honourable Society of Cymmrodorian*, 18 (2012), 10–21.

—— 'Married women, crime and the courts in late medieval Wales', in Cordelia Beattie and Matthew Frank Stevens (eds), *Married Women and the Law in Premodern Northwest Europe* (Woodbridge: Boydell and Brewer, 2013), pp. 71–90.

Jones, Karen, *Gender and Petty Crime in Late Medieval England: The Local Courts in Kent, 1460–1560* (Woodbridge: Boydell and Brewer, 2006).

Jones, Karen, and Michael Zell, 'Bad conversation? Gender and social control in a Kentish borough, c. 1450–c. 1570', *Continuity and Change*, 13 (1998), 11–31.

Jussen, Bernhard, '"Virgins – Widows – Spouses": on the language of moral distinction as applied to women and men in the middle ages', *History of the Family*, 7 (2002), 13–32.

Kane, Bronach and Fiona Williamson (eds), *Women, Agency and the Law 1300–1700* (London: Pickering and Chatto, 2013).

Karras, Ruth Mazo, 'The regulation of brothels in later medieval England', *Signs*, 14 (1989), 399–433.

—— '"Because the other is a poor woman she shall be called his wench": gender, sexuality and social status in late medieval England', in Sharon A. Famer and Carol Braun Pasternack (eds) *Gender and Difference in the Middle Ages* (Minneapolis: University of Minnesota Press, 2003), pp. 224–225.

Keene, Derek, *Survey of Medieval Winchester*, 2 vols. (Oxford: Clarendon Press, 1985).

Kelleher, Marie A., 'Later medieval law in community context', in Judith M. Bennett and Ruth Mazo Karras (eds), *The Oxford Handbook of Women and Gender in Medieval Europe* (Oxford: Oxford University Press, 2013), pp. 133–147.

Hatcher, John, *Plague, Population and the English Economy 1348–1530* (London: Macmillan, 1977).

—— 'Women's work reconsidered: gender and wage differentiation in late medieval England', *Past and Present*, 173 (2001), 191–198.

Hatcher, John and Mark Bailey, *Modelling the Middle Ages: the History and Theory of England's Economic Development* (Oxford: Oxford University Press, 2001).

Hawkes, Emma, '"[S]he will ... protect and defend her rights boldly by law and reason ..."': Women's knowledge of common law and equity courts in late-medieval England', in Noel J. Menuge (ed.), *Medieval Women and the Law* (Woodbridge: Boydell and Brewer, 2003), pp. 145–161.

Helmholz, Richard H., 'Married women's wills in later medieval England', in Sue Sheridan Walker (ed.), *Wife and Widow in Medieval England* (Ann Arbor: University of Michigan Press, 1993), 165–182.

Herlihy, David, *Opera Muliebria: Women and Work in Medieval Europe* (New York: McGraw-Hill, 1990).

Hilton, Rodney, 'Lords, burgesses and hucksters', *Past and Present*, 97 (1982), 3–15.

—— 'Small town society in England before the Black Death', in Rodney Hilton, *Class Conflict and the Crisis of Feudalism*, revised edition (London: Verso, 1990), 19–40.

—— 'Towns in English feudal society', in Rodney Hilton, *Class Conflict and the Crisis of Feudalism*, revised edition (London: Verso, 1990), pp. 102–113.

—— 'Women traders in medieval England', in Rodney Hilton, *Class Conflict and the Crisis of Feudalism*, revised edition (London: Verso, 1990), pp. 132–142.

Holt, Richard and Nigel Baker, 'Towards a geography of sexual encounter: prostitution in English medieval towns', in Lynne Bevan (ed.), *Indecent Exposure: Sexuality, Society and the Archaeological Record* (Glasgow: Cruithne Press, 2001), pp. 201–215.

Howell, Martha, 'The gender of Europe's commercial economy, 1200–1700', *Gender and History*, 20 (2008), 519–538.

—— *Commerce before Capitalism in Europe, 1300–1600* (Cambridge: Cambridge University Press, 2010).

Hurl-Eamon, Jennine, 'Female criminality in the British courts from the middle ages to the nineteenth century', *Journal of Women's History*, 21 (2009), 161–169.

Hutton, Diane, 'Women in fourteenth-century Shrewsbury', in Lindsey Charles and Lorna Duffin (eds), *Women and Work in Pre-Industrial England* (London: Croom Helm, 1985), pp. 83–99.

Hutton, Shennan, '"On herself and all her property": women's economic activities in late-medieval Ghent', *Continuity and Change*, 20 (2005), 325–349.

—— *Women and Economic Activities in Late Medieval Ghent* (Basingstoke: Palgrave, 2011).

—— 'Property, family and partnership: married women and legal capacity in late medieval Ghent', in Cordelia Beattie and Matthew Frank Stevens (ed.), *Married Women and the Law in Premodern Northwest Europe* (Woodbridge: Boydell and Brewer, 2013), pp. 155–172.

Hyams, Paul R., 'What did Edwardian villagers understand by law?', in Zvi Razi and Richard Smith (eds), *Medieval Society and the Manor Court* (Oxford: Clarendon Press, 1996), pp. 69–102.

Ibbetson, David J., *A Historical Introduction to the Law of Obligations* (Oxford: Oxford University Press, 1999).

Ingram, Martin, 'Law, litigants and the construction of "honour": slander suits in early modern England', in Peter Coss (ed.), *The Moral World of the Law* (Cambridge: Cambridge University Press, 2000), pp. 134–160.

—— *Carnal Knowledge: Regulating Sex in England, 1470–1600* (Cambridge: Cambridge University Press, 2017).

Jewell, Helen M., 'Women at the courts of the manor of Wakefield, 1348–1350', *Northern History*, 26 (1990), 59–81.

Johnson, Lizabeth, '*Amobr* and *Amobrwyr*: the collection of marriage fees and sexual fines in late medieval Wales', *Transactions of the Honourable Society of Cymmrodorian*, 18 (2012), 10–21.

—— 'Married women, crime and the courts in late medieval Wales', in Cordelia Beattie and Matthew Frank Stevens (eds), *Married Women and the Law in Premodern Northwest Europe* (Woodbridge: Boydell and Brewer, 2013), pp. 71–90.

Jones, Karen, *Gender and Petty Crime in Late Medieval England: The Local Courts in Kent, 1460–1560* (Woodbridge: Boydell and Brewer, 2006).

Jones, Karen, and Michael Zell, 'Bad conversation? Gender and social control in a Kentish borough, c. 1450–c. 1570', *Continuity and Change*, 13 (1998), 11–31.

Jussen, Bernhard, '"Virgins – Widows – Spouses": on the language of moral distinction as applied to women and men in the middle ages', *History of the Family*, 7 (2002), 13–32.

Kane, Bronach and Fiona Williamson (eds), *Women, Agency and the Law 1300–1700* (London: Pickering and Chatto, 2013).

Karras, Ruth Mazo, 'The regulation of brothels in later medieval England', *Signs*, 14 (1989), 399–433.

—— '"Because the other is a poor woman she shall be called his wench": gender, sexuality and social status in late medieval England', in Sharon A. Famer and Carol Braun Pasternack (eds) *Gender and Difference in the Middle Ages* (Minneapolis: University of Minnesota Press, 2003), pp. 224–225.

Keene, Derek, *Survey of Medieval Winchester*, 2 vols. (Oxford: Clarendon Press, 1985).

Kelleher, Marie A., 'Later medieval law in community context', in Judith M. Bennett and Ruth Mazo Karras (eds), *The Oxford Handbook of Women and Gender in Medieval Europe* (Oxford: Oxford University Press, 2013), pp. 133–147.

Kermode, Jennifer I., 'Money and credit in the fifteenth century: some lessons from Yorkshire', *The Business History Review*, 65 (1991), 475-501.

Kermode, Jennifer and Garthine Walker (eds), *Women, Crime and the Courts in Early Modern England* (London: UCL Press, 1994).

Kerr, Margaret H., 'Husband and wife in criminal proceedings in medieval England', in Constance M. Rousseau and Joel T. Rosenthal (eds), *Women, Marriage and Family in Medieval Christendom* (Kalamazoo, MI: Medieval Institute Publications, 1998), pp. 211-251.

Kittell, Ellen E., 'Women, audience, and public acts in medieval Flanders', *Journal of Women's History*, 10 (1998), 74-96.

—— 'The construction of women's social identity in medieval Douai: evidence from identifying epithets', *Journal of Medieval History*, 25 (1999), 215-227.

Kittel, Ruth, 'Women under the law in medieval England, 1066-1485', in Barbara Kanner (ed.), *The Women of England: From Anglo-Saxon Times to the Present* (London: Mansell, 1980), pp. 124-137.

Klerman, Daniel, 'Jurisdictional competition and the evolution of the common law: an hypothesis', in Anthony Musson (ed.), *Boundaries of the Law: Geography, Gender and Jurisdiction in Medieval and Early Modern Europe* (Aldershot: Ashgate, 2005), pp. 149-168.

Kowaleski, Maryanne, 'Women's work in a market town: Exeter in the late fourteenth century', in Barbara A. Hanawalt (ed.), *Women and Work in Preindustrial Europe* (Bloomington: Indiana University Press, 1986), pp. 145-164.

—— *Local Markets and Regional Trade in Medieval Exeter* (Cambridge: Cambridge University Press, 1995).

—— 'An introduction to town courts in medieval England', in Richard Goddard and Teresa Phipps (eds), *Town Courts and Urban Society in Late Medieval England* (Woodbridge: Boydell and Brewer, 2019), pp. 17-43.

Kuehn, Thomas, '*Fama* as legal status in Renaissance Florence', in Thelma Fenster and Daniel Lord Smail (eds), *Fama: The Politics of Talk and Reputation in Medieval Europe* (Ithaca: Cornell University Press, 2003), pp. 27-48.

Lacey, Kay E., 'Women and work in fourteenth and fifteenth century London', in Lindsey Charles and Lorna Duffin (eds), *Women and Work in Pre-Industrial England* (London: Croom Helm, 1985), pp. 24-82.

Lambert, Tom, *Law and Order in Anglo Saxon England* (Oxford: Oxford University Press, 2017).

Lansing, Carol, 'Conflicts over gender in civic courts', in Judith M. Bennett and Ruth Mazo Karras (eds), *The Oxford Handbook of Women and Gender in Medieval Europe* (Oxford: Oxford University Press, 2013), pp. 118-132.

Laughton, Jane, 'Women in court: some evidence from fifteenth-century Chester', in Nicholas Rogers (ed.), *England in the Fifteenth Century* (Stamford: Paul Rogers, 1994), pp. 89-99.

—— 'The alewives of later medieval Chester', in Rowena E. Archer (ed.), *Crown, Government and People in the Fifteenth Century* (Stroud: Alan Sutton, 1995), pp. 191–208.

—— *Life in a Late Medieval City: Chester 1275–1520* (Oxford: Oxbow, 2008).

—— 'The control of discord in fifteenth-century Chester', in Richard Goddard, John Langdon and Miriam Müller (eds), *Survival and Discord in Medieval Society: Essays in Honour of Christopher Dyer* (Turnhout: Brepols, 2010), pp. 213–229.

Lewis, C.P. and A.T. Thacker, *A History of the County of Chester Volume V: The City of Chester* (Woodbridge: Boydell and Brewer, 2003–2005).

Lipscomb, Suzannah, *The Voices of Nîmes: Women, Sex and Marriage in Reformation Languedoc* (Oxford: Oxford University Press, 2019).

Loengard, Janet S., 'Legal history and the medieval Englishwoman revisited: some new directions', in Joel T. Rosenthal (ed.), *Medieval Women and the Sources of Medieval History* (Athens, GA: University of Georgia Press, 1990), pp. 210–236.

—— '"Which may be said to be her own": widows and goods in late-medieval England', in Maryanne Kowaleski and P.J.P. Goldberg (eds), *Medieval Domesticity: Home, Housing and Household in Medieval England* (Cambridge: Cambridge University Press, 2008), pp. 162–176.

—— 'What is a nice (thirteenth-century) English woman doing in the King's courts?', in Linda E. Mitchell, Katherine L. French and Douglas L. Biggs (eds), *The Ties that Bound: Essays in Medieval British History in Honor of Barbara Hanawalt* (Farnham: Ashgate, 2011), pp. 55–70.

Madden, Philippa C., *Violence and Social Order: East Anglia 1422–1442* (Oxford: Clarendon Press, 1992).

Marcombe, David, 'The late medieval town, 1449–1560', in John Beckett (ed.), *A Centenary History of Nottingham* (Manchester: Manchester University Press, 1997), pp. 84–103.

Mason, Rebecca, 'Women, marital status and law: the marital spectrum in seventeenth-century Glasgow', *Journal of British Studies*, 58 (2019), 787–804.

Mastoris, Stephen N., 'The boundary between the English and French boroughs of mediaeval Nottingham: A documentary survey', *Transactions of the Thoroton Society*, 85 (1981), 68–74.

—— 'Regulating the Nottingham markets: new evidence from a mid-thirteenth century manuscript', *Transactions of the Thoroton Society*, 90 (1986), 79–83.

Mate, Mavis E., *Daughters, Wives and Widows after the Black Death: Women in Sussex, 1350–1535* (Woodbridge: Boydell and Brewer, 1998).

—— *Women in Medieval English Society* (Cambridge: Cambridge University Press, 1999).

McGibbon Smith, Erin, 'The participation of women in the fourteenth-century manor court of Sutton-in-the-Isle', *Marginalia*, 1 (2005), http://www.marginalia.co.uk/journal/05margins/smith.php (accessed 23 November 2018).

McIntosh, Marjorie Keniston, *Controlling Misbehavior in England, 1370–1600* (Cambridge: Cambridge University Press, 1998).

―― 'The benefits and drawbacks of femme sole status in England, 1300–1630', *Journal of British Studies*, 44 (2005), 410–438.

―― 'Women, credit, and family relationships in England, 1300–1620', *Journal of Family History*, 30 (2005), 143–163.

―― *Working Women in English Society, 1300–1620* (Cambridge: Cambridge University Press, 2005).

McNamara, Lawrence, *Reputation and Defamation* (Oxford: Oxford University Press, 2007).

McSheffrey, Shannon, 'Men and masculinity in late medieval London civic culture: governance, patriarchy and reputation', in Jacqueline Murray (ed.), *Conflicted Identities and Multiple Masculinities: Men in the Medieval West* (New York: Garland, 1999), pp. 243–278.

―― *Marriage, Sex and Civic Culture in Late Medieval London* (Philadelphia: University of Pennsylvania Press, 2006).

―― 'Detective fiction in the archives', *History Workshop Journal*, 65 (2008), 65–78.

―― 'A remarrying widow: law and legal records in late medieval London', in Kim Kippen and Lori Woods (eds), *Worth and Repute: Valuing Gender in Late Medieval and Early Modern Europe: Essays in Honour of Barbara Todd* (Toronto: Centre for Reformation and Renaissance Studies, 2011), pp. 231–252.

Mills, Judith, 'The Nottinghamshire History Lecture 2009 Stevenson Revisited: A fresh look at Nottingham's borough records, 1400–1600', *Transactions of the Thoroton Society*, 113 (2009), 55–72.

―― 'Continuity and change: the town, people and administration of Nottingham between c.1400 and c.1600', Unpublished PhD thesis, University of Nottingham, 2010.

Milsom, S.F.C., *Historical Foundations of the Common Law*, second edn (London: Butterworth, 1981).

de Moor, Tine and Jan Luiten Van Zanden, 'Girl power: the European marriage pattern and labour markets in the North Sea region in the late medieval and early modern period', *Economic History Review*, 63 (2010), 1–33.

Müller, Miriam, 'Conflict, strife, and cooperation: aspects of the late medieval family and household', in Isabel Davis, Miriam Müller and Sara Rees Jones (eds), *Love, Marriage and Family Ties in the Later Middle Ages* (Turnhout: Brepols, 2003), pp. 311–329.

―― 'Social control and the hue and cry in two fourteenth-century villages', *Journal of Medieval History*, 31 (2005), 29–53.

―― 'Peasant women, agency and status in mid-thirteenth to late fourteenth-century England: some reconsiderations', in Cordelia Beattie and Matthew Frank Stevens (eds), *Married Women and the Law in Premodern Northwest Europe* (Woodbridge: Boydell and Brewer, 2013), pp. 91–113.

Muldrew, Craig, 'The culture of reconciliation: community and the settlement of economic disputes in early modern England', *The Historical Journal*, 39 (1996), 915–942.

—— *The Economy of Obligation: The Culture of Credit and Social Relations in Early Modern England* (Basingstoke: Palgrave, 1998).

—— '"A mutual assent of her mind"? Women, debt, litigation and contract in early modern England', *History Workshop Journal*, 55 (2003), 47–71.

Mullan, John, 'Mortality, gender and the plague of 1361–2 on the estate of the bishop of Winchester', *Cardiff Historical Papers* (2007/8), 1–41.

Musson, Anthony, *Public Order and Law Enforcement: The Local Administration of Criminal Justice, 1294–1350* (Woodbridge: Boydell and Brewer, 1996).

—— 'Appealing to the past: perceptions of law in late-medieval England', in Anthony Musson (ed.), *Expectations of the Law in the Middle Ages* (Woodbridge: Boydell and Brewer, 2001), pp. 165–179.

—— (ed.), *Expectations of the Law in the Middle Ages* (Woodbridge: Boydell and Brewer, 2001).

—— *Medieval Law in Context: The Growth of Legal Consciousness from Magna Carta to the Peasants' Revolt* (Manchester: Manchester University Press, 2001).

—— 'Social exclusivity or justice for all? Access to justice in fourteenth-century England', in Rosemary Horrox and Sara Rees Jones (eds), *Pragmatic Utopias: Ideals and Communities, 1200–1630* (Cambridge: Cambridge University Press, 2001), pp. 136–155.

—— (ed.), *Boundaries of the Law: Geography, Gender and Jurisdiction in Medieval and Early Modern Europe* (Aldershot: Ashgate, 2005).

—— 'Crossing boundaries: attitudes to rape in later medieval England', in Anthony Musson (ed.), *Boundaries of the Law: Geography, Gender and Jurisdiction in Medieval and Early Modern Europe* (Aldershot: Ashgate, 2005), pp. 84–101.

Musson, Anthony and W. Mark Ormrod (eds), *The Evolution of English Justice: Law, Politics and Society in the Fourteenth Century* (London: Macmillan, 1999).

Neville, Cynthia, 'Common knowledge of the common law in later medieval England', *Canadian Journal of History*, 29 (1994), 461–478.

Nightingale, Pamela, 'Money and credit in the economy of late medieval England', in Diana Wood (ed.), *Medieval Money Matters* (Oxford: Oxbow, 2004), pp. 51–71.

Paul, Tawny, 'Credit, reputation, and masculinity in British urban commerce: Edinburgh, c.1710–70', *Economic History Review*, 66 (2013), 226–248.

Penn, S.A.C., 'Female wage-earners in late fourteenth-century England', *Agricultural History Review*, 35 (1987), 1–14.

Phillips, Kim M., *Medieval Maidens: Young Women and Gender in England, 1270–1540* (Manchester: Manchester University Press, 2003).

Phipps, Teresa, 'Gendered justice? Women, law and community in fourteenth-century Nottingham', *Transactions of the Thoroton Society*, 118 (2015), 79–92.
—— 'Misbehaving women: trespass and honor in late medieval English towns', *Historical Reflections/Réflexions Historique*, 43 (2017), 62–76.
—— 'Creditworthy women and town courts in late medieval England', in Elise Dermineur (ed.), *Women and Credit in Pre-Industrial Europe* (Turnhout: Brepols, 2018), pp. 73–94.
—— 'Female litigants in medieval borough courts: status and strategy in the case of Agnes Halum of Nottingham', in Richard Goddard and Teresa Phipps (eds), *Town Courts and Urban Society in England, 1250–1550* (Woodbridge: Boydell and Brewer, 2019), pp. 77–92.
—— 'Coverture and the marital partnership in late medieval Nottingham: women's litigation at the borough court c.1300–c.1500', *Journal of British Studies*, 58 (2019), 768–786.
Pollock, Frederick and Frederic W. Maitland, *The History of English Law before the time of Edward I*, 2 vols. (Cambridge: Cambridge University Press, 1895, 1898).
Post, J.B., 'Crime in later medieval England: some historiographical limitations', *Continuity and Change*, 2 (1987), 211–224.
—— 'Jury lists and juries in the late fourteenth century', in J.S. Cockburn and Thomas A. Green (eds), *Twelve Good Men and True: The Criminal Jury in England, 1200–1800* (Princeton: Princeton University Press, 1988), pp. 65–78.
Postles, David, 'An English small town in the later middle ages: Loughborough', *Urban History*, 20 (1993), 7–29.
Power, Eileen, *Medieval Women*, ed. Michael M. Postan (Cambridge: Cambridge University Press, 1975).
Razi, Zvi and Richard Smith (eds), *Medieval Society and the Manor Court* (Oxford: Clarendon Press, 1996).
—— 'The historiography of manorial court rolls', in Zvi Razi and Richard Smith (eds), *Medieval Society and the Manor Court* (Oxford: Clarendon Press, 1996), pp. 1–35.
Rees Jones, Sara, 'Women's influence on the design of urban homes', in Mary C. Erler and Maryanne Kowaleski (eds), *Gendering the Master Narrative: Women and Power in the Middle Ages* (Ithaca: Cornell University Press, 2003), pp. 190–211.
Reynolds, Susan, *Kingdoms and Communities in Western Europe 900–1300*, second edn (Oxford: Oxford University Press, 1997).
—— 'Medieval law', in Peter Linehan and Janet Nelson (eds), *The Medieval World* (London: Routledge, 2001), pp. 485–502.
Riddy, Felicity, '"Burgeis" domesticity in late-medieval England', in P.J.P. Goldberg and Maryanne Kowaleski (eds), *Medieval Domesticity* (Cambridge: Cambridge University Press, 2008), pp. 14–37.
Rigby, Stephen H., *English Society in the Later Middle Ages: Class, Status and Gender* (Basingstoke: Macmillan, 1995).

―― 'Gendering the Black Death: women in later medieval England', in Pauline Stafford and Anneke B. Mulder-Bakker (eds), *Gendering the Middle Ages* (Oxford: Wiley, 2001), pp. 215–224.

Robb, Hannah, 'Reputation in the fifteenth century credit market; some tales from the ecclesiastical courts of York', *Cultural and Social History*, 15 (2018), 297–313.

Rodziewicz, Janka, 'Order and society: Great Yarmouth 1366–1381', Unpublished PhD Thesis, University of East Anglia, 2008.

―― 'Women and the hue and cry in late fourteenth-century Great Yarmouth', in Bronach Kane and Fiona Williamson (eds), *Women, Agency and the Law, 1300–1700* (London: Pickering and Chatto, 2013), pp. 87–97.

Roffe, David, 'The Anglo-Saxon town and the Norman Conquest', in John Beckett (ed.), *A Centenary History of Nottingham* (Manchester: Manchester University Press, 1997), pp. 24–42.

Sagui, Samantha, 'The hue and cry in medieval English towns', *Historical Research*, 87 (2014), 179–193.

Schofield, Phillipp R., 'Credit and debt in medieval England: Introduction', in Phillipp R. Schofield and Nicholas J. Mayhew (eds), *Credit and Debt in Medieval England, c.1180–c.1350* (Oxford: Oxbow, 2002), pp. 1–18.

―― 'The social economy of the medieval village in the early fourteenth century', *Economic History Review*, 61 (2008), 38–63.

―― 'Trespass litigation in the manor court in the late thirteenth and early fourteenth centuries', in Richard Goddard, John Langdon and Miriam Müller (eds), *Survival and Discord in Medieval Society: Essays in Honour of Christopher Dyer* (Turnhout: Brepols, 2010), pp. 145–160.

Schofield, Phillipp R. and Nicholas J. Mayhew (eds), *Credit and Debt in Medieval England, c.1180–c.1350* (Oxford: Oxbow, 2002).

Seabourne, Gwen, 'Assize matters: regulation of the price of bread in medieval London', *The Journal of Legal History*, 27 (2006), 29–52.

Sharpe, J.A., *Defamation and Sexual Slander in Early Modern England: The Church Courts at York*, Borthwick Papers no. 58 (York, 1980).

―― 'The history of crime in late medieval and early modern England: a review of the field', *Social History*, 7 (1982), 187–203.

Shepard, Alex, 'Manhood, credit and patriarchy in early modern England c.1580–1640', *Past and Present*, 167 (2000), 75–106.

―― 'Crediting women in the early modern English economy', *History Workshop Journal*, 79 (2015), 1–24.

Sims, R.J., 'Secondary offenders? English women and crime, c.1220–1348', in Christine Meeks and Catherine Lawless (eds), *Studies on Medieval Women 4: Victims or Viragos?* (Dublin: Four Courts Press, 2005), pp. 69–88.

Skinner, Patricia, 'Disputes and disparity: women in court in medieval southern Italy', *Reading Medieval Studies*, 22 (1996), 85–103.

Smail, Daniel Lord, *Consumption of Justice: Emotions, Publicity, and Legal Culture in Marseille, 1264–1423* (Ithaca: Cornell University Press, 2013).

Smith, Llinos Beverley, 'Towards a history of women in late medieval Wales', in Michael Roberts and Simone Clarke (eds), *Women and Gender in Early Modern Wales* (Cardiff: University of Wales Press, 2000), pp. 14–49.

Spence, Cathryn, 'Women and business in sixteenth-century Edinburgh: evidence from their testaments', *Journal of Scottish Historical Studies*, 28 (2008), 1–19.

—— '"To Content and Pay": women's economic roles in Edinburgh, Haddington and Linlithgow, 1560–1640', Unpublished PhD thesis, University of Edinburgh, 2010.

—— '"For his interest"? Women, debt and coverture in early modern Scotland', in Cordelia Beattie and Matthew Frank Stevens (eds), *Married Women and the Law in Premodern Northwestern Europe* (Woodbridge: Boydell and Brewer, 2013), pp. 173–190.

—— *Women, Credit, and Debt in Early Modern Scotland* (Manchester: Manchester University Press, 2016).

Stevens, Matthew Frank, *Urban Assimilation in Post-Conquest Wales: Ethnicity, Gender and Economy in Ruthin, 1282–1350* (Cardiff: University of Wales Press, 2010).

—— 'Anglo-Welsh towns of the early fourteenth century: a survey of urban origins, property-holding and ethnicity', in Helen Fulton (ed.), *Urban Culture in Medieval Wales* (Cardiff: University of Wales Press, 2012), pp. 137–162.

—— 'London women, the courts and the "golden age": a quantitative analysis of female litigants in the fourteenth and fifteenth centuries', *The London Journal*, 37 (2012), 67–88.

—— 'London's married women, debt litigation and coverture in the court of Common Pleas', in Cordelia Beattie and Matthew Frank Stevens (eds), *Married Women and the Law in Premodern Northwest Europe* (Woodbridge: Boydell and Brewer, 2013), pp. 115–132.

Stretton, Tim, *Women Waging Law in Elizabethan England* (Cambridge: Cambridge University Press, 1998).

—— 'The legal identity of married women in England and Europe 1500–1700', in Andreas Bauer and Karl H.L. Welker (eds) *Europa und seine Regionen: 2000 Jahre Rechtsgeschichte* (Cologne: Böhlau, 2006), pp. 309–322.

—— 'Coverture and unity of persons in Blackstone's commentaries', in Wilfred Prest (ed.), *Blackstone and his Commentaries: Biography, Law, History* (Oxford: Hart, 2009), pp. 111–128.

Stretton, Tim and Kesselring, Krista J. (eds), *Married Women and the Law: Coverture in England and the Common Law World* (London: McGill-Queen's University Press, 2013).

Stuard, Susan Mosher, *Considering Medieval Women and Gender* (Farnham: Routledge, 2010).

Thomas, Keith, 'The double standard', *Journal of the History of Ideas*, 20 (1959), 195–216.

Titow, J.Z., 'The decline of the fair of St Giles, Winchester, in the thirteenth and fourteenth centuries', *Nottingham Medieval Studies*, 31 (1987), 58–75.

Tucker, Penny, 'Historians' expectations of the medieval legal records', in Anthony Musson (ed.), *Expectations of the Law in the Middle Ages* (Woodbridge: Boydell and Brewer, 2001), pp. 191–202.

Turning, Patricia, 'Women on trial: piecing together women's intellectual worlds from courtroom testimony', *Medieval Feminist Forum*, 46 (2010), 66–73.

—— *Municipal Officials, Their Public, and the Negotiation of Justice in Medieval Languedoc* (Leiden: Brill, 2013).

Vickery, Amanda, 'Golden age to separate spheres? A review of the categories and chronology of English women's history', *The Historical Journal*, 36 (1993), 383–414.

Walker, Garthine, 'Expanding the boundaries of female honour in early modern England', *Transactions of the Royal Historical Society*, 6 (1996), 235–245.

—— 'Just stories: telling tales of infant death in early modern England', in Margaret Lael Mikesell and Adele F. Seeff (eds), *Culture and Change: Attending to Early Modern Women* (Newark, Delaware: University of Delaware Press, 2003), pp. 98–115.

—— *Crime, Gender and Social Order in Early Modern England* (Cambridge: Cambridge University Press, 2008).

Walker, Sue Sheridan (ed.), *Wife and Widow in Medieval England* (Ann Arbor: University of Michigan Press, 1993).

—— 'Litigation as personal quest: suing for dower in the royal courts, circa 1272–1350', in Sue Sheridan Walker (ed.), *Wife and Widow in Medieval England* (Ann Arbor: University of Michigan Press, 1993), pp. 81–108.

—— 'Order and law', in Rosemary Horrox and W. Mark Ormrod (eds), *A Social History of England, 1200–1500* (Cambridge: Cambridge University Press, 2006), pp. 91–112.

Walker, V.M., 'Mediaeval Nottingham: a topographical study', *Transactions of the Thoroton Society*, 67 (1963), pp. 28–45.

Wilkinson, Louise J., *Women in Thirteenth-Century Lincolnshire* (Woodbridge: Boydell and Brewer, 2007).

Williamson, Fiona, 'Public and private worlds? Social history, gender and space', *History Compass*, 10 (2012), 633–643.

—— 'Space and the city: gender identities in seventeenth-century Norwich', *Cultural and Social History*, 9 (2012), 169–185.

Wood, Diana (ed.), *Medieval Money Matters* (Oxford: Oxbow, 2004).

Woodbine, George E., 'The origins of the action of trespass', *Yale Law Journal*, 33 (1924), 799–816.

Youngs, Deborah, *The Life Cycle in Western Europe, c.1300–c.1500* (Manchester: Manchester University Press, 2006).

—— 'The townswomen of Wales: singlewomen, work and service, c.1300–1550', in Helen Fulton (ed.), *Urban Culture in Medieval Wales* (Cardiff: University of Wales Press, 2012), pp. 163–182.

Zemon Davis, Natalie, *Fiction in the Archives: Pardon Tales and Their Tellers in Sixteenth-Century France* (Cambridge: Cambridge University Press, 1988).

Index

abduction 116, 140–143
affray 25, 26, 29, 37, 153, 155, 157–165
  married women 160–162
ale *see* brewing
amercements 34, 37
assault 33, 121–122, 123–124
assize of ale 90, 93, 97, 98–105
assize of bread 90, 93, 97–98
attachment 31
attorneys 35, 58, 61

baking 31, 97–98
  women's roles 98
Black Death 54, 64, 75, 121, 167, 170, 195
bloodshed 26, 154–155, 157, 158, 159, 162, 164, 168
borough courts *see* town courts
Bracton 9
bread *see* baking
brewing 31, 56–70, 71, 93, 94, 97, 98–105
  aletasters 91
  married women 99, 100–102, 103, 104
  women's fines 99, 100–101, 103
Brigstock 64
burgess status 31

Caernarfon 11
Chester 5, 22, 23, 30
  assize of ale 102–104
  borough charters 30
  Crownmote 30
  debt litigation 61–64
  femmes sole 76
  Palatine 23, 63
  Pentice Court 30
    records 35, 36
  Portmote 30
  St Peter's Church 30
  trading offences 98
Colchester 121, 166
common law 8, 9, 26, 27, 28, 65, 73, 114, 115
court records 5, 7, 22, 24, 26, 32, 35–40, 48–49
  formulae 38, 39, 40
  language 39
  scribes 38, 40
  structure 37–38
  voices of litigants 38–39
coverture 8–12, 28, 56–57, 65–68, 73, 74, 76, 78–79, 80–82, 100–101, 104, 109, 131–132, 136, 140, 191–197
credit 33, 46–47, 49, 56, 60, 64, 81–82, 118, 132, 134

damages 34, 37
  in trespass pleas 114, 116, 125, 128, 130, 131, 134, 139, 140–141
Danelaw 23
daughters 140, 141
debt 14, 26, 32–33, 45–90, 121
  married women 65–79
  value of debts 65
defamation 33, 113, 116, 118, 120, 129–133
detinue 14, 49, 77
distraint 31
Dyffryn Clwyd 11, 141
  Ruthin 50, 64, 65, 115, 123

Edinburgh 6
essoins 31, 73, 78, 128
Exeter 7, 32, 50, 51, 64, 79, 106, 121

felony 26, 114, 116
femmes sole 7, 12, 51–52, 65, 71, 75, 78–79, 103, 192

INDEX

food production 93
forestalling 93, 94, 96, 105–108

game-playing 177–178
Ghent 50, 57, 74
Great Yarmouth 11, 99, 167

hamsocn 127–129
honour 113–114, 117, 119, 120, 130–132
households 92, 97, 108, 128, 143–144, 178
   brewing 101, 105
housewife (as legal status) 103, 106
hucksters 95–96, 106
hue and cry 128, 142, 157, 165–171
   married women 169
   as tool for women 165–166

imprisonment 124
Ipswich 72
Ireland 23

juries 34–35, 37, 51, 90, 117

Kent 13, 121, 124, 129, 136, 138, 164, 173

larceny 116
leet jurisdiction 25, 32, 37–38, 155
London 5, 7, 10, 50, 51, 65, 68, 69, 79
Loughborough 50, 64

manor courts 11, 12, 50
marriage
   and debt litigation 54–55, 56–57, 62, 65–79
   and trespass litigation 136–139
   see also coverture
married women 65–79, 106–108, 136–140, 188–189, 191–196
migration 23

Norwich 72, 141
   hue and cry 165
Nottingham 5, 22, 23–24
   assize of bread 97–98
   borough charters 29
   borough court 24, 25, 29
      foreign pleas 29, 53
      records 35–36
   castle 23–24
   Common Hall 29, 161
   coverture 193–194
   debt litigation 52–58
   decennaries 29, 153, 156
   hue and cry 170
   Mayor's Court 29–30, 156
      jurors 96
      officials 29
      trading offences 94–97, 106–107
   nuisances 25

paraphernalia 77
Pollock and Maitland 9
poll tax 22–23
prostitution 8, 174, 175–177

Ramsey (Cambridgeshire) 167
rape 140–142
   see also abduction
regrating 93, 105–106

scolding 8, 129, 171–175
   as gendered offence 172–173
Scotland 6, 11, 28
   debt litigation 51
   married women 29, 74, 79
   jus mariti 28
   town courts 28
servants 60, 127, 138, 141, 142, 189
slander *see* defamation

theft 33
   see also trespass
town courts 5, 21, 22, 24–25, 31
   burgesses 24–25

221

INDEX

town courts (*cont.*)
  custom 26
  hue and cry 165
  jurors 25
  love day 34
  officials 22, 24, 25
  procedure 31–32, 34–35
trading offences 25, 29, 90–109
  licenses to trade 100
  as licensing 93, 96–97, 108, 109
  married women 92, 94
  records 91–92
trespass 15, 33, 37, 48, 113–146, 157
  animals 144
  married women 136–140
  nature of pleas 115–116
  numbers of women in pleas 120–123
  procedure 117–118
  property 133–134
  receiving stolen goods 164–165
  theft 134–135, 140–141, 143, 158, 164–165
  verbal attacks 129–133
  violence 123–129
  weapons 126–127, 158, 159, 163–164
  whore (as insult) 130–131
  women's honour 119–120, 130–131

violence 26, 29, 31, 153–154, 156, 157–165
  domestic violence 161–162, 170
  gendered patterns 119
  women as victims and perpetrators 158–159
  see also affray; assault; bloodshed; trespass

Wales 11, 23 27
  Welsh law 27
  see also Dyffryn Clwyd
Westminster 32
widows 9, 55, 57, 58, 63, 74, 77, 104–105
  remarriage 75
Winchester 5, 22–23, 30–31
  Ancient Usages 31
  assize of ale 100–102, 105
  assize of bread 98
  City Court 24, 30, 31, 156
    records 35, 36, 37
  guildhall 30
  hue and cry 166–171
  trading offences 94, 95, 107

York 54

EU authorised representative for GPSR:
Easy Access System Europe, Mustamäe tee 50,
10621 Tallinn, Estonia
gpsr.requests@easproject.com